£30-00

Restructuring: Place, Class and Gender

Restructuring: Place, Class and Gender

Paul Bagguley
Jane Mark-Lawson
Dan Shapiro
John Urry
Sylvia Walby
Alan Warde

SAGE Publications
London • Newbury Park • New Delhi

© Paul Bagguley, Jane Mark-Lawson, Dan Shapiro, John
Urry, Sylvia Walby, Alan Warde 1990
First published 1990

SAGE Publications Ltd
28 Banner Street
London EC1Y 8QE

SAGE Publications Inc
2111 West Hillcrest Drive
Newbury Park, California 91320

SAGE Publications India Pvt Ltd
32, M-Block Market
Greater Kailash – I
New Delhi 110 048

British Library Cataloguing in Publication data

Restructuring: place, class and gender.
 1. Lancashire. Lancaster. Human. geographical features
 I. Bagguley, Paul
 304.2769

 ISBN 0–8039–8214–3

Library of Congress catalog card number 89–069827

Typeset by Input Typesetting Ltd, London, SW19
Printed in Great Britain by Billing and Sons Ltd, Worcester

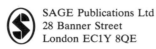

Contents

Preface

This book stems from the research initiative funded by the Economic and Social Research Council – *The Changing Urban and Regional System of the UK*. It involved the study of seven localities: south-west Birmingham, Cheltenham, Lancaster, Liverpool (outer estates), Middlesbrough, Swindon and the Isle of Thanet. We are grateful to the ESRC, to all the participants in the initiative, and to the coordinator Philip Cooke. We are grateful also to the staff of the Office of Population Censuses and Surveys and the Social Statistics Research Unit at City University for their help in making available to us data from the OPCS 1% Longitudinal Study. Crown copyright is reserved on all tables from the Longitudinal Study. Tables 4.7 to 4.9, 4.12 and 4.17 to 4.25 inclusive may not be reproduced without permission from OPCS.

Finally we would like to thank Anne Green who conducted some of the interviews reported in Chapter 4, and Maeve Conolly and Chris Quinn who helped us out with word-processing.

Lancaster Regionalism Group
Department of Sociology
Lancaster University

1
Introduction

A garden festival in Liverpool, Glasgow as a European centre of culture, the London docklands as the most desirable of places to live, Bradford and Wigan as highly successful tourist towns, Swindon as a centre for high tech industry – places in the 1980s are undergoing some extraordinary changes. The aim of this book is to make sense of these accelerating economic and social changes of recent years, changes which range from the local to the global. In particular we seek to understand both the diversity of place and the ways in which spectacular shifts can occur within given places: shifts in the nature and quantity of paid and unpaid work, in social and political mobilisation, in cultural and aesthetic experience, and in the built environment. Despite the focus on place, the causal processes that we describe cover every spatial scale – again, from the local to the global.

The theory that has gained the widest currency for focusing on the spatial aspects of this widespread economic and social change is that of 'restructuring'. The term is not that precise: more a label than a definition, and occurring in different versions with different emphases. There is, nevertheless, a major corpus of work and a core of writers that have developed the perspective. It is appropriate, then, to begin this book by specifying our relationship to aspects of 'restructuring theory'. We argue that disparate and sometimes contradictory elements have contributed to its development, so that there is no single consistent or comprehensive body of ideas against which our own positions can be mapped. We will review what we see as some of the main 'roots and branches' of 'restructuring' before describing the distinctive and additional elements that we place at centre stage. Rather than being a precise and detailed analysis of the development of the theory, this review is intended to set the background for our own work. The book is designed to evaluate the nature of 'restructuring' as a research programme: to consider whether it has progressive or degenerative features. Have the original clearcut formulations given rise, over a period of time, to a body of research findings and insights, and as a result established a hard core of assumptions, methods and theses (Lakatos, 1970)?

Roots and Branches of the Restructuring Perspective

Marxism

The influence of a revived and revised Marxist theory on many of the social sciences in the 1970s is the most important root of restructuring theory. It was central to the development, within the academic discipline of geography, of a critical reaction to orthodox, neo-classical or empiricist industrial location theory. Massey (1984: 3–17) describes the growing dissatisfaction with the 'confrontation of maps' approach, in which one spatially distributed phenomenon is 'explained' by reference to correlations with other spatially distributed phenomena, but without reference to the qualitative processes and dynamics of changing capitalist *production* and changing class relations and struggles.

The Marxist alternative emphasised the *space economy* – the manner in which capital *makes use* of particular places for varieties of production in the pursuit of accumulation; and the way that, as production processes are transformed, these uses change and force corresponding changes on the places that 'host' them. The focus here, then, was on the ways in which places become the *victims* of capital: how they are called into being, transmuted and destroyed in the pursuit of accumulation. This produced, from Massey, one of the clearest and strongest statements of restructuring theory: that – 'the social and economic structure of any given local area will be a complex result of the combination of that area's succession of roles within the series of wider, national and international divisions of labour' (1978: 116). We have previously dubbed this a 'geological metaphor', describing as it does the ways in which these divisions of labour overlie each other to constitute distinct regions and localities (Warde, 1985a).

For this model, although many factors go into creating locational advantages for different kinds of capital, *labour* plays a prominent role. The divisions of labour, the labour markets and the labour processes to be found in particular localities are simultaneously:

1   products of the previous activities of capital – of previous 'rounds of victimisation';
2   key factors in capitals' strategies of location. Locational advantage is largely seen as composed of the presence of labour in appropriate quantitites, with requisite skills, at the minimum price, and willing to comply with the dictates of the current labour processes. Obviously, these are rarely simultaneously available. This is the basis for other major insights of restructuring theory, such as the subdivision of activities within firms into

part processes which are located in different places (Massey, 1984); or *product cycle theory*, describing the relocation of activities from core to periphery as they age from innovative to established processes (Hymer, 1975). It is in this context that the *transnational* character of advanced capitalist production, and the debates about the significance of the 'new international division of labour' (Fröbel, Heinrichs and Kreye, 1980), assumed prominence;

3 sources of independent struggle and resistance, as the labour that is assembled, collectivised and schooled in class conflict through the agency of capital, organises autonomously around its own interests.

When these factors are combined with a further notion – that capital is much more spatially mobile than labour – then they yield insights into the sources and the dynamics of what it is that is *particular* to different places, defined primarily around labour process changes and industrial class struggle. Institutionally, this perspective was fostered in the UK by participants in the Conference of Socialist Economists (CSE) Regionalism Group.

Realism
In a related but separate development, there was a growing interest in realist theories of the social sciences (Sayer, 1984; Keat and Urry, 1982, postscript). Realist models of the social world distinguish between relatively enduring social entities which have causal properties, and specific, contingent events to which the social entities give rise. The relations between causal entities are highly complex, however, in that the *realisation* of their causal properties is not guaranteed but often depends upon the realisation, or partial realisation, of the causal properties of other entities; or, indeed, upon the *blocking* of the realisation of the causal properties of other entities whose effects may otherwise be contrary. The way in which empirical phenomena arise, then, reflects the intricate relations between entities, with the mutual realisation, part-realisation or blocking of their causal powers.

It is interesting that realism seems to have exerted a greater influence in radical geography than in most of the other social sciences. Perhaps geography's necessary attention to spatial variability throws the inadequacies of more global theories and methodologies into sharper relief, while the absence of credible alternatives and the accident of the disciplinary affiliation of key individuals must have played some part. There have been two main effects. First, realism has provided a methodological vehicle for extending the principal causal elements beyond class relations. Realist-influenced models usually include some or other combination of relations of gender, race, state, generation and nation. Secondly, it has introduced a much greater sophistication in the way that causal relations and interactions are conceived, and hence in the way that socio-spatial relations can be 'modelled'.

The combination of theoretical realism and restructuring, emphasising the 'spatiality' of social phenomena, is especially powerful. It involves the recognition that amongst the other properties of significant causal entities engaged in social processes are the *spatial ranges* over which they operate and can exert their powers. A spatialised realism therefore renders a powerful way out of – or else, perhaps, an extension of – the 'structural' approach. The structuralism of the 1970s produced sweeping claims of a global character, with the laws of motion of capital given overwhelming causal supremacy. A spatialised realism, by contrast, with a plurality of causal elements, standing in a much more complex relation to each other and subject to spatial constraints in their operation, offers some chance that a structural perspective could after all generate systems of explanation more adequate to the evident complexity of the real world.

Time, Space and Society
Another 'subtext' in the development of the restructuring perspective concerns the *rapprochement* of sections of the academic disciplines of geography and sociology (Gregory and Urry, 1985). From spatial science as a point of departure, radical geographers have been drawn further towards an appreciation of social process, while some sociologists and social philosophers have become much more aware of the spatial features of, and constraints on, social phenomena (the best example of the latter is, of course, Giddens; see, in particular, 1981; 1984). What is significant here is that from both directions the novel insights have at first seemed sufficiently powerful and simple to hold out a *totalising* prospect. That is, they have looked temptingly capable of yielding a general theoretical framework, yet with detailed practical application, such that a large and diverse range of socio-spatial phenomena can be encompassed. The national and international division of labour, the nature and distribution of class struggles, the processes of job loss, the constitution of distinctive localities, social and political mobilisation: all these and more fall within the remit of the research agenda of 'restructuring theory'.

Agency

The strategies of accumulation pursued by capital in a global context unleash a very powerful set of processes, but there is nevertheless a limit to the extent to which places are just victims of these processes. At the least, they are not *passive* victims, and local struggles are also a key component of the particularities of place. From this has been born, especially in the UK, a renewed interest in questions of 'agency' – what has come to be styled the 'proactive' capacities of local groups, interests and coalitions. This has been most clearly recognised for class struggles in the workplace, but has also expanded to encompass local organisation around other kinds of social and political struggle (Urry, 1986). For example, Cooke explores the features of South Wales as one of Britain's 'radical regions', arguing that there are places where class practices 'are as capable of being dominated at the level of culture, also, to a marked extent, politically, and even, in limited ways economically, by the interests of labour, as they are by those of capital' (1985: 213).

In this the restructuring perspective has reflected broader developments in Marxist theory, in which an Althusserian structuralism of the 1970s, emphasising the passive way in which agents were the bearers of functions for capital, was superseded first by a renewed stress on class struggle and then – following Gramsci – by attention to the relations of *civil society* and, more generally, of agency. The developments in restructuring theory show a strong resemblance to parallel developments in debates on the labour process, in which the path-breaking work of Braverman (1974) was subsequently criticised, amongst other reasons, for ignoring the capacities of labour for organisation and struggle.

'Flexible' Accumulation

There are three distinguishable 'schools' concerned to develop the notion of 'flexibility': the French 'regulation' school, centring on the work of Aglietta (1987); the American 'institutionalist' school, centring on the work of Piore and Sabel (1984); and the British 'managerialist' school, centring on the work of Atkinson (NEDO, 1986). Common to all is the supposed contrast that is drawn between a 'Fordist' economic structure, with mass production articulated to mass consumption and a complex and hierarchical division of labour; and a 'post-Fordist' structure in which there is specialised production for differentiated 'niche' markets, but with a 'flexible', multi-skilled workforce.

Flexible accumulation has become increasingly allied with restructuring theory, as shown, for example, in the contributions to a recent special issue of the journal *Society and Space* (1988). One attraction of the thesis of flexible accumulation is that it holds out yet another 'totalising' prospect: this time in connecting the analysis of capital accumulation and labour process issues to the *qualitative* aspects of production and to consumption. Another attraction is that 'flexibility' appears to identify some of the most salient restructuring changes taking place during the 1980s, in part at least, in the UK, because of 'Thatcherism'. In Chapter 2 we take up both the potential and the deficiencies of the notion of 'flexibility'.

Postmodernism
The current wave of interest in 'postmodernism' has also hit restructuring theory. Postmodernist is distinguished from modernist culture in rejecting hierarchies which separate elite and mass culture and which venerate high culture as deriving from a coherent body of knowledge under the stewardship of an artistic elite. Thus the 'aura', distance, seriousness and uniqueness of the work is replaced by a democratic, immediate and convivial reproducibility; while the sense of an immanent, historical development is replaced by an eclectic, promiscuous pastiche and collage of 'stylised' pasts and presents. Compartmentalised boundaries between the aesthetic and the practical, art and life, the cultural and the real, high and low, work and play, duty and pleasure, all become blurred. Postmodernism does not only affect the spheres of culture, but enters deeply into the circuits of capital in production and realisation. This is partly because, as Baudrillard argues (1981), in 'consumer capitalism' we no longer consume products but *signs*. We live in a world of 'simulacra', or images and copies without any original progenitor, in which reality and image are 'imploded' into the 'hyperreality' of the spectacle. For producers, too, their inputs are increasingly composed of simulacra – images, information, and so on – rather than of more conventional raw material. The aesthetic and the commodity increasingly interpenetrate in the field of 'design', partly in the service of providing the postmodern social classes with the 'positional' goods which, according to Bourdieu (1984), compose their 'habitus'. But this also provides advanced capitalism with the avenues for specialised, targeted and high-value-added production, in which the pure image itself becomes an increasingly dominant vehicle of accumulation.

We argue in Chapter 5 that postmodernism as a body of theory remains largely inchoate, since its usages in philosophy, in social theory and in aesthetic criticism have developed at a hectic pace, but largely independently of each other. It follows that postmodernism can be introduced into restructuring in a variety of ways. In the work of Harvey (1987), for example, the postmodern is used – pejoratively, and following the work of Jameson (1984) and the earlier work of Lyotard (1984) – to denote a phase of almost hysterical hyperconsumption, created by and subordinated to the imperatives of capital. Here postmodernism is allied to flexible accumulation and largely subsumed in the service of an older body of theory. Elsewhere, as in Lash and Urry (1987), the postmodern is seen as paralleling economic, spatial and political changes, and the 'service class' is particularly emphasised in both creating and consuming postmodern culture.

While postmodernism liberates the cultural and the aesthetic, and reasserts a hermeneutic impulse in social theory (Vattimo, 1988), the subordination of production and other material processes to the sign risks a 'reverse reduction' to the renewed 'productivism' of flexible accumulation. We do not yet assent to Baudrillard's proclamation: 'The end of labour. The end of production. The end of political economy.' (Baudrillard, 1976: 20; Kellner, 1987). We take 'the postmodern', despite some important qualitative changes, to be an intensification and continuance of the modernist maelstrom in which there are very substantial remnants of 'unfinished business'. These include the older imperatives of accumulation, and the social and spatial restructurings which they engender; and an agenda of liberation in which those dominated through processes of class, gender, race and place continue to struggle against the multiple and complex sources of their subordination, and seek their own vehicles for political participation and cultural expression. One interesting consequence of the blurring of these boundaries, though, has been to bring back into prominence a *literary* approach to the particularities of place. The task has come to include the exercise of an aesthetic and empathetic sensibility – to tell a good story – and the work of writers such as Raban (1986) and Theroux (1984) is quoted in the same breath, and with as much weight, as academic texts (Cooke, 1987; Thrift, 1988a).

Locality
If these have been some of the roots and branches of the restructuring perspective, then studies of *locality* have been a major fruit. It suddenly became necessary to pursue detailed investigations of named places. This work does stand in need of some defence, not least because there is an unfortunate history in both sociology and geography of untheorised studies of 'communities' or 'real places' (Pudup, 1988). Savage et al. (1987) address the proliferation of such studies in recent funded research programmes in the UK, and

the ways in which they have needed to disentangle sets of related but non-congruent concepts: local and national, abstract and concrete, specific and general, micro and macro, agent and structure. Though it may be tempting to connect 'the local' to one side of these pairs, on examination both halves are equally pertinent to the study of the local, the national, or indeed any other spatial scale.

There are many impulses to local studies. At its simplest, spatial processes must find *some* kind of spatial expression, so that the locality suggests a means to tackle this through 'case studies'. At its best, such cases are chosen comparatively to reflect variations on some key dimension, though difficult problems of comparability will remain (Warde, 1985a). The emphasis on agency (local 'proactivity'), with its interest in whether particular social environments can modify the distribution and effects of major social and economic forces, also supposes some arena in which such struggles can be played out. At a more theoretical level, it is an interesting question whether spatially variable phenomena generate specific localised causal entities with their own distinct powers; or, more intensely, whether combinations of spatially variable phenomena fit together to create 'locality effects' (Duncan, 1986). Hence, it might be that, say, local labour market, local labour process and local political processes come together to generate a radically distinctive locality with pronounced causal powers. Concern with such questions is naturally heightened in the UK at a time of political polarisation, when the abandonment of national consensus politics has been matched by attempts at more focused resistance, and experimentation with new forms of political intervention and mobilisation in the local state. None of these, however, provides an adequate *methodological* defence of locality studies as currently practised, since none of them – including questions of local causal processes and locality effects – provides a specification of what the appropriate spatial scale will be. Just what is a 'locality', then, remains unclear. Our own view is that the locality study as a *method* has arisen from the attempt to address the complexity of spatially intersecting causal processes, and we consider the issues of complexity and the definition of locality below.

Place, Class and Gender

Diversity and Complexity
We have highlighted seven elements which form the background and substance of 'restructuring theory'. These elements have an

understandable relation to each other in terms of their temporal succession and the ways in which interest in one feeds into interest in others. By the time these elements are combined, however, their terrain has become quite vast and in some respects incompatible. There would seem to be little that integrates them beyond a loose 'post-Marxist' affiliation. 'Restructuring' does still denote a particular concern for the *spatial* aspects of social phenomena, and gives a certain privilege to the dynamics of, and in reaction to, capital – but little more precision is possible. These remain the hard core of the research agenda of restructuring.

An analysis of the processes and strategies through which capital seeks expanded accumulation is thus at the core of restructuring theory. Even here, however, we think that the full complexity of the system has usually gone unrecognised. Suppose that a very simple model is drawn up, reflecting current debates on the environment of accumulation on six key dimensions: state regime, labour market, input/purchase market, product market, technology, and work organisation; and that some very skeletal elements and conditions within each of these dimensions are set out. This theoretical scheme, which is relatively clear in its basic elements, yields a vast and bewildering degree of complexity when pursued in detail: the number of possible combinations is well over 100 000 (Shapiro, 1987a). Even when these have been sifted to exclude unlikely combinations of strategies, over 5000 remain. It is important to recognise that these do not represent just a set of empirical permutations – there is no empirical element to it at all – but a set of theorised and plausible combinations of 'restructuring strategies' facing a unit of capital. This should make it clear how problematic it is to appeal to a 'logic of accumulation' as accounting for an observed empirical trend such as technical change or plant closure.

The current phase of locality studies originated in the rediscovery, on a new and much more satisfactorily theorised base, of spatial specificity. But a consequence of looking again at 'real places' has been to force the recognition that they are even more 'particular' than at first suspected. A greater diversity of significant social phenomena – cultural, political, aesthetic and even personal (Rustin, 1987) – finds 'place' within them, and these both show spatial diversity and patterns of organisation in their own right and enter into complex interrelations with other socio-spatial forces. From a relatively stark and clear starting point in spatialised class relations – the dynamics of capital and labour – restructuring theory has, then, swelled. This totality has at one level become much more *graspable* through the rapprochement of social and spatial perspectives, but has also become almost infinitely complex. This complexity is not just a matter of 'individual' variations around broad abstractions; it is a complexity in the relations among the abstractions themselves! As this proliferates, the objective of using the locality as a manageable testbed for a realist synthesis inexorably recedes. A paradoxical result is that the more one 'knows' about places, the less 'knowable' they become: a key theme in our work is hence the contradictory and relatively unpredictable character of local change.

In the face of these problems of the heterogeneity and complexity of restructuring theories, our study will not attempt a chimerical 'totality' of significant socio-spatial processes within a locality – what one might call a 'full-blown realism' of place. We shall instead try to develop the insights and avoid the pitfalls of the various elements in order to explore the delicate connections between and within disparate social phenomena. In our conclusion we will consider the degree of theoretical coherence and integrity that emerges.

However, this project does not only deploy the various existing elements of restructuring theory. We also seek to generate some distinctive additional elements in trying to *develop* the research agenda. The most important elements that we seek to elaborate are *gender relations*, *civil society*, *political mobilisation*, and the restructuring of *services*. Throughout the book we show the centrality of gender relations for the analysis of restructuring. In Chapter 5 we elaborate some tools with which to approach the relations of civil society. In Chapter 6 we explore the complexities of local political mobilisation. And in Chapter 3 we examine the distinctive aspects of the restructuring of services.

What is 'Locality'?

We have repeatedly invoked the 'local' and the particularities of place without yet specifying what is meant by these much used but most troublesome terms (Duncan, 1986; Savage et al., 1987; Urry, 1988b). We derive our sense of the local from a realist perspective, by paying attention to the *spatial ranges* of the many causal elements that impinge on any chosen area. We describe in Chapter 5 how we extend our interest to the elements of civil society, and when these are added to more familiar causal elements we arrive at a very large set of substantive entities and social collectivities, each of which possesses its own spatial shape and range. This list includes households; housing or 'neighbourhood' communities; school catchment areas; ethnic and religious communities; classes at local, regional, national and international scales; political party districts at various scales; factory catchment areas; local (and supra-local) labour markets, spatially differentiated by class, race and gender; the state at district, county, regional and national scales; firms at all spatial scales and of all shapes; extra-local patterns of connection between ethnic, religious, class and migratory populations; and voluntary organisations and social movements.

All of these overlie each other and can enter into substantive relations where they overlap, involving sometimes the same and sometimes different collections of individuals and other subjects. Social reality, from this perspective, is made up of the totality of these significant interrelationships over space, and 'restructuring' can be conceived as the spatial and temporal dynamics that they embody. Considered globally, the number of these interrelationships is as good as infinite and, as we suggested earlier, much of the impetus for locality studies may stem from the search for a more manageable object. A 'locality' is simply a ring drawn around one set of these intersections of elements, and is therefore unavoidably *arbitrary*. It does not, of course, follow that one is concerned only with elements whose spatial range is equal to this local unit; the significant elements at larger scales, right up to the global, which impinge on the locality, and significant elements at smaller scales within it, must all be included. What is meant by 'significant' will, in turn, depend on the substantive issues in question.

A locality therefore offers the possibility of examining a more rounded set of processes and interrelations of causal entities in different spheres – in the formal economy, civil society and the state. Its size remains unspecified – it too depends on the substantive issues in question – but the kinds of locality actually chosen in the current wave of UK research projects (Savage et al., 1987), that is, 'towns' and hinterlands of roughly local authority district and travel-to-work-area (TTWA) size, offer some advantages. Since many civil struggles focus around the local state, it would be strange to pick an area smaller than the smallest significant unit of the local state. Similarly, although labour markets vary in size and are specific to class, gender and sectoral groups, a locality on this scale comes closest to covering the employment opportunities common to much of a given population, and the market for much labour shared by a given set of employers. There is also a less tangible, 'informational' sense in which most people can know something about many of the significant elements within such a locality. To some degree this makes it a meaningful unit to them, and one in which subjects can pursue relatively well informed struggles.

Lancaster

It is in this sense of 'locality' that we have tried to focus our discussion through the use of Lancaster as a case study. Our interest is always centred on the more general processes or issues, but pursuing the spatial logic of these processes dictates precisely that they cannot be studied in a vacuum, only in the context of real interactions. Lancaster serves as an example, then, but it is obvious from what has gone before that there can be no such thing as a neutral example. Its web of connections is probably unlike that of anywhere else. Lancaster turns out, we think, to be a fascinating place – but so should anywhere if studied in such depth. It also shows very clearly the dilemmas of the time. It was a place of manufacturing industry, but is hardly so now. It has become a public service centre, and is embroiled in the political turmoil currently surrounding public services. It has many of the features of a first-rate 'historic town', but is only now feeling its way towards exploiting its 'heritage'. It seeks a future in private services, but with uncertain prospects. These are, of course, shorthands for *contested* projects in which local interests are opposed: political life, after decades of slumber, is stirring. It is a place 'on the brink'.

Temporal Change

In order to make sense of any such place it is important that the historical dimension is not forgotten. Indeed, the geological metaphor does contain a notion of temporal change in the model of overlying rounds of accumulation, with residues from previous rounds persisting into the present. It is, though, not very clear what constitutes a *round* of accumulation, and whether the round applicable to, say, a particular industrial sector necessarily draws other local phenomena into its ambit. When 'the locality' is broken down into fine gradations of causal elements, as we propose, then a finer and more discriminating sense of corresponding temporal changes, and their interactions, is also required. There is a need to consider the different means by which the past exerts a force upon the present, and the application of these means to different causal elements in the local scene.

We can distinguish, first, the physical environment: capable of change by human agency, but relatively enduring. This will affect both the possibilities for material production in a place, and the constitution of the subjectivities within it. This is also so with the built environment, enshrining as it does certain enduring possibilities, but capable too of reconstruction and changes of use. Thirdly, there is an institutional environment, in which regularities of association, specialised functions and patterns of organisation may facilitate collective action, which can be reproduced across changes of personnel and which will be endowed with certain organisational resources and capacities. Fourthly, there are the continuities of individual lived experience, with the capacity to make critical contrasts with other times and other places, and including the formative experiences through which individual subjects are constituted. Finally, there are individual and collective processes and projects through which these other elements of past and present are symbolically appropriated and understood. Thus, Patrick Wright (1985) explores the different ways in which the past and present of Stoke Newington are understood by its various 'inhabitants' – 'old' white working-class, black working-class, middle-class radical and middle-class 'yuppie' gentrifiers, local authorities – and how these contrary 'histories' and 'memories' are used in constructing current projects. Locality will, then, be experienced in terms of these material continuities and changes, but also through *invented* traditions (Hobsbawm and Ranger, 1983) and in communities that are necessarily, though to varying degrees, *imagined* (Anderson, 1983).

This book is organised around an apparent reductionism. We start with the restructuring of manufacturing industry in Chapter 2 and the restructuring of service industries in Chapter 3. We then move to a discussion of local labour markets and people's longitudinal experiences in Chapter 4, and of culture, civil society and transformations in urban form in Chapter 5. Lastly, in Chapter 6, we discuss political mobilisation and change. This 'reductionism' is partly real – the result of acknowledging the crushing force of the dynamics of economic restructuring which are both nationally and globally organised. But the book is mainly organised like this because the research agenda of 'restructuring' has typically viewed causal relations as running in this way, from the economy to social life and to politics. In our examination of restructuring, part of what we shall evaluate is precisely this causal thread. One conclusion that the locality study of Lancaster convincingly demonstrates is that not only does place matter, but that social life and politics are bound up in most complex ways with economic change. Indeed, since such change is, as we shall see, partly cultural, then the elements in question are mutually interdependent and causally interconnected. Overall, while we will maintain that 'restructuring' has been a most fertile or progressive research programme, some of its central features such as economic reductionism have now to be firmly jettisoned. Lancaster's history incontrovertibly shows that.

2
Economic Restructuring and Labour Market Change: the Case of Manufacturing

In this chapter we shall critically examine some recent theories of economic restructuring, and use a modified version of these theories to examine the processes of changing employment in the manufacturing sector of the Lancaster economy from the 1960s to the 1980s. We pay particular attention to the work of Massey (1978; 1979; 1984) and Massey and Meegan (1982), whose work has provided an exceptionally influential framework for examining changes in local economies. A further area of theory relating to changes in manufacturing employment that we shall examine is variously known in terms of 'flexibility', 'post-Fordism' or 'flexible specialisation'. It has been argued that new flexible working practices in manufacturing constitute the new round of economic restructuring during the 1980s, following on from the processes of the 1960s and 1970s discussed by Massey and Meegan. We shall briefly identify and critically develop the insights of three broad schools of flexibility theory: the French Marxist regulation school as exemplified in the work of Michel Aglietta (1987); Piore and Sabel's account of the crisis of mass production and the subsequent emergence of flexible specialisation as part of a distinctive North American institutionalist school of flexibility theory (Piore and Sabel, 1984; Sabel, 1982); and Atkinson's account of the flexible firm, part of what we consider to be a distinctive British managerial theory of flexibility (Atkinson, 1986).

Following on from this critical discussion we develop some theses of our own with respect to the analysis of restructuring. First, we shall argue that discussions of economic restructuring have been hampered by an insufficiently detailed account of gender and race relations, and that it is necessary to theorise a variety of forms by which labour is structured. Secondly, from the perspective of particular firms we shall show that a much wider range of restructuring strategies is possible than some analyses have allowed for. Furthermore, this contingency is so great that we do not think it possible to develop a general predictive account of economic restructuring (Shapiro, 1987a). Rather, it is preferable to develop a theoretically informed classification of restructuring strategies from the perspective of the individual firm. We shall then treat this as a heuristic device to analyse how the various strategies of restructuring work out empirically in specific sectors of local labour markets. Finally, we examine these strategies and processes of restructuring in the context of the manufacturing sector of the Lancaster economy.

Theories of Economic Restructuring

The Restructuring Thesis
The restructuring thesis provides a set of theoretical propositions about regional development and the spatial patterns of class relations (Massey, 1978; 1979), and goes on to specific analyses of employment decline (Massey and Meegan, 1982) and the concrete analysis of the development of specific regions (Massey, 1984).

There are three basic elements to the thesis. First, there is the geological metaphor (Massey, 1978; 1979; Warde, 1985b), which is used to reveal how general processes of economic and social change have specific empirical outcomes in particular localities and influence the location decisions of capital. The second is an account of how the internal class structure of the capitalist enterprise is spatially organised – that is, how the class structure comes to appear as spatial divisions of labour. This is initially presented by Massey (1978: 116–19; 1979: 237–9) in the schematic form of an empirical generalisation of an emergent spatial division of labour. However, she later develops it into a more sophisticated account outlining several possible spatial divisions of labour (1984: 30–62, 70–93). Thirdly, there is the account of employment decline examined through the mechanisms of *intensification, investment and technical change*, and *rationalisation* (Massey and Meegan, 1982).

The starting point for the geological metaphor is the geographically uneven spread of those factors which affect the profitability of production processes. New rounds of investment will be geographically patterned in response to the pre-existing spatial pattern. The nature of capital's response to this pre-existing pattern will vary both between sectors and over time within sectors, as the conditions of production within it change. Furthermore, the spatial pattern of new rounds of investment is the outcome of the interaction between the existing geography of production and the emergent requirements of production.

To the changing needs of the leading sectors of capitalist production Massey adds two more directly spatial factors which influence the location of production. First, changes in the transport and communications systems of a given territory may occur between rounds of restructuring. Secondly, changes may occur in the needs for production in a particular sector, or there may be an overall shift in investment between sectors at a more aggregate level where those sectors have different locational needs (Massey, 1978: 115). These processes of restructuring have locally specific consequences.

This new distribution of economic activity, produced by the evolution of a new spatial division of labour, will be overlaid on, and combined with, the pattern produced in previous periods by different forms of spatial division. The combination of successive layers will produce effects which themselves vary over space, contributing to a new form and geographical distribution of inequality in the conditions of production, as a basis for the next round of investment (Massey, 1978: 116).

The geological metaphor, although it has been extensively criticised, provides a powerful explanatory mechanism to describe how national and international cycles of accumulation produce spatially uneven effects as a result of pre-existing economic and social uses of space (Warde, 1985b). The metaphor is developed through Massey's account of spatial differentiation as a competitive resource – the search for spatial advantage. As traditional constraints on location are overcome (transport, communication, energy sources and so on), companies can seek spatial advantage by discriminating between different types of available labour in different local labour markets. Enhanced potential for mobility means that companies have been able to differentiate the production needs and organisation of different functions. Such differentiation has produced a spatially realised form of the hierarchical division of labour, with different functions located in appropriate local labour markets. Looking at the period 1965–80, Massey documents this process.

In Massey's general model of the spatial form of capitalist functions, control and research and development functions were located in large urban centres such as London; skilled work was located in older provincial urban centres with well established supplies of skilled labour; while semi- and unskilled work was located in areas with pools of surplus labour, low wages and no tradition of militancy among the labour force.

This example of an emerging spatial division of labour is elaborated in Massey's later work as one instance of three spatial structures of production (1984). The emerging spatial division of labour in leading sectors such as electronics is described as a 'part-process' spatial structure. The other two spatial structures of production that Massey discusses are, first, the locationally concentrated type with no intra-firm hierarchies – that is, all control, R and D and production take place on the same site; and secondly, the cloned branch-plant pattern. In this latter case there is a central site where all control, R and D and production are located, but the company also has branch plants which are total production sites in themselves but with limited control and R and D functions, if any (Massey, 1984: 70–82).

While the first two elements of Massey's thesis form a fairly coherent framework for understanding spatial restructuring, the third element, that of employment decline, is less clear in its particular spatial implications. Three alternative strategies are identified as underlying shifts in employment and unemployment: rationalisation, intensification, and investment and technical change. Rationalisation involves the loss of jobs through the simple reduction of productive capacity. Job loss through intensification occurs where the productivity of labour is increased by changes in the social organisation of production (without any significant technical change), with the goal of achieving greater effort and output from employees. Investment and technical change involve the purchase of significant new plant and machinery that results in the reduction of the labour force whilst maintaining or improving output. The different processes have different general spatial implications. Intensification tends to produce employment decline *in situ*; rationalisation involves employment decline *in situ*, but may also involve concentrating production at lower levels of capacity in fewer sites; whilst investment and technical change offer the most dramatic spatial possibilities by closing capacity in one place and investing in new plant and machinery in a new site elsewhere (Massey and Meegan, 1982). In general, however, the spatial dimension is rather more contingent in this aspect of restructuring theory compared with the analysis of the geological metaphor or the spatial divisions of labour and structures of production.

We have a number of significant reservations with these models as an approach to understanding spatial development. Some of the major ones concern rather abstract methodological problems. These have been characterised as involving 'pseudo-concrete' analysis (Sayer, 1985; Shapiro, 1987a). The problem is that empirical outcomes of 'concrete' events are either *reduced to* a few abstract theoretical categories, or that the 'concrete' *represents* in some unmediated way the abstract causal factors. The result is that crude stereotypes such as technical change or branch plant economies tend to be used as total explanations. This oversimplifies the 'openness' of empirical events. Consequently, forms of restructuring such as flexibility are overlooked (Cooke and Morgan, 1985), and local agglomerations of mutually interdependent firms as

sources of job growth are also ignored. Massey and Meegan's original account in terms of technical change, intensification and rationalisation, although developed to exemplify a particular mode of
analysis, has tended to be reified and rigidified. The way to develop
restructuring theory is to pursue a strategy of further, more
detailed, concept formation.

The level of the 'concrete' is more complex, and requires a wider
range of concepts to grasp this complexity in an empirical analysis.
One way in which some restructuring writers have responded is to
analyse contemporary restructuring in terms of flexibility and a
broad shift to a new economic form – post-Fordism. This theoretical
shift has occurred both because some perceive a genuine shift in
the patterns of capital accumulation (Cooke and Morgan, 1985;
Harvey, 1987) and because of the new theoretical possibilities of
particular analyses of some schools of post-Fordist analysis – in
particular, the regulation approach (Jessop, 1988). In the light of
the current vogue for the analysis of labour flexibility, we shall
consider the arguments of what we consider the key texts in this
debate.

Post-Fordism and Labour Flexibility
Increasingly during the 1980s, analysts of contemporary capitalism
have been writing of a transition from Fordism to post-Fordism
(Aglietta, 1987; Piore and Sabel, 1984; Atkinson, 1986). These can
be divided into three schools: the institutionalist school (Piore and
Sabel); the regulation school (Aglietta); the managerialist school
(Atkinson).

The central element of a Fordist economic structure is the articulation of mass production to mass consumption. Large volumes
of the same product are produced, using specialised machinery
dedicated to the one product. Jobs are largely semi- or unskilled
and arranged in complex hierarchies of control, and are subject to
detailed 'Taylorist' organisation. In the most extreme forms of
Fordist production literally thousands of simple detailed jobs are
created, so generating an extremely fragmented division of labour.
As Henry Ford himself boasted:

> The lightest jobs were again classified to discover how many of them
> required the use of full faculties, and we found that 670 could be filled
> by legless men, 2637 by one-legged men, two by armless men, 715 by
> one-armed men, and ten by blind men. Therefore, out of 7882 kinds of
> job . . . 4034 did not require full physical capacity. (Henry Ford, 1922,
> quoted in Littler, 1985: 15)

To the standard product, made using dedicated flow-line technology under a Taylorist organisation of work, was allied the

phenomenon of high wages and the reshaping of working-class culture and patterns of consumption.

Whereas speciality and fragmentation at work and uniformity in consumption might be the central features of Fordism, broad job descriptions and labour flexibility allied with the fragmentation of mass markets constitute the essence of post-Fordism. From the point of view of production, post-Fordism refers to the shift within both manufacturing and services to developing flexible systems capable of producing a range of different products. Flexible manufacturing systems allow plant to be used to produce several different types of products or to produce short runs of increasingly customised products. Service industries, as well, are moving towards increasingly high-value-added and customised products (NIER, 1986; Urry, 1987c). These changes are reflected in the demand for flexibility of labour. The emphasis is on breaking down rigid job classifications both horizontally between functions and vertically within the hierarchy of authority, implying 'multi-skilling' on the one hand and participation on the other. In the realm of consumption greater choice and variety are preferred; gone is the option of one version of one model. In that Fordist industry *par excellence*, automobiles:

> the clientele increasingly show preferences for quality and well-designed cars within particular price segments. Moreover, car manufacturers are tending to develop new and highly specialized models such as mini-vans, mini pick-up trucks and four-wheel-drive vehicles. This is a case of cars being produced not in great numbers, but for niches of the market where there is low competition. (Volpato, 1986: 193–4)

The broad claim that unites the three approaches to post-Fordism and flexibility is that workforces and firms are having to become more flexible to meet new competitive environments. We shall now critically consider the claims of this broadly conceived post-Fordist view, beginning with Aglietta's analysis of capitalist regulation.

Aglietta develops a theory of neo-Fordism, which he sees as an intensification of Fordist principles in relation primarily to new technology in production line manufacturing industries. He analyses a succession of regimes of accumulation. 'Extensive accumulation' is the period when relative surplus value is increased by modifying traditional modes of organising the labour process. Employers merely put more of the same machines under the same roof. Labour power is reproduced in a traditional, uncommodified manner with little state intervention in civil society (Aglietta, 1987: 71). 'Intensive accumulation' develops with the extensive commodification of social life, and a 'consumption norm' is formed based on the earnings of the working class. The focus of capitalist development moves from a concern with transforming the labour process to a concern with the reproduction of labour power. Accumulation occurs in the context of shorter hours, high wages and mass consumption, in contrast to intensive accumulation which operates with long working hours and low wages. Intensive accumulation becomes most developed as Fordism (Aglietta, 1987: 116–17).

For Aglietta, Fordism is a twofold deepening of an already existing Taylorism. First, semi-automatic assembly lines are developed which move materials between work stations, with dedicated machines for specific tasks. Secondly, semi-skilled jobs emerge where the workers are fixed to a specific narrow range of tasks whose pace and rhythms are set by machines (Aglietta, 1987: 118–19). However, there are definite limits to this continued fragmentation of work, which creates a crisis for Fordism.

Aglietta describes the crisis of Fordism as essentially a crisis of the reproduction of the wage relation – that is to say, a crisis of the methods and goals of production and mode of life. The solution to the crisis, according to Aglietta, is the development of neo-Fordism. Machines that control their own operations, organised and planned as a total system, are characteristic of neo-Fordism (Aglietta, 1987: 123–5). The increased use of microelectronics in production enables a new *flexibility* within manufacturing systems. This flexibility enables the *centralisation* of the planning of production, but the *decentralisation* of the units of production. These, in part spatial, processes result in an increasing fragmentation of the working class among smaller units of production. In contrast to the other post-Fordist writers considered here, Aglietta treats re-emerging job flexibility not as multi-skilling, but as a further intensification and extension of de-skilling (1987: 129).

Consumption is understood by Aglietta as the mainly private process of the reconstitution of human energies. Consumption uses labour time and involves the process whereby individuals come to recognise their roles in society. Aglietta sees consumption as being largely determined by developments in production (1987: 158). The emergence of mass production generates mass consumption which, he argues, involves the systematic restructuring of traditional working-class ways of life. Standardised housing and the automobile are the characteristic commodities of this mode of consumption.

The social consumption norm underpinning this does not, however, apply to blacks or to women. For blacks it does not apply because of racism, both in the labour market and more generally.

For women it does not apply because their principal role in society is in the process of privatised consumption in the household (Aglietta, 1987: 172). According to Aglietta, women work for a 'supplementary wage', since their role in the economy is determined by their role in the nuclear family. Women are considered to function as a reserve army of labour, under Fordism.

In our view, there are some important problems with Aglietta's approach. First, he tends to overgeneralise from his analysis of the labour process and its restructuring by capital. Fordism is treated not merely as a structure of economic relations and institutions but as a whole form of society, which means that social relations are almost entirely reduced to capitalist economic relations, specifically those of manufacturing industry. Moreover, whether considered at the level of the form of the labour process, or as his overgeneralised conception of a whole phase of capitalist *society*, Fordism is driven by an objective technological dynamic. These reductionist tendencies are further compounded by the way Aglietta ultimately attempts to explain phenomena in terms of the needs or actions of capital. Such technological and economic determinism, together with functionalism and class instrumentalism, were common drawbacks of a wide variety of 1970s Marxist discourse, and have been extensively criticised elsewhere (Jessop, 1982; Urry, 1981).

Moreover, neo-Fordism remains imprecisely defined. Aglietta seems at times to imply that it is simply an intensification of Fordist forms of production at a higher level of technological development with more intensified de-skilling. Unlike many writers on labour flexibility, such as Piore and Sabel (1984), Aglietta does, however, make some attempt to consider gender relations and to explain women's labour market position. This attempt is extremely problematic, since he tries to explain gender divisions in terms of the needs and actions of capital while failing to consider patriarchal power. Similarly, he attempts to analyse 'racial' divisions in terms of racist ideologies constructed by capital, where white fractions of the working class play only a passive receptive role.

The problem of overgeneralisation is perhaps most acute in the way in which Aglietta ignores the role and restructuring of the service sector. For the service sector is important not only in terms of employment (as Chapter 3 shows), but also because of its distinctive patterns of labour flexibility, especially women's part-time employment. We shall return to this problem as a more general drawback of many accounts of economic restructuring, in Chapter 3.

Piore and Sabel, by contrast, write about a putative transition from mass production to 'flexible specialisation', which they term the 'second industrial divide' (Sabel, 1982; Piore and Sabel, 1984). Major differences exist between Aglietta's thesis and that of Piore and Sabel. The latter emphasise the market as the primary causal factor in the development and crisis of Fordism, and see social struggles as shaping technological change and the institutions of regulation in Fordism. Piore and Sabel also make an important distinction between large firms that move towards flexibility and the emergence of small firms producing short batches. This last case is what they term 'flexible specialisation'. Their focus is on the institutional matrix within which different forms of economic development can be either encouraged or blocked (Sabel, 1982: 195).

The development of flexible specialisation requires certain general conditions. First, the development of microtechnology and its application to production enable flexibility to develop (although flexibility is not inherent in technical change – the possibilities of microelectronics have only been utilised in this flexible way because of the fragmentation of markets). Secondly, competition must be organised in such a way that flexible specialist firms remain flexible and innovative and are not fixed to their niche markets. To avoid the 'rigor mortis' of small flexible firms, Piore and Sabel recommend forms of social regulation: regional agglomerations of firms; federations of firms; the development of 'solar firms' (where important parts of the production process are subcontracted to firms with which the core company has a more or less permanent relationship); or a system of 'workshop factories'. What these four forms share is a *social* regulation of competition, cooperation, prices, wages and training.

Some critics have argued that their model is overdrawn. Murray (1987), for example, examining the same Italian regions and economic sectors as Piore and Sabel, shows that Fordist firms still dominate economic relations. Furthermore, he points out that much production was always carried out in non-Fordist organisations. Equally important, Murray argues that Piore and Sabel play down the exploitative aspects of flexible specialisation and the way in which the high-quality jobs go to white middle-aged men.

Piore and Sabel effectively ignore relations of gender and race, within both the labour process and the labour market and also within the institutional forms that regulate economic processes. Labour market legislation on both working hours and social security benefits is highly gendered, and this influences significantly the conditions under which men and women enter the labour market and, consequently, who is offered what type of flexibility. Furthermore, many of the community institutions that control access to skills are, or have been, frequently used to exclude categories of the population around gender and racial cleavages. Piore and Sabel's analysis presents this in a partly positive light, referring to the role that flexible specialist industrial districts have had in the United States in reinforcing the ethnic identities of immigrant communities (1984: 291).

In Britain the managerialist analysis of flexibility has been principally developed by Atkinson (1984). Like Aglietta and Piore and Sabel, Atkinson sees some form of functional task flexibility as an important new development in the organisation of contemporary labour processes. However, unlike them, Atkinson also sees the emergence of part-time and temporary employment as highly significant.

Atkinson builds his model of the 'flexible firm' on dual labour market analysis (Doeringer and Piore, 1971). This is most evident in the way that he identifies a core and a peripheral labour force. The core workers are on permanent contracts, are highly skilled or multi-skilled and are essential to the organisation's activities. The periphery contains two types of flexibility – numerical flexibility in the form of part-time or temporary work, and what Atkinson refers to as 'distancing', which is principally the subcontracting of functions previously carried out in house. Numerical flexibility is primarily concerned with employers' strategies for matching the durations of labour inputs to demands for that labour (part-time employment to cover peak hours of demand in consumer services, for example, or temporary seasonal work in hotel and catering). Finally, he discusses pay flexibility, which refers to the ability of firms to use pay to encourage functional flexibility, reward scarce skills or tie pay to individual performance.

In Atkinson's account, changes in both production and consumption underlie the shift towards flexibility. Diversity and uncertainty in product markets, the attempt to consolidate the productivity gains in manufacturing of the early 1980s, and advanced technical change, are all seen as forms of restructuring which management relates to increased flexibility. Furthermore, unemployment has shifted the balance of power in industrial relations in favour of management, who have then taken the opportunity to introduce new work practices. More recently, Atkinson argues, there has been a shift on the part of employers from an initial concern to break down particular demarcations and eradicate restrictive practices towards an attempt to incorporate the active participation of employees and to encourage the workforce to take increased responsibility for its effectiveness (1989).

The flexible firm is a deceptively simple model, and critics such as Pollert (1987) and MacInnes (1987) have criticised its overgeneralisation, its tendency to ignore gender relations and its slippage between the description of and prescription for a new managerial ideology for the 1980s. Pollert, particularly, criticises the apparent overemphasis on temporary employment and subcontracting in the flexible firm model. Furthermore, she correctly stresses the importance of some of these 'innovative' strategies in the public sector which Atkinson does not consider. The core/periphery generalisation is also problematic as an analytical tool, given the difficulties of operationalising it empirically (Pollert, 1987: 16–18; Walby, 1987: 6–9).

One issue that we have not yet considered is the spatial implications of the putative transition from Fordism to post-Fordism. Atkinson has nothing to say on this, whilst for the other issues quite contradictory claims appear to have been made. For example, Sabel (1982: 220–6) discusses the *decentralisation* of production in Italy as part of the emergence of what he refers to there as neo-Fordism. However, this seems to be decentralisation at the level of the unit of production through subcontracting, rather than some decentralisation of already existing concentrated industry. The effect at the level of the spatial distribution of units of production and employment seems to be a reconcentration of production following on from a decentralised pattern under Fordism. 'Peripheral' branch plants are closed, whilst production is concentrated in highly automated plants surrounded by a series of subcontractors. This pattern is suggested both theoretically by Piore and Sabel (1984) as the re-emergence of 'industrial districts', and empirically for, especially, car manufacturing (Oberhauser, 1987) but also for the US motion picture industry (Storper and Christopherson, 1987).

The clearest statement of the locational logic of post-Fordist manufacturing industries has been developed by Scott (1983; 1986). He provides an analysis of the spatial and locational implications of the vertical and horizontal integration and disintegration of capitalist production. Vertically disintegrated production is small-scale and labour-intensive, in contrast to the more familiar mass production of capital-intensive vertically integrated enterprises.

Vertically disintegrated production occurs because of continuous product differentiation or the market uncertainties of small-batch specialised production. Further, Scott considers relations of subcontracting to be central to the understanding of the logic of horizontally and vertically disintegrated production complexes (1983: 237). He distinguishes two forms of subcontracting. 'Concurrent subcontracting' corresponds to horizontal disintegration, where a cloning of the same kind of firms occurs as individual firms subcontract orders that exceed their normal productive capacity. 'Complementary subcontracting' generates vertical disintegration, since it involves work which is not usually part of the activities of the firm. Both kinds of subcontracting ensure wage discipline and balkanise the workforce, according to Scott, following the broad arguments of dual labour market theory (1983: 243–4). Subcontracting, vertical and horizontal disintegration collectivise the uncertainties of the product market for capital, and in this sense Scott's model comes close to Piore and Sabel's flexible specialisation in industrial districts. In Scott's account, the large-scale production units of Fordist mass production, his vertically and horizontally integrated firms, can locate literally anywhere since they have reduced product market uncertainties, and this leads to the decentralisation of production and employment. In contrast, industries which are characterised by vertical and horizontal disintegration are highly centralised in large urban complexes.

> we should expect locational convergence or clustering of plants to occur where production processes are labor intensive and vertically disintegrated, ie. where plants are small, outputs highly variable in shape and form, and where inter-plant linkages are labyrinthine. Clustering is reinforced where production is subject to much uncertainty. (Scott, 1983: 248)

The locational logic of firms in Scott's model is driven not by the search for the right kind of labour, as in Massey's account of restructuring, but by the search for the right kind of firm to be close to for reasons of inter-firm linkages.

However, other authors such as Perrons (1986: 251) have suggested that the smaller flexible production units could be located on a more decentralised pattern. Furthermore, Lipietz (1987) has analysed the emergence of 'peripheral Fordism' in the industrialising of the less developed countries, again suggesting some form of geographical decentralisation as part of the resolution to the crisis of Fordism. Clearly there is much confusion over what is meant, in geographical terms, by centralisation and decentralisation. Such meaning depends on the spatial scale that is being referred to, and this is not always made clear by some of the writers concerned. The districts of Emilia-Romagna in Italy and Baden-Württemberg in West Germany have an infrastructural system of institutions aimed at balancing competition with cooperation through a sharing of work and information via regional and municipal channels. In the UK, where inter-company relations are notoriously weak and where local authorities have largely lost the power and the financial ability to provide institutional support, industrial regions are unlikely to be developed (or recreated) quickly (Hirst and Zeitlin, 1988).

At the level of *national* economies it does seem that production is becoming more concentrated within their boundaries. In the UK much has been made of the urban–rural shift of the 1960s, discussed above, which might be seen as coinciding with the era of Fordist mass production and its initial crises. Subsequently, as the crisis deepened in the late 1970s and early 1980s branch plants closed in peripheral areas, resulting in a broad arc of 'affluence' north and west of London – the 'sun-belt'. However, such accounts cannot explain sectoral differences in patterns of location, and the manufacturing industries to which they refer are no longer central to the employment prospects of many local labour market areas. As with many of the broad claims of post-Fordism, there is a tendency to overgeneralise from a few cases.

We have criticised the three approaches to the analysis of flexibility along a variety of dimensions, and these are summarised in Table 2.1. All the approaches have specific drawbacks, but they are all inadequate in terms of their analysis (or lack of it) of gender and race issues in relation to flexibility.

Table 2.1   *Central problems with main approaches to flexibility*

Problem	Regulation school approach (Aglietta)	Institutionalist school approach (Piore and Sabel)	Managerialist school approach (Atkinson)
Gender	Reduced to needs of capital	Totally ignored	Treated descriptively
Primary causal factor	Technology (forces of production)	Changes in markets	Eclectic
Principal methodological error	Functionalist and reductionist	Institutionalist	Descriptive/ prescriptive (ideological)
Analysis of service sector	None	None	Ignores public services
Empirical validity	Overgeneralised	Overgeneralised	Overgeneralised
Race	Reduced to needs of capital	Weakly analysed	Ignored
Part-time employment	Ignored	Ignored	Descriptive

Gender Restructuring

We argued in Chapter 1 that gender relations are central to an adequate understanding of restructuring. There are two aspects to this. On the one hand, pre-existing sets of gender relations in particular places are an important consideration in understanding how places change. Gender relations infect and alter class relations and are importantly linked to workplace organisation. It has been shown elsewhere that one cannot understand the uneven spatial spread of particular types of class relations and workplace organisation without looking at variations in gender relations (Savage, 1987a; Mark-Lawson, 1988; Mark-Lawson et al., 1985; Walby, 1986b; Warde, 1988b). At the same time gender relations in particular places are themselves altered by the process of restructuring. Consider, for instance, the impact of the restructuring of cotton textiles in Lancashire in the interwar period, which saw rationalisation and closure impacting highly unevenly on skilled women workers, in some cases breaking down local traditions of household structure and domestic relations (Mark-Lawson, 1988). Understanding the spatial development of new manufacturing industry in the same period, as Glucksmann (1986) argues, depends on an understanding of the pre-existing forms of gender relations in different areas. Closer to home, the lifetime experiences of working women in Lancaster have been altered by the virtual disappearance of manufacturing work for women, as later chapters will show. In this section we briefly consider the approaches to gender taken by the authors already discussed, and the way in which gender relations have been dealt with in terms of restructuring, of flexible accumulation and of post-Fordism. We go on to make a set of proposals concerning a more adequate approach to inserting gender relations into our understanding of restructuring.

In much of the work on spatial aspects of industrial change gender relations have, on the whole, been overlooked. The 'regional problem' is often seen as a problem of male employment; regions in which women had low levels of employment were not considered problematic. At the same time, where gender divisions in employment have been examined in depth it is unusual for authors to consider the spatial dimension. This has been true of the development of theories of women as a reserve army of labour (Beechey, 1977; 1978; Braverman, 1974), and in accounts of occupational segregation (Cockburn, 1983; Hakim, 1979). Hence, as theories of gender developed it was often implicitly assumed that patriarchal relations were constant across places (and often across time as well). In this sense writers on gender relations echoed an assumption within accounts of social class – that class relations were unaffected by the places in which they developed.

More recently, however, spatial variations in class relations have been identified as a valid theoretical area of interest; indeed, it has been argued that specific forms of class relations are inherently local. Gender relations, too, have been shown as rooted in place and subject to spatial variation, and such variation has been shown to have observable effects on occupational segregation (Bagguley and Walby, 1988), on local politics and on local class relations (Mark-Lawson, 1988; Savage, 1987a; Mark-Lawson et al., 1985). Indeed, it has been suggested that class relations locally cannot be understood without reference to gender relations and patriarchal practices. Such variations in gender relations in the workplace and in the sphere of political behaviour, it has been argued, can also be observed in the domestic sphere (although empirically investigating such a claim is highly problematic).

Massey (1984) and Massey and Meegan (1982) are relatively unusual in devoting some attention to gendered divisions in local labour markets (other exceptions include Townsend, 1986; Women and Geography, 1984). However, the restructuring thesis, in its consideration of spatial variation, limits its attention to *women* rather than *gender relations*. Where gender relations are considered – for instance, in looking at the sex-typing of jobs or the impact of domestic divisions of labour on women's workplace participation – they are taken as spatially invariant. Hence, although the work is significant in considering women, gender relations (unlike the labour factor) are not treated as an integral part of restructuring.

Let us examine in more detail the way in which gender is considered within the restructuring thesis. One important strand of Massey's argument is that women, especially married women, are a spatially specific reserve army of semi- and unskilled labour. As we discussed earlier, in order to describe the changes that have taken place over the last ten years Massey and Meegan divide the type of labour required by companies into three categories: 'best staff', doing research and development work, usually graduate and male; skilled manual craft workers, usually male; and semi- and unskilled workers, typically female. These forms of labour, it is argued, are unevenly spatially distributed: R and D staff are concentrated in the south-east (with some outliers – for instance, around Chester on the Welsh Borders, and around Edinburgh in 'Silicon Glen'). Skilled manual workers are concentrated in the old manufacturing heartlands in the midlands and north, while semi- and unskilled female labour is to be found in many areas but is historically utilised at different rates and different places.

Massey suggests that women are newly entering into capitalist wage relations and expanding the workforce. Married women, who once constituted a latent reserve army of labour, are now joining the workforce, albeit at different rates in different places: 'There are therefore locational advantages, so far as access to this kind of labour is concerned, where there are reserves of new workers coming on to the labour market for the first time. A number of areas of the country have such reserves, in particular of female labour' (Massey, 1984: 144). The factors that differentiate female from male labour, Massey and Meegan suggest, are threefold. First, there are sets of ideological beliefs which give rise to a view of women as having lower levels of skill and capability than men (Massey, 1984: 25, 35, 140, 141). Secondly, there is the sexual division of labour outside the workplace, especially the greater responsibility for paid work and its restrictions on daily mobility. Finally, there is the fact that women receive less support than men do from trade unions (Massey, 1984: 141).

A final aspect of the treatment of gender in the restructuring thesis concerns the significance of occupational segregation by sex. Massey and Meegan (1982) suggest that changes in the female activity rates are linked to changes in the availability of jobs which have been sex-typed as 'female'. While recognising that such sex-stereotyping is a social construction rather than an inherent feature of the work itself, sex-stereotyping is nevertheless treated as constant across time and place in the analysis. This means that increases in the levels of women's employment can be treated as determined by increases in those occupations and industries that have traditionally employed women.

There are several problems with the account of gender provided by the restructuring thesis, which limits its explanations to a concern with particular aspects of women's employment and which fails to go beyond that to look at gender *relations*. First, the account given of gender relations in the restructuring approach is unduly static. It cannot, for instance, explain the very significant spatial differentiation in the female participation rate which has existed in the past in the UK and which still exists within the European (and indeed within international) labour markets. The restructuring thesis would need to explain this by changes in capitalist relations and by the search for spatial advantage. But for the UK it is unclear why capital has not attempted to use reserves of female labour in the past, nor why there have been such marked variations in the use of female labour in different places. Historical evidence shows that the late twentieth century is by no means the first period in which women have entered capitalist social relations, and that women have laboured in different places and at different times under different sets of patriarchal and capitalist relations and with different degrees of fit between the two sets of relations (Mark-Lawson and Witz, 1988). Savage (1987a), for instance, showed that local forms of gender relations have significant effect on local forms of collective action.

Secondly, the approach to gender taken by the restructuring thesis treats the sex-typing of occupations as fixed, overlooking the intense struggles that have taken place in the past over whether men or women fill particular occupational slots (Cockburn, 1983; Walby, 1986b; Witz, 1988). Such struggles constitute a significant part of the restructuring process; indeed, in spatial terms, where employers have attempted to redefine the sex-typing of occupations (as Massey herself shows), this has often involved spatial relocation of functions in order to avoid conflict.

Thirdly, it is worth pointing out that Massey's account rests on an assumption that women do work that is semi- or unskilled, reflecting the focus on manufacturing industry in this account. In the next chapter we discuss the general problems faced by the restructuring thesis because of its focus on manufacturing industry. Here let us just note that the work which employs nearly half of all women workers – namely, clerical work – is entirely absent from these accounts. What is significant here is not whether clerical work is 'skilled' but the fact that it has a completely different spatial distribution from semi- and unskilled manual work (Walby, 1986b).

Finally, the concept of women as a reserve army of labour is fundamentally flawed; indeed, arguments about women as a reserve army have now been more or less abandoned (for a refutation see Walby, 1986b: 74–80). Women do not 'flow' on to the labour market when there are shortages, precisely because of pre-existing segmentation by gender in both local and national labour markets. As Walby has argued elsewhere:

> [a] model of a neat fit between the interests of capitalists and men underlies many of the discussions on the use of women as a reserve army of labour . . . this position underestimates the conflict between patriarchy and the capitalist mode of production and presents an inaccurate picture of historical stasis. Rather, the relations between patriarchy and capital should be seen as historically and spatially variable and riddled with conflict. (1985: 162)

It is only once gender is treated as a set of social relations that are spatially and historically varied that analysis can turn to shifts in patriarchal relations which alter the forms and relations under which women labour, both in the household and in the workplace. These shifts constitute the core of social restructuring.

In the above account we have concentrated on the approach taken by the restructuring thesis to gender, precisely because those authors discussed are relatively unusual in paying attention to this aspect of social change. Debates on flexibility and post-Fordism, as Table 2.1 shows, have almost entirely ignored relations of gender and race. Yet there is an apparent paradox in the attempts of employers to improve the flexibility of labour, a paradox in which gender relations are centrally implicated. One of the motivations behind a move towards flexibility is the removal of labour market rigidities that impede the efficient utilisation of labour. Occupational segregation by sex constitutes a significant labour market rigidity in the UK (Hakim, 1979). Looking at the degree of segregation at socio-economic group level, we see that such segregation increased between 1971 and 1981. In 1981 more men were working in SEGs that were at least 90 per cent male and more women in SEGs that were 70 per cent or more female than was the case in 1971 (Bagguley and Walby, 1988: 26–37).

What this highlights is the contradiction between the two major forms of flexibility. Numerical flexibility, with its heavy emphasis on the use of part-time females, has been highly significant in its increase over the last twenty years or so. Yet this increase would appear to have been accompanied by a parallel increase in occupational segregation and hence a deepening of labour market rigidities which prevent full functional flexibility from developing. Functional flexibility is designed to remove demarcation and hence segmentation. This form of flexibility has been applied largely to those groups of workers who, in the past, have been most successful at imposing demarcation within the workplace – that is, skilled craft workers, who are usually male. Functional flexibility has not led to a loosening of sex-typing of occupations, nor has it removed demarcation by sex. This is not surprising when we consider that, in the UK at least, women have been unsuccessful in using trade union organisations to pursue favourable demarcation strategies. Furthermore, companies have often had to manage the change to functional flexibility, where it has been introduced, in a highly circumspect way, offering benefits to those male workers affected by the changes. It has been highly unlikely that attempts would simultaneously be made to break down traditional gender segregation.

It is worth pointing out, moreover, that the jobs women fill are often already functionally flexible – which is exactly the reason why they are so often treated as 'unskilled'. The history of demarcation, which was often partly a strategy to keep women out of particular occupations, would not lead us to expect that women would be experiencing functional flexibility. Pre-existing gender relations and patriarchal forms of control over labour make functional flexibility for women's occupations, as a managerial strategy, unnecessary.

Restructuring Restructured

The previous discussion has identified a number of significant theoretical developments in the literature on restructuring. Such developments included a diversity of forms of restructuring, and the importance of 'labour' and the ways in which specific regions or localities are reorganised in terms of rounds of restructuring – the 'geological metaphor'. At the same time we identified some difficulties with the literature: a neglect of those social forces affecting 'restructuring processes' that are not reducible to 'capital', such as social relations of gender and race; a tendency towards pseudo-concrete analysis which takes insufficient account of the multitude of possible strategies that could be pursued, and tends to exaggerate some tendencies (for example, flexibility); a neglect of services (which we will discuss in the next chapter); and a tendency to economic and technological reductionism (considered further in Chapters 5 and 6).

One reason for these difficulties for our analysis is the variety of different analytical objectives we wish to achieve (and which differ from the objectives of much of the literature examined). Our aim is to seek, first, to explain changes in the pattern of location of a given sector, as a partly unintended outcome of the various strategies that firms adopt in the pursuit of accumulation, especially those with effects on, or caused by, available categories of labour – that is, the class, gender and racial composition of various segments of the total available labour force.

Secondly, we wish to describe and explain how or why given firms choose a particular restructuring strategy. For this there is no general answer, but a grammar of options, whereby we can express the constraints operating in particular circumstances that predispose firms to choose from among those options. This implies that we generate a typology of the most important restructuring processes and their constraints. The key constraints that we wish to emphasise are struggles between groups and resistance of social groups – that is, *resistance* of labour in general, trade unions, informal workgroups and local communities. *Capacity for resistance* is determined by the nature of relationships between (1) groups within labour – unions versus non-union, men versus women, white versus black, white-collar versus blue-collar – and between (2) labour and capital, particularly the intersection with the control element (factory regime) of managerial strategies, and (3) the state, capital and labour.

Thirdly, we are concerned to describe and explain the consequences of current strategies of industrial restructuring for class, gender and race within given places. Finally, we aim to describe and explain how the labour force in a given locality, region or nation is restructured. This in part depends not just upon capitalist forces and the strategies pursued by firms and within industries, but also upon labour and the state and upon struggles *between* genders and races – a process that we will term 'social restructuring'.

Bearing these partly contradictory objectives in mind, we will now set out a number of minimal theoretical propositions. Industrial restructuring is best understood as the outcome of managerial strategies pursued to improve accumulation, and results from competition between capitals. This is a fairly permanent condition, but it is enhanced at times of economic crisis – of the individual firm, the industry, the national economy or the regime of accumulation. Such strategies arise in particular economic, social and political environments, which include the firm's competitive location in the sector; its level of technology; its industrial relations; the labour market conditions; the intersection of wider social structures of class, patriarchy and racism – that is, 'social restructuring'; state policy/legislation, and so on.

There are three main sets of possibilities which influence the strategy employed by a particular firm: technical change, reorganising production and spatial relocation. The factors mentioned above determine the relative strength of these possibilities.

Central to the 'restructuring thesis' is the claim that the labour factor is particularly important to industrial location. However, labour is conceived of 'abstractly', as an abstract category counterposed to capital. Labour should be viewed, rather, as fragmented, comprising different sets of collective agents who may pursue different objectives and have conflicting interests. Fragmentation by class is an obvious example, but other equally important social relations are patriarchal social relations by which men benefit, directly or indirectly and to a greater or lesser extent, from the subordination of women. Such relations are in part sustained by a variety of forms of closure, and are challenged by attempts at usurpation. Social relations between ethnic groups may also involve closure and attempted usurpation (Witz, 1988).

Distinguishing between industrial restructuring as a strategy pursued by a given firm following a logic of accumulation, and the restructuring of a given sector which is a partially unintended outcome of an exceptionally diverse range of determinants (including again the processes of social restructuring) is an essential first step. In relationship to gender, for instance, the principal form taken by patriarchal relations within the sphere of production is that of occupational segregation. Such segregation is the outcome of social struggle between men and women organised around interests which are not reducible to the logic of capital accumulation. The observable empirical outcome within a given industrial sector will, hence, reflect interests, struggles and collective agents which significantly constrain and channel the attempts by firms to pursue competitive advantage.

It is possible to identify patterns in the industrial restructuring of manufacturing which are empirically common and which derive from the three sets of possibilities outlined earlier:

Technical Change
1   Investment and technical change: heavy capital investment with new means of production and sometimes new products, at times resulting in considerable job loss, highly unequally distributed through space. Technical change can be minimally classified into the following forms:
(a)   product innovation;
(b)   innovation in the processes of production;
(c)   conventional technical change: for example, the introduction of traditional mechanisation;
(d)   advanced technical change involving the use of microelectronics, for example.

Production Reorganisation
2   Intensification: increases in labour productivity through managerial or organisational change, with little or no new investment or loss of capacity.
3   Rationalisation: closure of capacity with little or no new investment or new technology.
4   Flexibilisation: so that the supply of labour can be closely tied to the volatility of demand – which can take two forms:
(a)   functional flexibility where job demarcations are weakened or dissolved;
(b)   numerical flexibility where the amount of labour time is varied on a daily, weekly or longer-term basis.

Spatial Relocation
5   On a 'decentralised' pattern: moving into areas where labour/ property/land is cheaper both within and between nation states. In the case of labour this may result from enduring patterns of occupational segregation.
6   On a 'concentrated' pattern: the spatial centralisation of companies, particularly because of the attraction of other compan-

ies that are vertically and/or horizontally disintegrated. This involves vertical and horizontal disintegration: subcontracting elements of the labour process to firms providing specialised products or components, thereby distancing the cash and risks involved.

In order to examine the effects of industrial restructuring patterns within a given region or locality, it is necessary to consider (1) that there is a much wider range of possible forms (at least six general types, rather than two or three in the case of manufacturing) than most writers have countenanced; (2) that these forms result from a set of determinants of 'social restructuring' which may itself be spatially variable; and (3) that the effects on and within the region or locality are the complex, unintended outcome of a whole set of struggles between collective agents, some within interests unconnected with strategies of accumulation.

Deindustrialising Lancaster

Now we shall apply the arguments developed in the previous section to an analysis of the deindustrialisation of Lancaster's economy. We begin by providing an overview of sectoral changes in employment, before moving on to case studies of particular industries where we shall draw out the interactions of the various processes of restructuring.

The core manufacturing sectors of the Lancaster economy were laid down as follows. During the mid-nineteenth century the major oilcloth producers (manufacturing linoleum and table baize) developed, and the local economy quickly became dependent on them for employment. This labour market dependence was the material basis for the peculiar quiescence of labour in Lancaster (Warde, 1989). The middle years of the twentieth century saw further major rounds of investment in textiles (specifically artificial fibres) and chemicals. During the 1960s, when the older sectors began their precipitous decline, further new investment occurred in clothing and footwear, employing many more women in direct production than the older sectors had.

The early 1980s saw the most rapid sectoral change in employment in Lancaster (see Table 2.2). In the three years 1981–4 the decline in manufacturing employment was twice as fast as during the previous ten years. The particular plant closures and forms of restructuring involved in this are discussed below. In complete contrast, the construction and utilities sector grew almost twice as

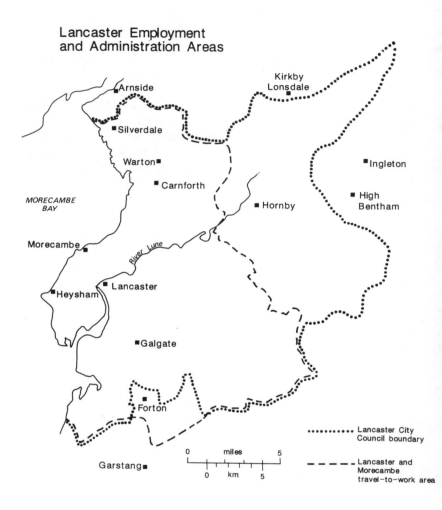

Figure 2.1   *Lancaster employment and administration areas*

fast during the 1981–4 period, compared to the 1970s. This is largely due to the impact of the construction of the Heysham nuclear power complex, and to a lesser degree to the development of the Morecambe Bay gas field base. The primary sector of employment resumed growth, albeit from a very low base, during the 1980s, and the service sector experienced continued growth in financial services, hotels and catering, in retailing and in the health sector.

Table 2.2   *Lancaster: total employment by sector, and percentage changes in employment by sector 1971–81 and 1981–4*[1]

	1971		1981		Change 1971–81
	No.	%	No.	%	%
Primary	1,092	2.6	852	1.9	−22
Manufacturing	11,227	26.4	9,640	21.8	−14
Construction and utilities	3,437	8.1	4,487	10.1	31
Services	26,848	63.0	29,258	66.1	9
Total	42,604	100.0	44,237	100.0	4

	1981		1984		Change 1981–4
	No.	%	No.	%	%
Primary	746	1.8	790	1.8	6
Manufacturing	9,094	21.4	6,549	14.8	−28
Construction and utilities	4,380	10.3	6,770	15.3	55
Services	28,328	66.6	30,053[2]	68.1	6
Total	42,548	100.0	44,162	100.0	4

[1]The data for 1971–81 use 1968 Standard Industrial Classification, those for 1981–4 the 1980 SIC, hence the discrepancies in figures for 1981.

[2]The 1984 Census of Employment failed to cover one of the largest public sector service employers in Lancaster and indeed the whole of Lancashire. We have corrected the service sector data for 1984, using our own information from the employer concerned. Other users of the 1984 Census of Employment should note that the problem applies to Lancashire as a whole (Lancashire County Planning Department, 1988).

Source: NOMIS, Census of Employment

The sectors that have been centrally involved in the deindustrialis-ation of employment in Lancaster have been chemicals, textiles (mainly the production of man-made fibres) and linoleum pro-duction. In 1961 these sectors accounted for over 80 per cent of all manufacturing employment in Lancaster; by 1984 they accounted for 35 per cent (see Tables 2.3 and 2.4). Textiles and chemicals have all but disappeared, and the remnants of the linoleum firms produce various kinds of plastic-coated rubber products, as well as wallpapers.

Table 2.3   *Manufacturing employment by sector, Lancaster TTWA and Great Britain, 1971–81*

Sectors		1971 No.	%	1981 No.	%	Change %
Order[1] III	Lancaster	416	4	216	2	−48.1
Food, drink and tobacco	GB (000s)	743	9	630	11	−15.2
Orders IV–V	Lancaster	1,336	12	385	4	−71.2
Chemicals	GB (000s)	480	6	430	7	−10.4
Orders VI–XII	Lancaster	1,121	10	1,935	22	72.6
Metals and engineering	GB (000s)	4,121	52	3,066	52	−25.6
Order XIX	Lancaster	3,189	28	3,073	35	−3.6
Linoleum etc.	GB (000s)	331	4	251	4	−24.2
Order XIII	Lancaster	3,219	29	901	10	−72.0
Textiles	GB (000s)	582	7	315	5	−45.9
Orders XIV–XV	Lancaster	1,175	10	793	9	−32.5
Clothing and footwear	GB (000s)	476	6	296	5	−37.8
Order XVII	Lancaster	193	2	127	1	−34.2
Timber and furniture	GB (000s)	265	3	216	4	−18.5
Orders XVI and	Lancaster	578	5	1,277	15	120.9
XVIII Miscellaneous	GB (000s)	890	11	723	12	−18.8
Total	Lancaster	11,227	100	8,707	100	−22.4
Manufacturing	GB (000s)	7,888	100	5,927	100	−24.9

[1]Orders of the 1968 Standard Industrial Classification.

Source: NOMIS, Census of Employment

Lancaster deindustrialised relatively early, contrary to what might have been expected given its industrial structure and 'small town' image (Murgatroyd and Urry, 1985). Manufacturing employment in Lancaster declined by over 32 per cent between 1961 and 1971, compared to a decline nationally of just over 10 per cent, but during the 1970s, especially after 1976, it seemed that the fortunes of manufacturing employment in Lancaster were no worse than nationally (Bagguley, 1986a). Some of the large firms responsible for the earlier job losses appeared to have restructured successfully, the ex-linoleum producers for example. Furthermore, during the late 1970s a number of new start-ups in metals and engineering and miscellaneous manufacturing may have been encouraged by Lancaster's assisted-area status and by subcontracting work from the nuclear power complex at Heysham.

Table 2.4   *Manufacturing employment by sector, Lancaster TTWA and Great Britain, 1981–4*

Sectors		1981 No.	%	1984 No.	%	Change %
Category[1] 20	Lancaster	449	5	358	5	−20.3
Food, drink and tobacco	GB (000s)	669	11	587	11	−12.3
Category 10	Lancaster	786	9	675	10	−14.1
Chemicals	GB (000s)	359	6	330	6	−8.1
Categories 8,	Lancaster	2,268	25	1,736	27	−23.5
12–19	GB (000s)	3,124	52	2,629	50	−15.8
Metals and engineering						
Categories 9, 25	Lancaster	3,046	33	1,757	27	−42.3
Other manufacturing	GB (000s)	509	8	498	9	−2.2
Categories 11,	Lancaster	888	10	581	9	−34.6
21	GB (000s)	292	5	247	5	−15.4
Textiles						
Category 22	Lancaster	777	9	595	9	−23.4
Clothing and footwear	GB (000s)	335	6	314	6	−6.3
Category 23	Lancaster	125	1	102	2	−18.4
Timber and furniture	GB (000s)	214	4	206	4	−3.7
Category 24	Lancaster	755	8	745	11	−1.3
Miscellaneous	GB (000s)	509	8	479	9	−5.9
Total	Lancaster	9,094	100	6,549	100	−28.0
Manufacturing	GB (000s)	6,011	100	5,290	100	−12.0

[1]Categories of the 1980 Standard Industrial Classification.

Source: NOMIS, Census of Employment

However, during the early 1980s deindustrialisation and job loss in manufacturing returned to Lancaster with a vengeance. Between 1981 and 1984 employment declined in the manufacturing sector more than twice as much as nationally. With the exception of the 'miscellaneous' category, employment in each of the sectors declined in Lancaster *between twice and twenty times* as much as was the case in the rest of the country. The further decline in the fortunes of the 'other manufacturing' category of former lino firms and a variety of late-1970s new start-ups account for much of this decline.

In complete contrast to the collapse of employment in mar ˍfac-
turing, the number of production firms in Lancaster rapidly
increased in the 1980s – at a rate twice that found nationally – by
31.8 per cent (see Table 2.5, based on VAT registrations). The
table also shows, though, that production sector firms remain a
smaller proportion of the total in Lancaster than nationally, and
the overall growth in registrations in Lancaster is lower than is
found in the rest of the country. Local economic intervention by the
City Council played some role in this, by focusing on encouraging
indigenous small firms (Urry, 1987a). However, the extensive
redundancies and the new opportunities offered by subcontracted
work for the nuclear power and offshore gas and oil industries have
also played a part.

Table 2.5   *VAT registrations in production sector and all
registrations, Lancaster District and Great Britain, 1980–5*

	1980		1985		Change
	No.	%	No.	%	%
LD					
Production	148	4.9	195	6.1	31.8
Total	3,021	100	3,205	100	6.1
GB					
Production	120,964	9.3	138,157	11.1	14.2
Total	1,287,918	100	1,426,900	100	10.8

Source: Business Statistics Office

We will now provide a brief account of the industrial restructuring of the three sectors which have experienced dramatic falls in
employment in the local manufacturing economy: floor and wall
coverings, textiles and clothing, and footwear (see Murgatroyd and
Urry (1985) for an account of chemicals). We shall consider services
in more detail in the following chapter. Underlying the deceptively
simple changes in the sectoral composition of the local labour
market are sets of diverse processes of restructuring which, we will
show, combine concretely in quite complex ways with local relations
of gender and race.

Floor and Wall Coverings
The largest employers in Lancaster since the nineteenth century
have been those producing linoleum (Williamsons) and oilcloths
(Storeys). This sector, along with rubber and plastics production,
is classified under 'other manufacturing' in the 1968 Standard Industrial Classification (SIC) while the firms themselves now produce
plastic-coated products. These factors, alongside the development

of several small rubber and plastics companies in the area during the 1970s, make the interpretation of employment data difficult.

Much of the 1960s deindustrialisation in Lancaster took place as a consequence of decline in this sector, with employment falling by some 2000. Table 2.3 shows that the 1970s were a period of relative stability, with a decline of only 3.6 per cent compared to a national decline of over 24 per cent between 1971 and 1981. However, the experience of the early 1980s was a total reversal of this situation, with employment in Lancaster declining a phenomenal *twenty times* the rate of the national decline.

Two major companies had dominated this sector since the nineteenth century – Williamsons (now Nairns) and Storeys (now part of Wardle Storeys). Both were formed in the mid-nineteenth century to produce oilcloths and, later, linoleum. In the late 1940s and early 1950s Storeys restructured successfully into the production of PVC plastic-coated products, while Williamsons continued the production of linoleum (Christie, 1964: 203–7).

During the 1950s Storeys changed their products and processes dramatically, pursuing a strategy of intensification and technical change. A new twenty-four-hour, seven-day shift work system was introduced, and the new strategies were reflected in an employment decline in the sector of 37 per cent for men and 45 per cent for women. Women textile workers were particularly badly hit. Concentrated in the spinning and weaving of cotton backing fabrics for lino, a process which became redundant with the move to PVC products, the female-employing cotton spinning and weaving plant was gradually closed down. The textile sector in Lancaster generally suffered a decline in employment between 1961 and 1971, with women's employment declining by 66 per cent and men's by 30 per cent. Hence a sector that had traditionally provided skilled manufacturing work for women all but disappeared in the period.

These events in Lancaster illustrate the importance of considering restructuring in relation to gender. Women's segregation into certain types of work in this sector, combined with legislation restricting their hours of work, meant that the processes of restructuring led to women being expelled from the industry. In terms of our typology of restructuring outlined above, this sector experienced both product and production process forms of technical change. Products, in particular, were highly advanced technically for this sector in relation to international competitors. Given that Storeys were such a technically advanced and dynamic firm during the 1960s, why did the subsequent collapse occur? The company hardly fits the stereotype of the ageing backward British manufacturer.

Storeys were taken over by the Manchester-based firm of Turner and Newall in 1977 after a slump in profits of over 30 per cent. By the early 1980s, when Storeys employed around 1200 people in Lancaster, there had been several rounds of redundancies, and a £4 million loss was made in 1980–1. From interviews with management and newspaper reports there appears to have been a collapse in demand in the early 1980s. Rationalisation was the main strategy pursued to reduce costs – by reducing stocks, cutting out shifts and, finally, after a string of redundancies, by closing the largest of the three sites in Lancaster.

The owners of Storeys, Turner and Newall, experienced a major profitability crisis in the early 1980s. In the first six months of 1982 they suffered a pre-tax loss of £4.5 million on sales of £329 million, compared to a pre-tax profit of £8.5 million on sales of £303 million in the same period of 1981 (*Financial Times*, 10.12.82). The value of their shares collapsed, falling by 56 per cent during 1982 (*Financial Times*, 23.12.82). Their response to this crisis was to dispose of unprofitable subsidiaries. As one of these, at the time making an annual loss of £2 million a year, Storeys was sold to Wardles, a company manufacturing similar products at Earby in East Lancashire.

When the market for linoleum collapsed in the early 1960s, the other major employer in this sector, Williamsons, was forced into a merger with its major rival, Nairns of Kirkcaldy, and a series of redundancies followed (Martin and Fryer, 1973; Murgatroyd and Urry, 1985). The company also pursued a strategy of diversification, producing vinyl-coated wallpaper, plastic floor coverings, knitted and tufted fabrics and paper-backed carpets for export, although the latter two products had disappeared by 1980. Nairns, as the company had become known, was acquired in 1975 by the multinational, Unilever. By 1982 the company employed only 630 staff, and further contraction followed a decline in export markets. In May 1985 the company (now down to 550 employees) was sold to a Swiss-based chemicals multinational.

The main factor underlying changes in employment in the linoleum sector in Lancaster has been rationalisation and technical change in product and process innovation. The most successful response on the part of the companies has been diversification. Now this seems to imply the first of Piore and Sabel's forms of flexible specialisation, that of large corporations producing a more diverse range of products. Such diversification has been facilitated by the fact that the plant in this sector has always been sufficiently flexible to produce a diverse range of general products. It is simply a matter of changing the inks and patterns for printing. However, this product market strategy has not been accompanied by the development of multi-skilled flexible work in the labour process. Work is still largely semi-skilled, with employees still specialising on one or two machines. Companies in this sector have flirted with participation schemes such as 'quality circles', and are considering flexibility in the area of maintenance crafts. However, interviews with management suggest no clear indication of a more general managerial strategy of decentralisation of authority and job flexibilisation.

Textiles
Employment in Lancaster's textile sector saw a dramatic decline between 1961 and 1981, with the loss of almost 5000 jobs, and in the early 1980s a further 300 jobs were lost. Textiles made up over 35 per cent of local manufacturing employment in 1961, but by 1984 it accounted for only 7 per cent. The major employer in Lancaster textiles was a large integrated producer of man-made fibres which located in the area during the 1920s.

The restructuring of this sector in Lancaster has had a highly uneven impact on men's and women's employment. The latter declined much more rapidly and earlier than that of men (66.7 per cent compared to 30 per cent between 1961 and 1971). As a result, an increasing proportion of the workforce was male. A major part of this shift in the gender composition of the weaving sector in Lancaster took place in the early 1970s. Whilst women's full-time employment declined by 16.8 per cent between 1971 and 1976, men's full-time employment *increased* by 163 per cent. Furthermore, women's part-time employment in this sector disappeared in the early 1970s. This is largely attributable to changes in the patterns of shift work in weaving, which involved employers seeking numerical flexibility by introducing night shifts for men to replace women's part-time employment (Bagguley, 1986a).

The decline in the production of man-made fibres accounted for the loss of some 2000 jobs in Lancaster during the 1970s. Between 1971 and 1981 50 per cent of employment in man-made fibres in Lancaster was lost. The Lansil plant had originally been constructed by the Cellulose Acetate Co. Ltd in 1928, and in 1962 it was acquired by the Canadian-based multinational, Monsanto, through its subsidiary, Chemstrand Ltd (Murgatroyd and Urry, 1985). In 1973–4 Courtaulds took over the plant, reputedly after pressure had been put on central government by local politicians in the midst of rumours that Monsanto was considering the closure of the plant. With the recent large-scale redundancies in the linoleum industry (Martin and Fryer, 1973), the decline of traditional manufacturing industry had become a significant political issue in Lancaster. Part of the take-over deal that had attracted Courtaulds (according to former managers of Lansils) was the 40 per cent capital grant that became available for re-equipping the plant as a result of the intermediate development-area status of Lancaster at the time.

According to the former management, the new equipment introduced during the mid-1970s at Lansils by Courtaulds had a dramatic effect on employment levels. In the spinning sheds, for example, before the introduction of the new machinery there used to be a hundred men per shift producing 10-ounce bobbins. Afterwards, fifteen men per shift produced 4-kilo bobbins. In some instances the new technology eradicated the need for whole sections of the workforce. The Lancaster careers officer recalls placing about ten 'boys' each year with Lansils in the early 1970s, to file down the 'burrs' of aluminium that bunched up at the edge of the bobbins as the yarn was wound on. In the mid-1970s a machine was installed that performed the same task automatically. Much of this investment in conventional technical change in the production process took place in the spinning sheds. The restructuring of the Lancaster textile industry through technical change, giving rise to heavy job loss, reflects the fortunes of that industry nationally. Dicken shows that most of the job losses in the UK textile industry during the 1970s were due to changes in labour productivity through technical change (1986: 251).

Lansils closed in the autumn of 1980. Courtaulds claimed that it had to rationalise because of overcapacity and that the Lancaster plant could not compete with Courtaulds' similar plant at Spondon in Derby. After closure, some of the more modern machinery from Lancaster was transferred to the Derby site. In textiles, then, it seems that the major process underlying changes in employment has been rationalisation and technical change.

A management buy-out of parts of Courtaulds now employs around a hundred and fifty people. Here the management talk of a 'new realism' in industrial relations. However, their description of full 'functional flexibility' in terms of 'people doing what needs doing' does not fit easily their description of the rigid segregation of shifts and labour processes by race and gender. For example, their warping process in the mid-1980s was staffed by 80 per cent women on day shifts. The three-shift knitting processes were all male and 30 per cent Asian. Furthermore, one young Asian man referred to by management was working in the warping area, but wanted to transfer to knitting to be 'back with his mates'.

Flexibility in this company seemed to be constrained in its everyday practices by gender and racial segregation in the workforce.

Informal workplace solidarities continued to limit managerial discretion, despite the 'new realism' in industrial relations. In terms of market strategy the company clearly seemed to pursue a flexible specialisation strategy, producing some eighty different products and introducing two or three new ones each week. Like the other examples of flexible product market strategies that we have been discussing, this is an instance of product differentiation rather than diversification. In another sense, flexibility here might simply be a function of size. Since there are relatively few maintenance workers, is it really surprising that production workers should do some maintenance and that craftworkers should be multi-skilled?

Clothing and Footwear
The clothing and footwear sector was an important source of employment for women in the manufacturing sector in Lancaster during the 1960s and 1970s, employing in 1971 more women than any other manufacturing sector in Lancaster. Total employment there increased by over 61 per cent between 1961 and 1971, but during the 1970s and 1980s the sector went into steep decline, and reductions in employment were much greater in Lancaster than in the country as a whole.

Footwear production expanded in Lancaster during the 1950s, whereas clothing manufacture expanded principally during the 1960s. The subsequent declines in employment were apparently due to rationalisation and the bankruptcy of firms, as international competition intensified during the late 1970s and early 1980s (Bagguley, 1986a: 34–9). However, this rationalisation has had profoundly uneven effects on the workforces. Women's part-time employment declined much faster than the full-time employment of both men and women. Between 1981 and 1984 women's part-time employment declined more than twice as much as women's full-time employment in Lancaster.

In one clothing company part-time employment was simply 'phased out' through natural wastage, with the rise in unemployment and intensifying competition (interview with management, 1987). In contrast to the 1960s when the company used part-time employment, nurseries and a playgroup to ensure that women could be attracted into work, overtime became used more frequently to meet specific customer demands. This company pursued a 'flexible specialisation' strategy in relation to market demands. The market was described as sophisticated and highly competitive, and the company aimed to provide whatever customers demanded. The company specialised in customised company uniforms which are short-run one-off products. Here production was 'driven' by market demands, but it would be misleading to describe it, according to Atkinson's criteria, as a 'flexible firm', or as a full-blown flexible specialist, as described by Piore and Sabel.

The company retained very traditional clothing sector management practices, with what they described as a 'traditional' authority structure – no semi-autonomous work groups here – and conventional industrial relations and productivity pay structures. Functional flexibility and multi-skilling did not mean much to this company; the flexibility lay in product range design and use of machinery, whilst work practices were those traditional to the clothing sector. What this history of workplace nurseries and part-time employment exemplifies is the importance of domestic and workplace gender relations in shaping managements' numerical flexibility strategies.

Another clothing company in Lancaster was, in comparison, rather inflexible in terms of its product range. This company was dependent on one large retail chain for buying its products, and so was competing with a range of regular subcontractors rather than a niche market. The aim for this company was stability and long-term planning. A wide and varying range of designs of the same basic products was produced with modern versions of the traditional sewing machines. The 'stability' of having one main buyer meant that there was little demand for numerical flexibility, with only a few, stable, part-time women employees. Men, in contrast, worked on the knitting side of the business on a shift system.

In footwear the decline in levels of employment since the late 1970s was principally attributed by management to a decline in orders, with total employment declining by almost half in the early 1980s. One firm interviewed in the mid-1980s had pursued a strategy of functional flexibility through multi-skilling amongst its women machinists. As one manager put it, 'We used to be flexibile within reason, but now we're very flexible.' This refers to the women's machinist grades A to C (from most to least skilled). Grade A workers are trained on all machines in the section. The varying detail in the product requires task flexibility, in that skilled workers occasionally worked on less skilled jobs. Initially there were some 'trade union gripes' about grade A workers doing less skilled work, but now 'people feel flexibility keeps their jobs secure', according to management (interview with management, 1987). There are only two part-time employees, since none were taken on during the long period of natural wastage. In this instance functional flexibility has followed substantial cutbacks in the workforce, and involves highly skilled employees working on less skilled tasks, rather than multi-skilling around the same level.

In the clothing and footwear sector of Lancaster the decline in employment has been due principally to rationalisation. Subsequent moves to flexibility have concentrated, on the one hand, on product market flexibility with little consequence for major restructuring of the labour process, and, on the other, on downward functional flexibility utilising an already existing skill structure. All firms have shown a decline in numerical flexibility in the form of part-time employment because of the way in which redundancies have been implemented and the move to overtime working. Flexibility in this sector is by no means a 'revolution', frequently involving as it does only the evolution of earlier 'traditions' of work organisation. Furthermore, it is clear that gender relations significantly influence both the form of flexibility (part-time work for women, shifts for men) and the boundaries of functional flexibility. *We found no instances of workers being functionally flexible across the boundaries of sex-typed occupational groups.*

Conclusion

Restructuring theory has contributed major advances over previous attempts to explain economic change and industrial location, primarily by identifying underlying causal processes and considering the significance of labour and its conflict with capital. We have identified several variants of this theory, from the classic statements by Massey to the recent debates on flexibility, where writers draw on the labour process literature and debate the role of the market, 'consumption', institutions and management in the move from 'Fordism' to 'post-Fordism'.

A number of problems were identified as common to all these writers. In particular, they largely ignore gender relations and so fail to deal with one of the single most important forms of employment change in the postwar West. The recomposition of the labour force, with women now making up nearly half of the paid workforce, is a most dramatic shift in the social relations of employment in this period. The refusal of most previous accounts to describe or explain such changes also leads to an inability to understand the shifting relationship between a divided workforce and capital. We have argued that in addition to the relation between capital and labour we must analyse patriarchal relations, and indeed those of ethnicity. We have developed a number of arguments concerning restructuring, distinguishing between its industrial and social forms. Within the former we have considered a variety of different forms that could be taken, and in the last section of the chapter we have analysed changes in the local Lancaster economy in terms of these various distinctions.

A further major problem with the restructuring literature is its overconcentration on the manufacturing sector at the expense of services. Manufacturing has been treated not only as the empirical site of the substantive studies, but as the source of determination of the whole economy – and, indeed, in some accounts, of the whole society. Yet manufacturing now employs far fewer people than the service sector. In the next chapter we will deal with the complex problems of the analysis of services.

3

The Restructuring of Services

The Growth of Services

It is common in much social science to assume that the analysis of service industries and occupations is relatively unimportant. This argument is based on one or more of the following claims: that services have been relatively insignificant in the historical development of most major societies; that their pattern of development is fairly simple to explain, since it derives from the logic of manufacturing industry; that service activities do not need much investigation of their constitutive social relations, since they do not result in important economic, social or political outcomes (unlike the predominantly male manufacturing industry); or that the investigation of service industries and occupations can be pursued simply by taking over modes of analysis developed to investigate manufacturing industry.

In this chapter we shall maintain that none of these claims is justifiable, and that one way to counter them is to begin to construct a sociology and geography of service activities. We shall concentrate in particular on the various forms in which different service industries may be socio-spatially reorganised, which is dependent in part on the important character of the service delivery to the consumer. The forms of restructuring occurring within different industries have important consequences upon the demand for different kinds of labour and upon the resulting balance of class and gender relations. Many of these forms of restructuring are spatially uneven in their impact, so the resulting local social structures will vary geographically, often in quite distinctive ways.

Considerable variation exists in the local patterning of labour markets – different occupations; different gender, racial and generational mixes; different types and levels of skill, and so on. What are important to many such locally specific labour markets are the diverse types not of manufacturing but of *service* employment, which accounts for around two thirds of employment in most local labour markets. Moreover, by 1981 services accounted for 63 per cent of the GDP of the USA and 55 per cent of the GDP of the

UK (Clairmonte and Cavanagh, 1984: 219; *Economic Trends*, Feb. 1986, No. 388: 29). However, we will not adopt a straightforward 'post-industrial' society thesis. In terms of *output* and international *trade*, manufacturing remains at a world level of profound importance – so important, indeed, that a recent report suggested that rather than entering a *post*-industrial age we are entering a *hyper*-industrial epoch (FAST, 1986: 32). According to Cohen and Zysman (1987), 'manufacturing matters'. Rather than shifting out of industry into services, we are moving from one kind of industrial economy to another, because much high-wage service work depends upon domestically based manufacturing employment.

However, there is no doubt that in terms of *employment* in local labour markets much of the First World is dependent upon services. In order to discuss this adequately, some preliminary distinctions need to be made. We will distinguish between service industry – in which the final product is a commodity which is in part, at least, immaterial or intangible; service occupations – forms of labour that do not involve manual work; and service functions – the specific uses that consumers derive from the outputs of both service and non-service industries (Gershuny and Miles, 1983). We will now analyse some problems involved in explaining the growth of service industry, by considering Gershuny and Miles's explanation in terms of five interconnected sets of processes (1983; Gershuny, 1986; Petit, 1986; Urry, 1987c):

1 'Engel's Law', whereby increasing wealth leads to proportionately lower demand for 'basic' goods and increasing demand for progressively more sophisticated service functions, changes;
2 'social innovation' changes, through the provision of services to households and through increased self-servicing by households;
3 'intermediate subcontracting' changes, in which activities which were (or might have been) part of the production process within one industry are subcontracted to intermediate producer service industries;
4 'productivity gap' (and hence price gap) changes, consequent upon low productivity growth and comparatively fast relative price increases in many final service industries, resulting from high labour input;
5 'occupational' changes in the employment structure within industries, which reduce the proportion of manual workers in the labour force. (Gershuny and Miles, 1983; and see Gershuny, 1986)

Gershuny and Miles suggest that much of the past growth in output (and employment) involved that part of the service sector which provides not final but intermediate services for producers, and that it is here that the best prospect for future growth, also, lies. The ten minimum list headings (MLHs) of non-public services in the United Kingdom to record the largest proportionate increases in employment between 1959 and 1981 are given in Table 3.1. Apart from 'other miscellaneous services', 'sport and recreation' and 'air transport', all the remaining fastest-growing sectors can be classified as 'producer services'. More recently (1981–4), however, many of the fastest-growing service sectors have been consumer-related, providing services for final consumers: a 73 per cent increase in employment in 'other tourism', a 29 per cent increase in 'renting consumer goods' and a 23 per cent increase in 'retailing footwear' (Marshall, 1988: 51).

Table 3.1 *The ten fastest-growing non-public service industries, 1959–81*

SIC[1]	Service	Increase 1959–81 %	SIC[1]	Service	Increase 1959–81 %
865	Other business services	332	882	Sport and recreation	122
899	Other miscellaneous services	193	864	Advertising	122
			862	Other finance	116
709	Miscellaneous transport	156	861	Banking	110
707	Air transport	139	879	Other professional and scientific services	83
863	Property	126			

[1]1968 Standard Industrial Classification.

Source: Marshall, 1985: 1157

This work by Gershuny and Miles is the most sophisticated contribution so far to our understanding of service employment change (although see Marshall, 1988, on producer services). Their account is, however, too concerned with relatively superficial determinants of demand and supply. It is insufficiently social, in the sense of ignoring both the *social* relations of capitalist production and the causes and consequences of diverse forms of social struggle. We will now consider two determinants that they ignore.

First, to demonstrate why investment has taken place in service production, it is necessary to consider the relative profitability of different economic activities. During the 1970s there was sharply declining profitability in manufacturing industry. In the UK the pre-tax net rate of return fell from above 20 per cent in 1960 to below 5 per cent in the early 1980s (Martin, 1988: 251). The share of total profits received by financial corporations rose from about

10 per cent in 1968 to nearly 60 per cent in 1980 (Van der Pijl, 1984: 280–2). Marked reductions were also to be found in the rate of profit in manufacturing industry in most of the other major Western countries, especially West Germany (Heap, 1980: 68).

It is also essential to recognise that service industries have become irreducibly internationalised. There are two aspects here: the growth in international trade in services, and the development of transnational service conglomerates. With the former, the proportion of world GDP in services that is exported rose from 7 per cent in 1970 to 11 per cent in 1980 (Clairmonte and Cavanagh, 1984: 224). This mirrors what has happened in the case of all goods and services where the proportion of exports rose over the same period from 16 per cent to 27 per cent (Clairmonte and Cavanagh, 1984). Not all countries, though, have shared in this increase in international trade in services. In 1981 the USA accounted for 20 per cent of all service exports, with the UK, France and Belgium accounting for a further 30 per cent. Countries that show a positive balance on service trade are the USA, the UK and Switzerland. Countries showing a negative balance are Canada, Japan and West Germany (Clairmonte and Cavanagh, 1984: 223–5).

There has also been a quite marked growth of transnational conglomerates in a variety of service industries. The single-line company has become much less common, and instead have developed large transnational corporations that deal in a wide variety of industries, sometimes involving a mix of services and manufacturing. We will very briefly note the difference between accountancy and tourist-related companies in this regard.

In the case of accountancy, there has indeed been a marked internationalisation. In the past decade or two a series of mergers has taken place which have created new, powerful Anglo-American firms (Leyshon et al., 1987). The total number of overseas offices operated by the leading twenty UK firms increased from 2000 to almost 4500 between 1975 and 1985 (Leyshon et al., 1987: 13–15). For example, Touche Ross International had in 1985 26,000 employees in 463 offices in a staggering ninety countries. However, these large conglomerates have in the main continued to provide essentially accountancy services, albeit with less emphasis upon auditing, and have not taken over or expanded into other non-financially related services. In the tourism/leisure industries, by contrast, a number of enormously powerful international conglomerates have developed, with a wide variety of interests. This has particularly occurred as airlines, especially in the USA after deregulation, have moved into car rentals, hotels, travel agency and holidays. One leading conglomerate in the UK is Grand Metropolitan, whose corporate empire includes retailing, alcohol and hotels, as well as tobacco manufacture (Clairmonte and Cavanagh, 1984: 252).

Gershuny and Miles also fail to analyse the consequences of diverse social struggles on levels of service sector employment. A number of such struggles can be noted here: the organisation of workers into trade unions and later into national confederations of labour, and the resulting counter-organisations of management and employers; the formation of social democratic parties and the pursuit of 'socialism' via the growth of extensive nationally organised institutions providing education, health and welfare services; the political organisation of immigrants, blacks and women seeking to extend citizenship rights via equal rights legislation and welfare provision and by increasing their ability to enter the labour force and hence to structure the patterning of job opportunities; the struggles that those employed in both public and private service institutions engage in to protect and enhance levels of employment, particularly reflected in high rates of public sector unionism; the changing relationship between production-based and consumption-based struggles, with the heightened importance of the latter and hence of diverse institutions involved in providing final services to consumers; an increased focus upon the 'household unit', and especially on attempts to extend the scope of individual households through increased self-servicing and by reducing dependence on final services from central agencies; and, finally, the growth of neo-liberalism, opposed to extensive public sector employment and especially to that found in various service sectors.

Thus far we have pointed to two particular determinants of service sector employment which Gershuny and Miles (1983) do not consider. Particularly problematic is their treatment of public service provision. Elsewhere Mark-Lawson et al. (1985), have argued that there are several modes of provision of a 'service function' to a given consumer. In relation to educational provision, childcare, medical attention or leisure provision there are at least five modes of service provision: (1) direct labour within households, especially of wives; (2) the market; (3) neighbourhood informal economy, either directly for money or indirectly for barter; (4) voluntary or charitable institutions; (5) the local or national state. They then show, first, that in interwar Britain it was in women's interests that certain service functions be transferred from (1) and (2) to (5); secondly, that where women were in paid work on a relatively equal fashion with men they were more able to organise in order to bring this about; thirdly, where they did so organise (as in Nelson in Lancashire) this resulted in much greater social welfare expenditure than in places where they were less able to do so, either because there was a very weak (and male-dominated) Labour movement (Lancaster) or a male-dominated, if strong, Labour movement (Preston); and, finally, that in places with a few employers able to dominate social and political life there was some shift from (1) and (2) to (4), as in Lancaster (as we show below). In at least some cases, higher welfare expenditure will have resulted in increased levels of public employment. This shows the complexity of the forces that account for the particular level of service provision in a locality in a given period. However, there is a further issue. These various localised struggles in the interwar period, partly under pressure from well organised women in some local Labour Parties, fed into the creation of a nationally centralised and essentially patriarchal welfare state in Britain in the period immediately after 1945.

We have argued that diverse struggles affect levels of service provision and levels of service employment. Such struggles will also affect the *type* of service sector employment. The political programme of radical Conservatism in the 1980s, which aims to shift service functions from the public to the private mode of delivery, will, *inter alia*, similarly shift service occupations into the sphere of private sector industry, changing the relations of production under which those in such occupations labour. But a further step in the analysis is necessary. It is not sufficient merely to identify the bases or causes of different social forces engaging in struggle; it is also necessary to analyse those processes which *transmute* such forces into structural consequences, into the particular balance between the different modes by which a given service function is met. It is that balance that produces employment consequences with medium-term implications for the trajectory of British societal development and for the place of service sector employment within this.

Services and Restructuring

We have so far talked rather generally of service industries, noting the possible differences between private and public services. However, this is only one basis of classification – there are at least five others. We will now set out various criteria by which the general category of 'services' can be more carefully distinguished:

1   *ownership*: whether the industry is predominantly publicly or predominantly privately owned. Further subdivisions within the 'public' sector in Britain relate to whether the service is organ-

ised nationally or subnationally, and whether it is subject to electoral accountability (organised by local authorities) or not (organised by a regional authority, as is health);

2 *nature of the market*: whether the demand for this service mainly comes from final consumers (for example, hairdressing), or from producers (for example, advertising), or from a mixture of the two (for example, laundries);

3 *nature of the product*: whether the service partly takes the form of a material product that can be bought, sold, stored, transported, and so on (computer software, take-away meals, educational programmes), or can only be consumed at the point of production (lecture, operation, haircut). In the former, the distinction between manufacturing and service production is rendered highly problematic (Walker, 1985: 50–1). In the latter, although physical proximity to the consumer is essential, there is further variation between services where the producer is mobile (surveyor), where the service user is mobile (university student), and where both are mobile (Bhagwati, 1987);

4 *degree of commodification*: whether the service is bought and sold on the market and its supply is dependent upon the conditions of profit maximisation (telephones); whether the service is marketed but where conditions of profit maximisation do not fully apply (railways); or whether the service is provided in relation to non-monetarily determined 'need' (acute healthcare);

5 *functions in the processes of production and circulation*: whether the service is concerned with services for management (accountancy), services for the workforce (education, health), or services to convey money and/or people and/or goods and/or information from place to place or from point of production to market, and so on;

6 *character of the service* involved and the nature of the object that is to be 'serviced'. There are significant differences in the service delivery between servicing material objects and servicing human beings. In the latter case the service is more likely to be closely monitored by the recipient, it will have to be provided at the point of consumption, and it will be much more difficult to 'store up' work to be completed when it is convenient for the producer.

Our aim in the following is to analyse the conditions that structure the way in which a given service function is met, in particular the conditions under which different service industries are restructured and the socio-spatial effects of such restructuring. In studying a variety of manufacturing industries (as discussed in Chapter 2), Massey (1978; 1984) and Massey and Meegan (1982) showed that the differential availability, price and organisation of the 'labour' factor was central to explaining the character of the restructuring found within a given sector. We shall now consider whether, even if Massey and Meegan were correct in their analysis of various manufacturing industries, it follows that the 'labour' factor plays a similar role in explaining restructuring in service industries.

First, it can be noted that there is a rather diverse set of factors that explain the restructuring pattern found. Thus new technologies or new products developed in manufacturing can affect the profitability or attractiveness of different service functions and sectors (and vice versa). For example, the development of the jet engine made possible the growth of European 'package tours', which have reduced employment in seaside hotels in Britain. Similarly, the development of 'automobility' has generated huge service industry employment in garages. Other determinants of the forms of restructuring include the changing location of consumers of the given function; the degree and forms in which groups of men and/or women are organised in a particular sector; the availability of land and/or buildings, especially away from the city centre (so permitting out-of-town hypermarkets); the changing patterns of demand from service employers to meet particular problems of variation of demand – by day, by week or by season; and the degree to which strategies of managerial reorganisation are actively fostered by central directives within a given sector (particularly true of public service provision).

Secondly, the 'labour' factor plays a different role in the location and organisation of much service industry compared with at least certain manufacturing sectors. We will return briefly to Massey here. In her account of *service* sector location, she almost entirely ignores the labour factor as explaining such a patterning (1984: 175–93). In considering why, for example, there is a spatial concentration of headquarters of major companies in the south-east, Massey refers to a number of determinants other than labour – personal contacts, nearness to the City of London and other sources of expertise, and superior communication facilities. It would certainly be difficult to argue that the relative *organisational* strength of labour was a likely determinant of the emerging spatial structure of service employment in Britain. Industrial disputes, and hence the threat of such disputes, reflecting the strength of labour, are fairly rare in most service industries, especially in the private sector. In the *1980 British Workplace Industrial Relations Survey* 92 per cent of service industry plants were wholly unaffected by industrial action in the previous twelve-month period (Daniel and Milward, 1984; and see discussion in Enderwick, 1984). Or, to put the point differently: the percentage of service industry plants experiencing industrial action by manual workers was 6.3 per cent in a year, compared with 45.7 per cent in manufacturing industry. Some changes are, admittedly, reported in the *1984 British Workplace Industrial Relations Survey*. Table 3.2 sets out such changes, particularly the enormous increase in strike action amongst non-manual workers in public services, where nearly two fifths of establishments reported a strike in the previous year. More recent and disaggregated data is presented in Table 3.3. This shows that there are two service industry sectors, transport and public administration, where industrial stoppages are fairly frequent. In most of the other service sectors, however, stoppages are extremely unusual, even where quite large employers are involved, as in the case of many hotels (Johnson and Mignot, 1982: 5).

Table 3.2 *Changes in industrial action by main industrial sector: establishments reporting a strike in a twelve-month period, %*

	Private manufacturing		Private services		Nationalised industries		Public services	
	1980	1984	1980	1984	1980	1984	1980	1984
Strike action by manual workers	21	10	3	4	24	30	10	9
Strike action by non-manual workers	3	1	1	4	16	9	9	38

Source: Adapted from Milward and Steven, 1986: Table 10.2

An interesting recent discussion of the industrial relations practices of a service industry is Marshall's analysis of the workplace culture of a large licensed restaurant (1986; and see the classic Whyte, 1948). He had expected that the combination of 'paternalism' and the opportunities for fiddles and pilferage would be sufficient to explain why most staff did not appear to resent either the long and demanding hours of work or the considerable wealth of the owner (on fiddles in waiting, see Mars and Nicod, 1984). However, Marshall argued that in fact such resentment failed to develop because most staff did not experience their work *as* paid work. Much of what they did consisted of activities that elsewhere would be classified as leisure. There was an erosion of the symbolic boundaries between what was work and what was play, what was work time and what

Table 3.3   *Incidence rates of work stoppages in Great Britain, 1986*

Industry grouping[1]	Working days lost per 1000 employees[2]
All industries and services	89
Energy and water	278
Manufacturing	203
Services	47
Agriculture, forestry and fishing	–
Coal extraction	767
Extraction and processing of coke, mineral oil and natural gas	–
Electricity, gas, other energy and water	20
Metal processing and manufacture	606
Mineral processing and manufacture	99
Chemicals and man-made fibres	48
Metal goods not elsewhere specified	88
Mechanical engineering	255
Electrical engineering and equipment	39
Instrument engineering	151
Motor vehicles	414
Other transport equipment	1,423
Food, drink and tobacco	52
Textiles	52
Footwear and clothing	75
Timber and wooden furniture	4
Paper, printing and publishing	118
Other manufacturing industries	31
Construction	33
Distribution, hotels and catering, repairs	3
Railways	3
Other inland transport	134
Sea transport	1,601
Other transport and communication	146
Supporting and miscellaneous transport services	55
Banking, finance, insurance, business services and leasing	2
Public administration, sanitary services and education	118
Medical and health services	8
Other services	2

[1]1980 Standard Industrial Classification.
[2]Based on the latest available mid-year (June) estimates of employees.

Source: *Employment Gazette*, Sept. 1987

was non-work time. This was reinforced by the fact that work rhythms were more like those of outside paid work; even poorly paid staff were 'free' to organise their activities according to their own designs. Much of the 'work' of the staff consisted of socialising with customers who were often friends from outside. And much of their 'leisure' involved spending time in the restaurant drinking after hours. The staff did not even use phrases such as 'going to work'; for most of them, according to Marshall (1986:42), it was a 'way of life' resulting from the physical proximity of employee and consumer, of 'work' and 'leisure'.

To the extent that other similar service establishments (privately owned, for final consumers, consumption at the point of production) possess similar features, then this will almost certainly prevent the emergence of widespread labour organisation. In a number of such establishments in Lancaster the management did not know whether the workforce were members of a union or not. Thus, in much of at least private service industry, spatial reorganisation will not be explicable in terms of the organisational strength of labour in different areas. Nor, since most service plants are fairly small, will the availability of large pools of labour be a likely factor that could possibly explain such developments. However, this is not to say that 'labour' is an unimportant consideration in service industry. There are four particular aspects of the 'labour' factor which are absolutely central to the analysis of services.

First, in many service enterprises labour costs represent a very high proportion of total costs – often between two thirds and three quarters – and so employers will certainly seek to monitor and, where possible, to minimise, such costs. A current example would be British universities, where staff costs are around 75 per cent of total costs. Most service establishments will not be able to lower labour costs in the manner achieved by McDonald's restaurants – to an extraordinary 15 per cent of the value of sales (Percy and Lamb, 1987). Moreover, it has been argued that many of the productivity gains achieved by manufacturing industry over the past ten years have depended upon the separating of service functions from manufacturing (Cornetz, 1988).

Secondly, since much service work is labour-intensive, adequate supplies of highly qualified labour may well be crucial to location. For example, the availability of particular kinds of skilled labour has been central to the development of the 'M4 corridor' and other parts of the south-east. In such cases, the adequate provision of appropriate houses (right price, size and style) is important in ensuring an adequate pool of qualified labour. The housing factor in industrial location will elsewhere be less significant, although it has recently resurfaced as an issue in the north-east, the question being whether there are adequate supplies of 'executive-style' housing to attract sufficient Japanese managers and the like. In the USA Noyelle notes how most of the large insurance banks have reorganised their systems divisions so that they are located in university towns or technology centres where there are adequate supplies of college graduates. Noyelle sees this as illustrating a general trend, that 'spatial reorganization is driven by the need for skilled labour' (1986: 20).

Thirdly, labour is to varying degrees implicated in the service *delivery*. This occurs as the intended outcome of a necessarily *social* process, in which some interaction occurs between one or more producers and one or more consumers and in which the quality of the interaction is itself part of the service being offered (Leidner, 1987). The consumers may (as in the case of a PhD student) or may not (as with the consumer of a McDonald's hamburger) be involved in joint production with one or more of the formal producers. The producers with whom the consumers come most into contact may or may not be those primarily responsible for the production of the service in question (lecturer on the one hand, waiter/waitress on the other). Nevertheless, because the production of the service is social, unless the service can be entirely materialised there has to be some spatial proximity between one or more of the producers and of the consumers. This is one important constraint upon location.

Fourthly, the social composition of the producers, at least those who are in the first line, may well be part of what is 'sold' to the customer. In other words, the 'service' consists in part of a process of production that is infused with particular social characteristics – of gender, age, race, educational background and so on. When the individual buys a given service, what is purchased is a particular social composition of the service producers (see Hochschild, 1983, on how this applies in the case of flight attendants). It should also be noted that in some cases what is also bought is a particular social composition of the other service *consumers*. Examples of this are to be found in tourism/transport where people spend considerable periods of time consuming the service in relatively close proximity to others, and hence part of what is being bought is the social composition of the other consumers. Holidaymaking is a classic example of a 'positional good', and the development of new and ever more exotic resorts stems from the desire to consume tourist services that are different from those being consumed by the 'masses' – that is, by people with social characteristics from which one is seeking to distance oneself.

Labour is itself part of the service product, and this poses particular difficulties for management. These difficulties are the more significant the longer and the more intimate the contact called for, and the greater the importance of 'quality' for the consumer of the particular service. It means that employees' speech, appearance and personality may all be treated as legitimate areas of employer intervention and control. Indeed, many services require 'emotional work' – in particular, a willingness to smile in a pleasant, friendly and involved way to the consumers (Hochschild, 1983). Marshall notes that in the restaurant that he studied, 'Staff were constantly encouraged to "cater for" the customers: to smile, exchange pleasantries, and, if there was time, longer conversations' (1986: 41). In the case of flight attendants Hochschild, however, notes that this emotional work has been made much more difficult with the intensification of work on the airlines since the mid-1970s: 'The workers respond to the speed-up with a slow-down: they smile less broadly, with a quick release and no sparkle in the eyes, thus dimming the company's message to the people. It is a war of smiles' (1983: 127).

Such a decline in quality is exceptionally hard for management to monitor and control, even if they are well aware that the attendants are no longer providing the complete service that the passengers expect. What is important here is that in many services the actual delivery is provided by relatively low-level workers who are badly paid (at least, relatively) and who have little involvement or engagement with the overall enterprise. They are also overwhelmingly female, except in older forms of transport or in societies where occupations like waiting have much higher status than in Britain. Overlying the interaction, the 'service', are particular assumptions and notions of gender-specific forms of behaviour. And yet for many consumers, what is actually consumed as a service *is* the particular moment of delivery by the relatively low-level service deliverers: the smile on the flight attendant's face, the pleasant manner of the waiter, the sympathy in the eyes of the nurse, and so on. The problem for management is how to ensure that these moments do in fact work out appropriately, while minimising the cost and an undesirably intrusive (and hence resented) system of management supervision, as well as minimising friction with other more highly paid workers backstage (Whyte, 1948). Jan Carlzon, the president of the Scandinavian airline SAS, terms these 'moments of truth' (1987). There are for SAS something like 50 million moments of truth each year, each of which lasts perhaps fifteen seconds when a customer comes into contact with an employee. It is, he says, these moments of truth that determine whether or not SAS will succeed or fail. He argues that the importance of such moments means that organisations have to be completely reorganised, with service to the customer as the primary objective. As a consequence, the actual service deliverers, the company's 'foot soldiers' who know most about the 'front-line' operations, have to be given much more responsibility to respond more effectively, quickly and courteously to the particular needs of the customer. This in turn means that the efforts of the front-line employees are much more highly valued. Since they are the providers of the 'moments of truth', their motivation is crucial. And, Carlzon argues, in such a service-oriented organisation individual decisions should be made at the point of responsibility, not higher up the hierarchy. The service deliverers have themselves to be the 'managers'.

It should also be noted that the production of many services is *context*-dependent: that is, they depend for their successful production upon aspects of the social and physical setting within which they occur. Examples include the hygienic cleanliness of a hospital; the style of furnishings in an office, reflecting an appropriate corporate image; the apparently safe interior of an aeroplane; the particular historically interesting assortment of buildings in a resort, and so on. In other words, the delivery of at least some services is very much connected with aspects of the environment, and especially with design and architecture. In certain cases the service cannot be received in an inappropriate physical or social context – part of the 'service', part of what is consumed, is in effect the context.

Finally, here it should be noted that since most people in Western societies are now service producers, many will have, intermittently at least, to provide some kind of 'emotional work'. Moreover, the huge increase in the range and quantity of services and the fact that everyone is now a service receiver means that the quality of services has become intensely contested. There are two reasons for this: first, because services meet an increasingly wide range of people's needs; and secondly, because their consumption often involves spending time (while consuming goods may take no time at all), especially since consumption has to occur serially, not simultaneously (Gershuny, 1987). The mass consumption of services has seen some consumers constituted as socio-political groupings of considerable influence – a reflection of how politics is being in part restructured towards so-called consumption issues, as a result of the widespread growth of service production. We will consider such themes further in Chapters 5 and 6.

In the previous chapter we noted that there were three sets of possibilities related to the explanation of which strategies of restructuring develop in particular industrial sectors. These three considerations are the possibilities of technical change, production reorganisation, and spatial relocation. In the case of services there is a fourth possibility: product transformation. These various possibilities yield thirteen different strategies of service sector restructuring, as we will now show.

Forms of Restructuring

Technical Change?
1   *Investment and technical change*: heavy capital investment within new means of production and, as a result, considerable job loss, which will generally be highly unequally distributed through space.
    (a)   private producer services, particularly through the development of the electronic office (Jarrett, 1984);
    (b)   higher education: in the UK there has been a relative shift in the distribution of students away from conventional universities to the 'distance learning pattern' of the Open University. This development has been made possible by the use of existing household equipment (TV and video cassette recorder) for the 'service delivery' (Gershuny and Miles, 1983: ch. 5);
    (c)   point-of-sale computer terminals in supermarkets and superstores, with important effects upon the scheduling of labour, clerical work and stock control (Sparks, 1981: 55–7). The resulting reduction of costs in larger stores will bring about the closure or run-down of smaller supermarkets and food stores.

Production Reorganisation?
2   *Intensification*: increases in labour productivity through managerial or organisational change, with little or no new investment or major loss of capacity.
    (a)   university education, where the number of degrees and diplomas produced by each member of staff in the UK between 1972 and 1982 increased by 2.5 per cent per annum (Marris, 1985). The proposal to increase the number of degree students in the UK by 50,000 without adequate funding to maintain the 'unit of resource' involves further drastic intensification;
    (b)   airlines: with deregulation, larger jets and the cheapening of air travel, work has been intensified. 'The cruise ship has become a Greyhound bus' (Hochschild, 1983: 124). The speeding-up of work has drastically shortened the time available for contact between flight attendants and passengers. As

we saw above, it is no longer possible to deliver appropriate 'emotional work'.

3   *Rationalisation*: closure of capacity with little or no new investment or new technology.

(a)   closure of cinemas in the UK in the 1960s and 1970s, mostly because of intense competition from household investment in TVs. Cinema attendances have only recently begun to increase, following extensive investment in new out-of-town multi-screen cinema complexes (as, for example, at Milton Keynes and Salford Quay).

4   *Commodification*: There are three main ways in which a service can be made subject to the dictates of the market:

(a)   market encirclement: that is, ensuring that a sector is forced to operate within a competitive environment. Recent examples include the deregulation of airlines in the USA, the shifting of UK university funding away from the state, the necessity for British Rail engineering workshops to *compete* for orders from British Rail, and so on;

(b)   budget centre fragmentation: that is, decentralising a sector so that different components are directly financially accountable. In the UK, recent examples include the reorganisation of the NHS and the treating of units as cost centres (following the Griffiths Report, 1984); and, in universities, the proposal to regard departments as budget centres (following the Jarratt Report, 1985; in Lancaster this is known as the 'cash economy' approach);

(c)   privatisation: that is, selling off to the private sector all or part of a given industry where this also increases 'competition'. Recent examples would include British Airways and British Telecom.

5   *Replacement of existing labour input* with cheaper female, young or non-white labour. This strategy depends upon there being patriarchal/generational/racist structures which confine large numbers of workers to exposed secondary segments of the labour market.

(a)   the specific recruitment of migrant labour by the large hotel chains. In some central London hotels 45 per cent of those employed are from 'black' racial groups; overall there are 115,000 employees in hotel and catering who are 'foreign nationals' (Bagguley, 1987: 35);

(b)   the recruitment of young workers by the fast-food industry. The 1986 Wages Act in the UK removed from workers under twenty-one all rights to a minimum wage rate or holiday pay (Percy and Lamb, 1987). Further 'liberalisation' of the labour market will take place according to the government's 1988 White Paper *Employment in the 1990s*.

6 *Flexibilisation of the labour input*, so that the supply of labour can be more closely tied to the volatility of demand, over a day, a week, a school term or a season.

(a) in the fast-food industry most workers work flexible hours, depending upon the work that is required. As a result the distinction between full- and part-time work is dissolved (see Percy and Lamb, 1987, on McDonald's, now one of London's five largest employers);

(b) most domestic work undertaken by women in hospitals is organised on a part-time basis. Interestingly, though, portering work, which has similar problems of shift organisation, is organised as full-time work – porters are male (see Beechey and Perkins (1987: 101) on how issues of gender enter into the very construction of part-time work for women).

Spatial Relocation?

7 *Decentralisation*: moving into areas where land and/or property and/or labour are cheaper. The availability of these cheaper locations is particularly important because much service work is labour-intensive and hence requires a lot of space. The resulting gender distribution of work will in part reflect patriarchal strategies of occupational closure.

(a) the removal of much office work ('back offices') out of central business districts, often to suburbs or surrounding satellite towns (Nelson, 1986);

(b) the establishment of out-of-town hypermarkets, DIY stores and cinema complexes (for example, Metrocentre, Gateshead; Salford Quay);

(c) the relocation of parts of the British Civil Service, especially in the 1960s and 1970s. This was often combined with other restructuring strategies, as in the case of the Driver and Vehicle Licensing Centre in Swansea. Winckler (1986) shows that concentration into one office (albeit not in London) and investment and technical change (that is, computerisation) were also part of DVLC reorganisation.

8 *Concentration*: the spatial centralisation of services in larger units and the closure or run-down of the number or scale of smaller units.

(a) the centralisation of all motor-licensing functions in the UK at DVLC in Swansea (see above and Winckler, 1986);

(b) the reorganisation of general practitioners in the NHS

into group practices with reduced levels of accessibility (Daniels, 1985: 128–34);
(c)   the reorganisation of hospital provision into larger units and the running down of smaller hospitals and clinics (see Whitelegg, 1982, on Blackburn, and below).

Product Transformation?

9   *Partial self-provisioning* of the service function and the resulting reduction in labour employed in existing labour-intensive service industry. One consequence is to increase the amount of unpaid work done in the home, especially that done by 'housewives'.
(a)   self-service in retail distribution – which is both more efficient than serviced shops and is often more popular with customers, who do most of the 'production' work (Levitt, 1976: 85);
(b)   self-servicing of the entertainment function through the development of TV, hi-fi, VCR and so on (Gershuny and Miles, 1983). However, this process is not costless, since such increasingly complex machinery has itself to be 'serviced', and this contributes to the 'harried' nature of modern life (Linder, 1970).

10   *Domestication*: the deliberate relocation of parts of the service to women's labour within households or hostels.
(a)   community care programmes in the NHS, which involve some relocation of patients from institutional care provided by the state to both privately owned welfare services and the patients' families. In each case there is a shift for women from paid to unpaid (or very badly paid) domestic labour (Finch and Groves, 1983).

11   *Subcontracting* or externalising elements of the service function to firms providing specialised services, thereby 'distancing' the costs and risks involved for the core firms (Atkinson, 1984).
(a)   'privatisation' of such functions as cleaning, laundry and catering in the NHS, using specialist private service companies (although this is sometimes resisted at the local level (see Bagguley, 1986b, and below));
(b)   development of private producer services that are both increasingly international *and* able to provide more customised services for their customer (Noyelle, 1986).

12   *Enhancement of quality of the service product*, through an improved labour input – that is, more skilled and/or better trained. Particularly important are improvements designed to bridge the typical divide between the company 'in here' and

the customer 'out there'.

(a)   the transformation of schoolteaching in the UK into an entirely graduate occupation;

(b)   the improvement in the treatment of mentally ill and handicapped patients, with the replacement of physical restraint by drug treatment in the 1930s and 1940s, and the introduction of non-pharmaceutical forms of therapy in the 1960s onwards (see Bagguley, 1986b, and below).

13   *Materialisation* of the service function so that the service product takes the form of a material object that can be bought, sold, transported, stored, or whatever.

(a)   the replacement of 'live' theatre, cinema and sport by TV and VCR (Gershuny and Miles, 1983);

(b)   the rapid development of 'take-away' food which has merely to be heated on the premises and not cooked by a chef when the customer requires it (see Percy and Lamb, 1987, report on McDonalds);

(c)   the use of 'cook and chill' techniques of cooking in hospitals and in larger hotels to even out the labour of highly paid chefs.

Thus far we have established a number of rather distinct patterns of 'restructuring'. In the following sections we shall attempt to elaborate on why particular patterns of restructuring are found in some sectors rather than in others. We will conclude here by noting some of the important recent changes in service employment in Great Britain (see Table 3.4).

Table 3.4   *Employment in services in Great Britain, 1974–84*

	1974	1984	Change %
Total employees (millions)	12.2	13.5	10
Men	5.9	6.2	4
Women, full-time	3.5	3.6	3
Women, part-time	2.7	3.7	36
Women, total	6.2	7.3	17
Distribution by sex (%)			
Men	49	46	−3
Women, full-time	29	27	−2
Women, part-time	22	27	5
Part-timers as % of total female employment	44	51	7

Source: NIER, 1986: 45

Table 3.4 shows that from 1974 to 1984 there was an increase in service industry employment of about 1.3 million. Almost all of this consisted of part-time women workers whose numbers increased by more than a third over the ten years. Part-timers now account for more than one half of the female labour force employed in services. With the exception of 'public administration', there was a marked increase in the percentage of female part-timers in all service sectors between 1974 and 1984. By 1984 the proportion of female part-timers within the total employment figure ranged from 12 per cent in banking, finance and wholesale distribution, to 48 per cent in hotels and catering. Even so, one fifth of all female part-time workers were to be found in retail distribution (NIER, 1986: 46).

Restructuring and the State

In this section we will briefly consider the role of the state in relation to various service industries. In 1981 33 per cent of all those in employment in the UK were to be found in the public sector, and almost all of these, with the exception of the utilities (*Economic Trends*, 1987: 201), were involved in the provision of services. Clearly, one restructuring strategy pursued by the Conservative government has been to effect 'commodification' via privatisation. It should be noted that only about one seventh of state employees are found in central government. Of the rest, most are employed in local government, in non-trading public corporations and in health provision.

How should this set of activities be understood? Is there a distinct set of restructuring strategies that is employed within the state? Our starting point here will be to examine the nature of these state activities (that is, those which are not directly marketed) in terms of the four considerations outlined on pages 62–7.

First, if we take *the possibilities of technical change*, we see that these are very limited. In the health sector, for example, technical change generally involves increased cost, either because the new technique enables the patient to be kept alive for longer, or because it involves increased nursing requirements, or both. The work in these sectors is necessarily highly labour-intensive, since there have to be moments of social interaction between producers and consumers.

Secondly, *the possibilities for reorganisation of the production process* are also rather limited. This is partly because the lack of a market for pricing services means that calculations cannot be easily made as to the likely productivity consequences of schemes of reorganisation, although the differences between this and large multinational private corporations should not be overemphasised (Offe, 1975; Shapiro, 1987b). Reorganisation may be unlikely because such services are normally organised by relatively highly paid groups of professionals, who are responsible for the definition of need and level of appropriate demand (Cousins, 1986: 93). Such professionals (for instance, NHS consultants) may be able to prevent substantial changes – particularly involving 'intensification' – from being fully implemented. Attempts may then be made to mimic a market through the introduction from 'above' of, for example, various performance indicators (Cousins, 1986).

Thirdly, *the possibilities of spatial relocation*: this too is rather limited, only being feasible in certain discrete cases, such as the concentration of vehicle licensing at Swansea. There are two very considerable constraints on spatial relocation. First, it would be impossible to shift much production of state-provided consumer services outside its national territory (although there may be imports of utilities, such as French-generated electricity). Hence, one of the favoured restructuring strategies pursued in parts of the private sector is not viable for the state. And secondly, since much of the state's activities consists of the provision of services to the population at large, these have to be organised on a widely dispersed basis – although there will be considerable contestation over the degree of dispersal (for example, over the closure of village schools, the run-down of cottage hospitals, the disappearance of sub-post offices, and so on).

Finally, *the possibilities of product transformation*: almost by definition, the state is concerned with providing services for 'general/mass' consumption, either for almost all of a given population (for example, schoolchildren) or for much of the less affluent sector (council housing). The state is rarely involved in producing 'specialised/niche' products, except in some aspects of higher education and in the procurement of specialised weapon systems (Shapiro, 1987b). The product market is also one that is unlikely to change very much. State service producers cannot move out of unprofitable product lines and develop new products. They have to provide service product(s) on a mass scale, and this is normally specified by Act of Parliament. The main possibilities for cost-saving arise from reductions in the quality of the service product.

Given these characteristics of state services, what forms of restructuring are likely to be found? Rationalisation and spatial relocation will be relatively uncommon; enhancement of quality will only be found where professional groups are powerfully placed (as in the British welfare state in the 1960s and early 1970s); and flexibilisation, replacement of labour input, materialisation, partial self-provisioning and subcontracting will all be found around the margins of the service in question. The four centrally important strategies for the restructuring of state services will be intensification, commodification, concentration and domestication. Intensification will result from the 'managers' in the organisation being given clearer, specific objectives and being expected to meet them by managing their unit, and especially their professional workers, more intensively; commodification will entail a variety of attempts to mimic markets, including the centralised specification of financial targets; concentration may well involve the relevant minister and/or outsiders to that service being much more powerfully placed to 'manage' it; and domestication will involve reducing the quality and hence the labour input provided by the state, while increasing that of unpaid women who will be providing 'a labour of love' (Finch and Groves, 1983).

We will now consider in detail an area of state service production particularly important in Lancaster – namely, health care.

The Health Sector

In the 1960s and 1970s this sector became an area of rapidly expanding employment. In Lancaster in the 1970s the number of health workers increased by nearly 40 per cent, and even in the 1980s the number employed in the NHS increased by nearly one fifth. There is a wide range of local provision: general NHS facilities (two hospitals); specialist NHS facilities, especially in mental handicap, psychiatric, dermatological, geriatric and eye areas; and two private hospital units (a Nuffield hospital and a hospice).

Lancaster inherited a health service that had been primarily shaped by a nineteenth-century spatial division of labour, in which Lancaster's role as the county centre made it an obvious choice for siting the county asylum (now the Lancaster Moor Hospital) in the 1830s. Furthermore, Lancaster's employers, in practising 'civic benevolence', contributed significant finance to the Royal Albert Hospital, which served a large portion of north-west England as a charitable hospital for the mentally handicapped. These hospitals existed in addition to the usual local provision, before the formation of the NHS. In 1951 health sector employment equalled 7.6 per cent of employment in the Lancaster borough, compared with 2.8 per cent in England and Wales as a whole. Within this total more men than usual were employed because of the large mental handicap and illness sectors – 39.2 per cent compared with 31.9 per cent nationally.

Overlying this legacy have been further important restructurings of the component labour processes and occupational hierarchies. To take one example within mental handicap, two particular strategies adopted were those of *technical change* and *enhancement of service quality*. The former has principally involved, starting in the 1930s, the use of drug treatments. This replaced mechanical forms of restraint as a means of controlling the symptoms of mental handicap (and mental illness). Such developments were followed, during the later 1960s and again during the late 1970s, by decisions to improve the quality of nursing care in mental handicap services. This resulted from the implementation of the Salmon Report on nursing (1964); from various national 'scandals' and subsequent investigations into the treatment of patients in mental illness, mental handicap and geriatric hospitals; and from the introduction of non-pharmaceutical forms of psychological therapy which are much more labour-intensive and require more highly trained nurses (Beardshaw, 1981; Martin, 1984).

These processes had three sets of employment effects during the 1970s and 1980s. The first was a clear separation of 'nursing' from 'ancillary' work on the wards, resulting in an increase in the latter, especially the work of part-time women cleaners in the early 1970s (Cousins, 1987: 111). A nurse who had worked at the Royal Albert Hospital for over seventeen years described the changes since he began work there as a nurse cadet:

> My main job was making beds, mopping floors and keeping the place neat and tidy, that's all any of the nurses did. Now mental handicap nursing essentially involves coordinating resources and activities around individuals to develop an individual mentally handicapped person's potential . . . The domestics did the catering and the laundry while we did everything on the wards. It used to be what you might call 'group care', with wards of fifty to sixty people looked after by four nurses. Now the largest wards have thirty people with four nurses, and in a few parts there are five residents with five staff. They're called residents or clients now, not patients – that's a word you never hear around here any more. (mental handicap nurse manager, 1986)

Secondly, the training of nurses improved, with a new syllabus, more tutors and new teaching aids. Thirdly, many more 'unqualified' nursing staff came to be employed at the Royal Albert during the later 1970s and early 1980s than was previously the case. The numbers rose from 90 (full-time equivalent) to 273 between 1975 and 1983, thus increasing, as a proportion of the nursing staff, from 29 per cent to 50 per cent (Lancaster DHA, 1984). Throughout this period the number of mental handicap residents was declining – from about 950 in 1979 to just over 700 by 1986 (Lancaster DHA, 1979; 1985). These medically 'unqualified' staff are involved in 'training' residents in social and occupational skills prior to their being 'returned to the community'.

A further important local effect was an increased number of ancillary workers in the early 1970s. This subsequently triggered a cost reduction strategy through the introduction of locally nego- tiated, productivity bonus schemes, drawn up to DHSS guidelines. By 1982 bonus schemes covering ten areas of ancillary work were operating. Most of these had been implemented that year, with estimated savings of over £67,000. At that time a further nine schemes were planned for other ancillary areas (Lancaster DHA, 1982: 35). However, by 1982 the estimated reductions in ancillary staff were only thirty (Lancaster DHA, 1982: 25) – unimpressive compared with increases elsewhere in the service. Probably the main effect, though, was a considerable intensification of the labour process, with more work being undertaken in the same number of hours with the same technology. Furthermore, the bonus schemes had a disorganising effect on local trade union organisation, as the shop stewards who had to negotiate the agreements on behalf of their members were in fact opposed to the schemes. In effect, such schemes introduced a degree of 'market rationality' into various labour processes, and the unions saw them as a prerequisite to a strategy of 'subcontracting' through the competitive tendering of ancillary service contracts, which was initiated by a government circular in 1983.

However, in Lancaster the management was slow to subcontract ancillary services to the private sector. Management tried to insist that all the tenders for contracts contain a fair wages clause in order to maintain the wages of the employees affected. This was overruled by the DHSS in London – which indicates the high degree of centralised control in the NHS over fundamental policy issues. A further indication of the unwillingness to subcontract locally was the fact that the privatisation programme was only completed at the end of 1986 – the deadline imposed by central government on all local health authorities. Furthermore, almost all of the local tenders were awarded 'in house', signalling management's concern to maintain close control over all that happens in their hospitals. It also reflects the fact that the large private sector companies that have successfully tendered elsewhere for hospital ancillary services concentrate their operations in the large conurbations and ignore 'peripheral' localities like Lancaster.

What have been the consequences of the privatisation pro- gramme for the workers concerned? A NUPE shop steward com- mented in the mid-1980s:

Another thing about the privatisation process of course is the assumption that if it's won 'in house', well that's OK, because to win it 'in house' the staff themselves usually willingly forgo bonus payments, and request management not to replace so 'n' so 'cos that's made 'em more efficient and they might win. So a lot of the 'in house' ones that are won, are won at such a cost that the service suffers because the people that are left simply can't do that much work.

A woman cleaner confirmed:

We've been knocked down to 25 [hours per week] . . . it's terrible, it's bad, you do a hell of a lot more in 25 hours, oh yes, it's gone down, definitely gone down. I mean there is supposed to be two to a ward, alright there is, but when you have had your days off, like I've had four off now, my mate will be on her own, and it is hard. (KI: 25)

Previously there had been relief domestics who covered for absentees, but these have now been dispensed with. The consequences for the mainly female cleaners are brought home in the following account of a day's work paid at the rate of £1.90 per hour:

I go in at eight o'clock, wash all the pots, cups and saucers, there's sixteen grown-ups on our ward every day here, it's a skin ward, and they are all good eaters, because they are not in because they are ill, it's because of their skin, and we do all the pots and then we have to do the day room and the smoke room, and then hoover the hallway, come back into the kitchen, for the odd pots . . . that have come in after time, get the trolley fixed, put that outside for the porter to take, do the wash basins in the ward, empty all the rubbish, and that brings you up to ten o'clock, then we have a break, ten minutes, then we come back, all the coffee pots are there then, and we do all the coffee pots again, set the trays up for dinner, then my friend goes into one end, and I go into the men's end and she goes into the ladies' end, she does the ladies' toilets, I do the men's toilets, do all the walls, side wards, sister's office, x-ray department, things like that and when you look at the clock it's ten to twelve. Dinner is at twelve then when you come back it's murder, you've to start then and it's like a full hour washing up and all the kitchen, mopping over the floor and everything, leaving everything clean and that brings you to half past four and you sometimes crawl out on your knees, because as I said if your mate is off you've to do it all on your own, the whole lot, it's terrible. I think Maggie Thatcher should get herself up here and have a look, in fact I would give her my end to do one morning, just to let her see what it is all about. (KI: 25)

The specific processes of restructuring in terms of technical change, enhancing the quality of some services, and subcontracting, have taken place in the context of a wider organisational restructuring in 1974 and 1982. These both involved increased centralisation and the introduction of private sector commercial management methods (Levitt and Wall, 1984; Cousins, 1987). In the earlier changes in 1974, management consensus teams were established consisting of a doctor, nurse, administrator and treasurer. One of the effects was to reduce the power of the hospital matron:

> it was the minute they got rid of Matrons. When there was the Matron in every hospital you respected the Matron, because she was the boss of everybody, cleaners included, and you were a team . . . you looked up to that lady. If you went out for a quiet puff, it was, 'oh – Matron's here', you'd die. You really would die, but today you've no respect, it's gone. (KI 25)

It is widely agreed that over the past decade there has been a very marked decline in goodwill amongst the NHS workforce, and especially in respect for and trust in the management. One ward clerk who had worked in the health service for a number of years said that management 'used to be more fatherly. Now the management is like factory management with a different attitude more like whizzkids. It's become a career' (KI: 8). A nurse who had left to work in the local private hospital felt: 'Relations between management and workers are dreadful. There's no respect for the people working on the wards and no clear attempt to solve day-to-day problems. That's why I left the health service and went to the Nuffield' (KI: 12). And a NUPE shop steward claimed: 'People are demoralised in the health service, absolutely bloody demoralised. Even a lot of lower-middle management feel the same sort of thing.' Interestingly, this demoralisation has made 'functional flexibility' *less* and not more likely to occur. A COHSE shop steward stated that:

> domestics and porters at one time were not averse to helping you out on the ward. If there was a domestic on duty she would come and tidy the patient for you if you were gone, so all that goodwill is retreating, because they just haven't got the time to do it 'cos they're doin' two people's jobs sometimes, they say 'sorry, haven't got the time' to do it. And so you're losing the comradeship that you did have with the other support services, a wedge has driven us apart, they're having their tea breaks somewhere else whereas at one time they all had their tea breaks together because they were like a family.

The managerial reorganisation in 1985 was based on the report by Roy Griffiths, the managing director of Sainsbury's. Its key theme was strong centralised managerial control with strict specific targets for savings, productivity and so on, but allowing considerable local autonomy over how these goals should be achieved: 'we believe that a small, strong general management body is necessary at the centre . . . to ensure that responsibility is pushed as far down the line as possible, ie, to the point where action can be taken effectively' (Griffiths Report, 1984: 2). This responsibility was vested not in a management team but in individuals – general managers at regional, district and unit (for instance, hospital) level, who were to be responsible for all aspects of management at their level. Griffiths highlighted in particular the lack of leadership in NHS management under the consensus system (Griffiths Report, 1984: 11). The new thrusting management style was to be achieved in two ways. First, the old health service managers were replaced by new general managers, and about 11 per cent of these were appointed from outside the health service (Cousins, 1987: 165). Only 3 per cent of district general managers are female, which means that the predominantly female nursing profession is now almost totally excluded from NHS management. By contrast, a nurse who had left the NHS for private health care said: 'I can go and talk to the matron . . . which I could never have done at the RLI [NHS hospital]: mind you my matron at RLI was a man and that may have something to do with it' (KI: 12).

Secondly, Griffiths proposed certain 'incentives' for the new management: 'There must be incentives for staff, through proper reward for performance and career prospects. The sanction of removing the inefficient performer must also be more easily available than at present' (Griffiths Report, 1984: 2). In practice this has meant that all general managers have been appointed on three-year fixed term contracts, are subject to regular efficiency assessments, and can be paid discretionary additions in proportion to their ability to implement change (that is, to make cuts).

A further strategy pursued in the Lancaster health service has been that of concentration, especially of the acute services, on to one site. This has resulted largely from National Health Service planning initiatives during the 1950s and 1960s, and these began to have significant employment effects in Lancaster during the 1970s. The growth of facilities in various acute specialities at the Lancaster Royal Infirmary resulted in nursing employment increasing from 299 in 1976 to 444 in 1981, and by 1986 the number had increased to 816. The Lancaster Royal Infirmary, with 360 beds, is the district general hospital for the Lancaster District and for South-East Cumbria. There is to be considerable capital investment, with 150 more beds by the early 1990s and further capital investment planned after that. There are one thousand people employed on the site. Two other local hospitals have seen a corresponding reduction in their functions and employment, and functions will be further concentrated at the Infirmary in future (Lancaster DHA, 1985).

Like much of the NHS nationally, the Lancaster District suffers from severe staff shortages. Severe shortages of qualified nurses have resulted in the need to close wards for short periods. There is a number of reasons for this: increased demand because of the reduction in weekly hours to thirty-seven; the policy of 'under-recruiting' – that is, not immediately replacing nurses until they are absolutely necessary; the high turnover because of relatively poor wages and conditions; and the counter-employment attractions of the Nuffield private hospital (opened in 1985), St John's Hospice, and many residential/nursing homes for the elderly in an area where the labour pool is small.

One further restructuring strategy that will have important effects in the next few years is that of *domestication*, of the implementation of community care programmes in both mental illness and mental handicap. Between 1983 and 1993 nursing employment within the former will have fallen locally by 25 per cent and in the latter by 50 per cent, together accounting for 450 lost posts (full-time equivalents) (Lancaster DHA, 1984). Small increases will occur in community psychiatric and mental handicap nursing. Ultimately, most buildings on both sites will be sold off, probably for office employment. Where the long-term patients from both institutions will go is somewhat controversial, since in the case of the mental handicap hospital over half were admitted before 1948 and only 10 per cent are classified by the health authority as 'Lancastrians'. This shows both the degree to which health services have been 'exported' from Lancaster, and the enormous problems that will be involved in the provision of care in the 'community' for elderly patients who no longer have a meaningful community to which to return.

Table 3.5   *Employment in Lancaster District Health Authority by sex and by full- and part-time working, 1976, 1981, 1985*

| | 1976 | | 1981 | | 1985 | | Increase 1976–85 |
	No.	%	No.	%	No.	%	%
Men, full-time	963	26.64	1001	24.98	1114	23.33	15.68
Men, part-time	29	0.80	25	0.62	129	2.70	344.83
Men, total	992	27.44	1026	25.61	1243	26.04	25.30
Women, full-time	1193	33.00	1404	35.04	1851	38.77	55.16
Women, part-time	1430	39.56	1577	39.36	1680	35.19	17.48
Women, total	2623	72.56	2981	74.39	3531	73.96	34.62
All	3615	100.00	4007	100.00	4774	100.00	32.06

Source: Lancaster DHA

Thus a number of restructuring strategies have been employed, especially technical change; intensification; commodification; concentration; domestication; and enhancement of quality, particularly under the direction of a centralised directive following the Griffiths Report. There has been relatively little subcontracting, replacement of existing labour or flexibilisation. Table 3.5 shows that most of the employment growth that did occur in Lancaster resulted from the increase in the numbers of full-time women workers (55 per cent in 1976–85) and not, as in many service sectors, from the increase in female part-time workers. However, such levels of full-time employment will almost certainly fall by the early 1990s, with the closure of hospitals and the predicted lack of financial resources. In the past there has been considerable union opposition to such changes. The closure of one local hospital in particular has been significantly delayed. It is doubtful if this 'success' will be repeated.

Tourist-related Services

In this section we will consider some of the employment changes that have occurred in the variety of mainly privately owned services concerned with tourism. In particular, we shall consider the development of the British seaside resort, dealing especially with the recent history of Morecambe. In many ways the rise and fall of resorts such as Morecambe reflect the changing fortunes of those manufacturing towns and cities from which most of its clientele derived. Such resorts, with their mass organised working-class pleasure provision, were, as important products of nineteenth-century industrialisation, just as important as the rapidly expanding industrial towns and cities. And the rotting piers, the boarded-up cinemas and theatres, the windswept amusement arcades – indicative of the current malaise in many resorts – are just as important, as icons of a deindustrialised Britain, as vacant mills or workless shipyards.

Explaining why large numbers of people no longer wish to consume tourist-related services within seaside resorts requires consideration – not only of changes in the political economy of the industries concerned, but of much more general developments in the very processes by which pleasure is formed and consumed in contemporary Western societies (Urry, 1988a). And this in turn depends upon changes in what people expect to do and see while away, particularly upon the meanings represented by the built environment. In Chapter 5 we will examine the implications of such meanings for contemporary tourism. For the present we will confine ourselves to analysing some of the more economic aspects involved in the restructuring of contemporary tourist-related industries. One initial point should be noted: namely, that for any particular resort there is no opportunity of spatial relocation. The resort *is* a particular place with a given physical and social infrastructure. The tourist-related services have to be both produced *and* consumed in that place.

The development of seaside resorts in Britain in the nineteenth century was one of the most marked manifestations of the emergence of mass tourism, which depended upon the development of 'work' as a relatively separate and organised sphere of social activity. Leisure (and tourism) appeared as similarly separate and organised, as the other side of the processes by which work had come to be rationalised. There was then a marked shift, from the individual traveller to the mass tourist, but this did not occur in any sense inevitably; nor did it necessarily involve the development of resorts by the seaside. We will make just a few points about how such resorts did develop historically in Britain (for further detail, see Urry, 1987b).

An important eighteenth-century development was the growth of a number of spa towns, which in many ways resembled 'life on a cruise or in a small winter sports hotel, where the company is small and self-contained' (Younger, 1973: 14–15). In such spas the professional classes both swallowed and bathed in the waters. The nineteenth century saw the striking development of seaside resorts in which the social exclusivity practised within the spa towns could not be maintained (Pimlott, 1947: 55). Such resorts showed faster rates of population increase than did many manufacturing towns (Lickorisch and Kershaw, 1975: 12). All such resorts attempted to improve or maintain their 'social tone' – that is, their social class composition. Those resorts which were less successful in this were those near to large working-class population centres with good rail links, and where land ownership 'on the front' was highly fragmented. Certain places developed into characteristic working-class resorts; and as this happened wealthier holidaymakers looked elsewhere for superior accommodation, a more attractive physical infrastructure and a higher social tone (Perkin, 1976). The working-class resorts thus developed alongside the growth, within the new urban centres, of 'self-regulating working-class communities'. Especially in the north, the voluntary associations played a key role in the financing and organising of regular holidays. Walton summarises:

> The factory communities, after early prompting by employers and agencies of self-improvement, thus created their own grassroots system of holiday oganisation in the later nineteenth century. Each family was enabled to finance its own holiday without assistance from above. The unique Lancashire holiday system was thus based on working-class solidarity in retaining and extending the customary holidays . . . whole

towns go on holiday, and find resorts able to look after their needs. (1978: 39)

And finally, different resorts came to attract holidaymakers from different towns (and from different social groups). Resorts that developed later often had to draw visitors from further afield. In the case of Morecambe it became the seaside resort for the West Riding, and known as 'Bradford-by-the-Sea'. It prospered, especially during the interwar and immediate post-Second World War years. Central to its prosperity were the following conditions: the extensive growth of paid holidays for manual workers; the importance of the railway, as opposed to the car or plane, in the mass transportation of holidaymakers; the perpetuation of the family household as the principal holiday-going unit; the maintenance of a regional or, at most, a national market for holiday sites, and the limited development of an internationalised tourist industry; and the lack of investment in, and attraction of, alternatives to the seaside. However, by the early 1960s concern was being expressed locally over the consequences of the 'holiday abroad' idea. By the early 1970s it was noted that Morecambe was not getting its fair share of foreign tourists, and that the resort needed a new image (Riley, 1974). Local government reorganisation in 1974 (which took place under Lancaster City Council), coinciding with the recognition in the 1970s of the tourist potential of Lancaster with its 'historic' sights, saw Morecambe receiving a declining sphere of public investment (*LG*, 16.2.73).

Since the early 1970s there have been dramatic changes in the social and spatial organisation of tourist-related industries in the UK. There has been a most significant increase in the provision of such services throughout the world, and specifically within the UK where they employ about 1.4 million people. Employment in hotels and catering increased by 54 per cent between 1971 and 1986. The number of overseas visitors increased from 8.5 million in 1974 to 14.5 million in 1985 (*Employment Gazette* (Feb. 1988): S63). Over the same period the number of domestic trips (excluding day trips) increased from 114 million to 140 million (Cabinet Office, 1985). And yet the places that in the 1960s possessed the most developed tourist infrastructure, the seaside resorts, are the very same places that have failed to capitalise on this expansion of demand. Why, one might ask, have many resorts gone into rapid decline, while almost everywhere else tourist-related services have been rapidly expanding?

For Morecambe, the following figures give some indication of the scale of decline. Between 1973 and 1987 the number of small hotels and boarding houses fell from 640 to 267, of self-catering establishments from 310 to 180, and of bed spaces from 12,340 to 7115 (*The Visitor*, 23.12.87). In just one week's advertisements in one local paper, 24 per cent of all hotels and 21 per cent of all guest-houses were up for sale (*Lancaster Guardian Property Guide*, 23.10.87). The Chair of one of the two associations of local hoteliers estimated that at any one time about one third of the hotels were 'on the market' (1986). A recent report states: 'In 1973 the resort boasted two piers, five cinemas, theatres, a dance hall, a wealth of live entertainment and many other attractions. Today the piers and cinemas have ceased operating, the theatres have closed and the range of live entertainment is extremely limited' (quoted in the *Lancashire Evening Post*, 23.12.87). It is estimated that in each year about 250,000 people stay in Morecambe (although often for less than a week, let alone a fortnight) and about one million visit it for a day (although the newly opened Frontierland attracted one and a half million visitors in 1987). Although these are substantial numbers, they are tiny when compared with those of Blackpool, which dominates the tourist market in the north-west. Just to take four indicators of the significance of Blackpool: there are 2700 hotels, tourism accounts for 12,000 jobs, 16 per cent of all short-break holidays in the UK are taken in Blackpool, and an incredible 25 per cent of day visitors have made at least *fifty* previous day trips to the resort (Lancashire County Council, 1987: 4/24).

But, of course, Blackpool is not the only competitor in the market. There have been a number of other crucial developments. First, there has been the exceptional internationalisation of the UK tourist industry: 22 million visits abroad from the UK in any year (*Employment Gazette* (Feb. 1988): S63). The emergence of the 'package holiday' phenomenon provides sun, sea, superior accommodation and the excitement of 'foreignness' at little more than the cost of an equivalent stay in Morecambe. This has transformed the working-class holiday market, although, of course, most workers in any year do not take a foreign holiday – only 12.5 per cent in 1985 and, in fact, over half took no holiday at all (*Political, Social, Economic Review*, 1986: 22). One reason why the package tour has had such an impact in Britain is because of the early emergence of integrated companies (the 'tour operators'). Through their use of new technologies (jets and computerised booking systems), and because of their immense bargaining power, they have managed to sell holidays equivalent to those sold in the rest of Western Europe at a considerably lower price. An EEC survey of fifty-seven hotels in Spain, Portugal and Greece showed that in 68 per cent the cheapest holiday was provided by a British tour operator and that in 70 per cent the most expensive was sold by a German company (Milner, 1987: 21).

Secondly, there has been a rapid development of new kinds of places to visit, most of which tend to be located away from the coast and, especially, away from 'working-class' resorts. A stunning 50 per cent of tourist attractions available to the public in 1983 had opened in the previous fifteen years (Cabinet Office, 1985). As they have opened, so they have provided stiff competition for the resorts, whose attractions are increasingly 'old-fashioned' and who are unable to secure sufficient public or private investment to develop new ones. We should note two examples here. First, there is currently an extraordinary growth in the number of museums, with about one new one opening each fortnight in the UK (see Urry, 1988a, on the postmodern museum culture). However, there are no museums in Morecambe, although three have recently opened in Lancaster and others are planned. Secondly, there has just opened in Sherwood Forest, Center Parcs, a Dutch-owned £34 million holiday village with tropical heat, palm trees and warm water lagoons. The seaside proper will have immense difficulty competing with such an artificial temperature- and environment-controlled 'seaside'.

Thirdly, there has been a change in the type of place that people wish to visit in Britain. With the increased interest in short breaks and day trips (as opposed to the week/fortnight's holiday), there is much visiting of historic places. Here not only have many of the pre-industrial towns and cities prospered (Cambridge, Canterbury, Edinburgh, Stratford, for instance), but also some of the places famous for 'industry'. People seem to find increasingly attractive, sites of industrialisation such as Ironbridge Gorge, Wigan Pier, the Beamish Museum and Bradford. This last has been singularly successful. As Bradford has deindustrialised, so tourists have stopped travelling in large numbers to Bradford-by-the-Sea (Morecambe). Instead, people from all over go to Bradford itself. It is now marketed as a 'Great English City Break', with special emphasis placed on visits to mills and mill shops.

Fourthly, there is a range of demographic and sociological processes that have reduced the likely demand for services in places like Morecambe. Factors here include the decline in the proportion of manual workers in the population; the decline of population in the large conurbations, especially in the north of England; the gradual shift of population to the south; the decline in the proportion of the population living in conventional family households; the increased importance of peer group rather than family for holiday and leisure activities; and the overwhelming importance of the car for most journeys (Urry, 1987b; 1988a). One hotel worker summarised thus the reasons for the decline of Morecambe: 'I just think it's part of the . . . north-west, the north/south divide, you know, everything is sort of moving down south and everybody is building that up and gradually up here it's just dwindling away' (KI 17).

Finally, these tendencies just mentioned are particularly import-ant in the case of overseas tourists. When overseas visitors come to Britain only one fifth include at least a day's visit to the seaside; and even Blackpool attracts very few such visitors (Medlik, 1982: 75). What is appreciated about the UK is that it is 'old', and that the places visited are associated with significant historic events and characters (Urry, 1988a). Seaside resorts have few such connections (except for Brighton and Lyme Regis).

However, it is interesting that one such seaside centre, the Isle of Man, now deliberately attempts to mobilise nostalgia in its TV advertisements. The message is 'You'll look forward to going back' (Granada, 2.1.88). And in the local Morecambe press there has been a lively debate as to whether Morecambe could be self-con-sciously redeveloped in this way as an Edwardian/1920s working-class resort (*LG*, 1987). But many people in the tourist trade see the issue differently. For them the objective is to attract private investment and to establish new entertainment complexes, with bright lights and advertising, and to have less in the form of 'nice, pretty developments and monuments' (leisure complex manager, 1986). The crucial point to note, though, is that the providers of existing and potential tourist services in such a place cannot but be concerned with the nature of the built environment, and hence also with issues of planning, design and modernisation. That this is the case will be reflected in the following discussion, where we will briefly summarise the main forms of restructuring found in tourist-related services, especially in Morecambe, where forms are signifi-cantly affected by constraints and possibilities embedded in the built environment. We will conclude by showing why other restructuring strategies (enumerated on pages 63–7) have not been of importance.

Technical Change?

1 *Investment and technical change*: we have already noted a wide variety of changes concerned with the high investment in foreign hotels; the development of the foreign, but not the dom-estic, package holiday by the large tour operators; and the invest-ment in inland historic sights. More specifically, the UK hotel industry has undergone some dramatic changes in its investment

location in recent years (for more detail on the following see Baggu-ley, 1986b).

The first point to note is that the proportion of overseas visitors is lowest in hotels located at the seaside and highest in hotels in London and small (inland) towns. Moreover, of all the regions in the UK the north-west attracts the lowest proportion of overseas visitors (7 per cent compared with an average for England of 25 per cent). Furthermore, taking all visitors, the average room occupancy rates were lowest at the seaside (47 per cent) and again highest in London (57 per cent) and small inland towns (56 per cent). Not surprisingly, these patterns are then reflected in new hotel building. In 1970 less than 10 per cent of planned hotels were in 'holiday areas', while 25 per cent were in London. Hotel building in 1981–4 had changed somewhat, with small towns accounting for 38 per cent of new hotels, the countryside 26 per cent and the seaside merely 9 per cent. Indeed, only 5 per cent of new hotel bedrooms were to be located at the seaside – which shows the relatively small-scale character even of new seaside hotels. There have been almost no large four-star hotels built at the seaside in recent years. In Morecambe, for example, ambitious plans to do so have now been abandoned; and indeed the largest hotels have only around fifty bedrooms. When Trust House Forte built a four-star hotel in the area it was located on the edge of Lancaster, close to the M6. Most of the well known hotel companies are rather under-represented in the resorts. In the case of Morecambe, only Best Western, of the leading hotel chains and consortia, has a local presence.

Production Reorganisation?

3 *Rationalisation*: we have already noted the closure of theatres, cinemas, hotels, guest-houses and self-catering accommodation in most seaside resorts. This reflects the decline in the number of visitors, particularly those who may stay for a week or a fortnight. In Morecambe's case the season is now only eight weeks long. And even then, some hotels have only a 32 per cent occupancy rate in peak season weeks (*Lancashire Evening Post*, 23.12.87). Much of the accommodation is now used to house DHSS claimants, people discharged from the large mental handicap/psychiatric hospitals into so-called 'community care', construction and other workers from the Heysham power stations, and old people. In 1983 there were 29 privately owned residential homes for the elderly in the Lancaster District, of which 18 had been opened in that year. By the end of 1986 there were 41, providing 655 places (Bagguley et al., 1989). This growth has generated considerable local concern about

whether too many of the seafront hotels are being converted into retirement homes.

Rationalisation has also affected the provision of entertainment services. For instance, Morecambe now boasts considerably poorer services than many other towns of comparable size, particularly as most places have seen recent rapid improvements in the provision of leisure/sports/entertainment services. It used to be the case that people had to go to the seaside in order to find concentrations of those services organised for the provision of 'pleasure' – now they would be better advised to stay at home.

6   *Flexibilisation of the labour input*: Table 3.6 sets out the main changes in the patterns of employment in the hotels and catering sector in Lancaster.

Table 3.6   *Employment in hotels and catering in Lancaster, 1971, 1976, 1981, 1984*[1]

| | 1971 | | 1976 | | 1981 | | 1984 | |
	No.	%	No.	%	No.	%	No.	%
Men, full-time	815	28.1	847	26.4	713	22.3	696	16.8
Men, part-time	234	8.1	372	11.6	413	13.0	540	13.0
Men, total	1049	36.2	1219	38.0	1126	35.3	1236	29.8
Women, full-time	1126	38.8	799	24.9	671	21.0	692	16.7
Women, part-time	728	25.0	1197	37.1	1399	43.7	2217	53.5
Women, total	1854	63.8	1996	62.0	2070	64.7	2909	70.2
	2903		*3215*		*3196*		*4145*	

[1]MLHs 884–7 (1968 SIC) for 1971, 1976, 1981; Activity Group 19 Hotels and Catering for 1984.

Source: NOMIS, Census of Employment

This table shows that there has been a marked increase in employment in this sector, particularly from 1981 onwards, but also that there has been a striking change in the character of the labour input. In 1971 only one quarter of the local labour force was made up of part-time women workers (compared with one third nationally). By 1984 the number of such workers had increased locally by 304 per cent. The number of full-time workers fell by 29 per cent over the same period. However, at the same time that there has been this heightened flexibility of the labour input (numerical flexibility), there has also been a pronounced functional flexibility of tasks. As one respondent described her part-time work:

> for the morning, serve the breakfast, clear it all away afterwards, clean the dining-room, and when I've set that up for dinner at night time, I start on the bedrooms, just go round the bedrooms and make sure the

beds are tidy, and tidy round the bedrooms and clean the sinks, and that's it, it's only a couple of hours. (KI 17)

Product Transformations?

9 *Partial self-provisioning*: in the case of domestic holidaymakers in England, the proportion of self-serviced nights increased from 54 per cent in 1974 to 63 per cent in 1984 (Bagguley, 1987: 18). In other words, almost two thirds of holiday nights were based in flats, caravans and tents, and only just over one third in hotels and guest-houses. In Morecambe there has been some shift to self-catering accommodation, but even here the number of such establishments fell by 42 per cent between 1973 and 1987.

12 *Enhancement of quality of the service product*: two particular features are increasingly found in hotels in the UK – first, the replacement of untrained family labour (spouse/children of the owner) by labour trained either within the larger companies or via hotel and catering courses; and secondly, the improvement in the quality of accommodation provided. On the first, there is relatively little evidence of this occurring in Morecambe. One hotel receptionist summarised thus the typical situation: 'To get me this job I wasn't asked for any qualification. I did have, I got four 'O' levels but they never inquired about that. The only thing they asked me for really was references' (KI 20). And even at the THF four-star hotel in Lancaster, the general manager commented: 'They don't need a single qualification as far as I'm concerned. That does nothing for me . . . I think this is one industry where if you've got the right attitude and the right ambition, you can do what you like . . . I have no formal qualifications.'

As far as the second point is concerned, the existing physical infrastructure of the typical terraced Morecambe hotel prevents much 'upgrading'. Indeed, most such properties were built as ordinary houses, not as hotels, and there is no space to expand. They cannot be easily upgraded with the provision of *en suite* facilities, which many holidaymakers now expect as a result of their experience of higher quality accommodation, the result of huge investments by overseas hotel owners.

For enterprises in existing resorts there are few other strategies available. There is little chance of much reorganisation of production or of spatial relocation, while changes in the nature of the service product would normally entail movement of facilities out of the resort. The minister with special responsibility for tourism, John Lee, summarised in 1988 the situation for resorts such as Morecambe. He maintained that what is crucially needed is the upgrading of facilities by private hotel owners. He noted that only two or three smaller Morecambe hotels had applied for funds for such upgrading. He maintained that people must decide whether to take an optimistic view of investment or 'whether they are going to shrug their shoulders, sink into their sea shells and gradually see the growing tourism spending power increasingly pass them by' (*LG*, 12.2.88: 13). In Chapter 6 we will consider the lack of political organisation of these individual enterprises and how they have to be organised, or, at least – and this point was made by the local tourism director – how their efforts need to be coordinated by the local Council.

In the following chapters we will consider what the effects have been of the various patterns of restructuring in both manufacturing and services. We will begin with the consequences upon the occupational structure of the transformed pattern of industry.

4

The Experience of Restructuring

We have so far discussed a range of issues relating to structural changes and the locality. These processes of change affecting the quantities and the organisation of different kinds of productive activity will in turn affect, and be affected by, local social, political, cultural and aesthetic relations and practices, and we consider these in Chapters 5 and 6. Although most of our work is concerned to look 'directly' at the processes and relations involved in these connections, it is also the case that they are, at some level, mediated through the people who comprise the population of a locality. Structural changes affect individuals, and are reflected in aggregate measures of the characteristics (location, economic activity, household position, industry, occupation) of those individuals. Equally, facts revealed through these aggregate features (the changing class composition of a locality, for example) can help to illuminate a range of structural and other local social changes. There are complex and multi-faceted links between the structure of places generated in a local economy, the incumbents of those places, and the forms and effects of local social, political and cultural life. Such links in turn are 'resumed' in (normally strongly contested) representations of 'what a place is like': a place of 'history and character' or of 'industrial dereliction'; a place of 'dangerous ghettos' or of 'cosmopolitan colour'. These representations appear in their turn, in a bewilderingly short time, to have become (or perhaps to have gained recognition as) key determinants of the prosperity and prospects of a 'place'.

These features and prospects have both a coarse and a fine spatial structure. Thus Martin (1988) argues that despite local variations there is nevertheless a clear and incontrovertible (and very long-established) 'north–south divide' in the UK, whether measured by employment, sectoral distribution, unemployment, class distribution, business activity, disposable income, poverty or party preference. On the other hand, Townsend (1986) shows that, at the level of travel-to-work areas (TTWAs), examples of marked net job growth over the period 1978–84 occurred in a surprising diversity of places and in most regions.

In this chapter we apply various data sources – principally the Census of Population, the Census of Employment, the OPCS 1% Longitudinal Study (LS – see Appendix), and a data set of our own of work histories of three hundred women, alongside qualitative data from a series of 'key informants' (KI – see Appendix) interviewed in the Lancaster TTWA – to the question of how social changes 'impinge across' the inhabitants of a place. But it is worth first considering how in general such aggregate resources can relate to more qualitative concerns with the action of social processes, at a whole variety of spatial scales, on 'the locality'. These dimensions can be summarised in Figure 4.1.

1   *Evidence* for process
  1.1 *reflective* relation to process
  1.2 *intrinsic* relation to process

2   *Effects* of process
  2.1 *description*
  2.2 *inputs* for local processes
    2.2.1 *circulation* of population
        (spatial comparison less feasible)
      2.2.1.1 *base measure*
      2.2.1.2 *independent* local change
      2.2.1.3 *outcome* of labour market, restructuring
    2.2.2 *recomposition* of population
        (spatial comparison more feasible)
        2.2.2.1 *economic* activity
        2.2.2.2 *housing*
        2.2.2.3 *'standard of living'*

Figure 4.1   *Aggregate data and social process in the locality*

First, there is the use of aggregate data to provide *evidence* for supposed processes. Change in sectoral employment is used as evidence for processes of industrial restructuring, for example, or changes in the class composition of an area can be used to support a claim about the enhanced importance of the service class in local politics. Here the data are assumed to have a *reflective* relation to process. But there is another level at which the relationship between data and process is much tighter, to the point where it may be difficult to distinguish them. The concept of 'migration', for example, can be so closely tied to the quantitative data on the movement of people that it fails to engage with any external causal process – the phenomenon is, as it were, seeking to 'explain itself'. Similarly, the concept of 'local labour market' can be used to focus almost exclusively on data about the supply of and the demand for certain categories of labour in particular places. In this, the constitution of labour markets by *social* processes of the exclusion of workers by credentials, kinship, gender, race and so on – and hence by struggles within and between groups of workers and of employers around those exclusions – has disappeared from view (cf. Peck, 1989). While aggregate data on the incumbents of job positions can obviously connect with debates about such social processes, they should not be used to *displace* them. Here, the data could be said to have an *intrinsic* relation to the process or concept, such that it would be hard to imagine the process in the absence of this particular kind of data. This must nearly always be grounds for suspicion about the concept's explanatory power.

Secondly, aggregate data can be used to clarify the *effects* of processes. The same data on changes in sectoral employment, for example, can be used in the reverse direction to provide evidence of the effects of industrial restructuring on the quantity, quality and distribution of employment. It is clearly a problem if the same data are used to do both! This can again be divided into two aspects. At a first level there is the *descriptive* use of data to set out the effects of processes. So, for example, describing the fate of the incumbents of jobs destroyed or relocated through deindustrialisation would justify itself within a British empiricist tradition of documenting poverty and inequality. But at another level, the effects of certain processes are in turn treated as 'inputs' for other processes. In the locality, for example, the effects of economic restructuring can be considered from the point of view of their impact on local political movements, local class relations or the local state.

This second level, of effects as inputs for local processes, can again be split into two components. First, there is what could be termed the *circulation* of population, meaning 'migration' viewed as the effects of restructuring in expelling people from or attracting them to the locality. This will obviously involve *measures* of population, mostly drawn from the census. It is therefore helpful to distinguish three different aspects of the concern with population. First there is population as a 'base measure' of, for example, the number of married women of working age in the local labour market area, against which economic activity – the number of married women in employment – can be assessed and compared with other areas. Secondly, there are measures of significant local characteristics or local changes which are relatively independent of the labour market: for example, the size of the retired population, or the urban versus rural location of different social classes. And thirdly, there are postulated *outcomes* of labour market changes, such as rates of in- and out-migration by sex, class, age, sector, industry or occupation.

The point or interest of such questions is in the contribution of 'circulation' to 'remaking' a place. Local 'traditions' or sedimented practices in politics or in the labour movement, for example, are obviously vulnerable to significant relocations of the people engaged in them. Again, the characteristics of local civil society will be affected by processes of circulation. Savage and Fielding (1989), for example, have recently referred to the south-east of Britain as an 'escalator region', where people from all regions gain their first entry to the service class, but many of them later depart for other regions. One must then, in turn, consider the role of such (newly) 'metropolitan' service class immigrants in local civil society, in local cultural and aesthetic struggles, and so on. This issue is taken up, in the context of struggles over a local plan for Lancaster, in Chapter 5.

The purpose of a notion of 'circulation', therefore, is to forge a mediating link through which aggregate data on spatial relocation can work to connect the effects of processes of restructuring as 'inputs' to processes of local social change. The second, equivalent, notion is that of the *recomposition* of a population. This applies to significant shifts of experience – and hence, perhaps, of material interests and of organisational capacities – for particular local groups: where, for example, people move out of employment, or from full-time to part-time work, or from factory to office work, or from a private to a state employer, or from one neighbourhood in a locality to another. 'Recomposition' can also be subdivided into a number of aspects. First, one could distinguish the recomposition of economic activity: changes in the availability of full-time or part-time work broken down by sex, age, class, industry, and so on. Secondly, there is the recomposition of housing: changes in tenure, in cost, in 'style' and also in location as, for example, in the expulsion of the urban working class to penal outer estates in Glasgow or Liverpool. One could more generally here include the spatial recomposition of a locality, as in the separation of areas of industry and residence, or the break-up and redevelopment of areas, and the dislocation of people, of a particular class or occupational character, as in 1960s slum clearance. And thirdly, it is perhaps increasingly relevant to consider the 'standard of living' that obtains in particular areas or regions, as the balance of relative incomes and costs shifts rapidly and dramatically. It has recently been estimated, for example, that these relativities of costs and income – and especially housing and transport – produce a cost-of-living 'penalty' of 18 per cent for the whole of the south-east, and 25 per cent for London.

These notions of circulation and recomposition are not cut-and-dried distinctions; they intersect and contaminate each other in various ways. It must be stressed that the different dimensions discussed here relate to different *uses* of data rather than different data sources. In the relation of data to issues, the same sources can be employed in various ways. We made use of reflective evidence for restructuring, mostly from Census of Employment data, in Chapter 2, whereas here it is issues of circulation and recomposition that are salient. We use temporal and spatial dimensions to interpret the data, comparing 1971 and 1981, and comparing the Lancaster area usually with national averages for Britain or for England and Wales. There is, though, a difference between circulation and recomposition in the appropriateness of attempting spatial comparisons. It makes some sense for recomposition to compare rates of economic activity, for example, in one locality with another, or with a national average – though there are always potential pitfalls such as ecological fallacies in the way such comparisons are made. But it is more problematic for questions of circulation because there is no meaningful, rather than conventional, way to 'standardise' a spatial unit. One could, for example, try to compare the variation by region in the numbers who have relocated across a regional boundary between 1971 and 1981; but there would be no way of knowing that one was comparing like with like. This is paradoxical, since it is circulation – an inherently spatial concept – for which spatial comparisons are most fraught. Recomposition questions are not immune from such problems, which will in part depend on the characteristics of particular spatial units. The notion of travel-to-work area tries to capture such a standard – and, since 1984, does so on the basis of real data on journeys to work rather than on intuition – but with very variable success. Lancaster District is a fortunate example, since the administrative area and the TTWA correspond closely. It is also a remarkably self-contained labour market: in 1971 only 7.9 per cent of Lancaster residents in employment worked outside the district, while 7.8 per cent of those employed in the district lived outside it. For 1981 the corresponding figures are 7.9 and 6.8 per cent.

The Recomposition of Economic Activity

We focus here on the recomposition of economic activity, in particular on the relationship between industrial and occupational change. In this chapter we discuss the parameters of such change in Lancaster and its possible meaning for the incumbents of places in the Lancaster labour market. Chapters 5 and 6 look at the effects of such changes on social, cultural and political behaviour. Here we take a threefold approach to economic recomposition. First, we use aggregate data to improve the 'transparency' of the processes under investigation, and secondly we discuss what these processes might mean for individuals. In the following chapters we will attempt to close the conceptual circle by looking at the way that disparate individual experiences of change reflect back on places themselves.

One problem in achieving such transparency is the insensitivity of aggregate data to the multiplicity of ways in which gender and race inform occupational trajectories. This insensitivity has been most apparent in early postwar sociological analyses of class, which held that women had the same class position as their husbands or fathers (for critiques of this position see Acker, 1980; Delphy, 1984; Stanworth, 1984; Walby, 1986a). We have argued throughout that the recomposition of structures of patriarchal and racist relations is a crucial aspect of social restructuring. Yet if it is the case that the basis for this recomposition is underlain by economic recomposition (as is argued for class relations), then aggregate employment and industrial data will shed little light on the process because of the assumptions on which the collection of such data is based. For instance, the aggregate data presented in this chapter show that Lancaster appears to be an 'escalator' region for women: one in which women experience upward occupational mobility as a result of restructuring processes. This distorts significantly the way women experience occupational change, and the way that occupational data are collected is profoundly insensitive to women's occupations.

The evidence provided in earlier chapters showed that Lancaster experienced early deindustrialisation. However, we do not know whether individuals within the locality have themselves experienced this process. Cross-sectional data, even when it is presented in a time series, cannot provide information about individual trajectories. Such information can only be gathered via longitudinal studies. It is also the case that a number of theoretical questions can only be satisfactorily investigated by using longitudinal data. Some authors have pointed out that a meaningful understanding of class position will not be achieved by looking at an individual's immediate occupation, but must take into account that person's likely occupational trajectory. This has been demonstrated by Stewart et al. (1980) in relation to the class position of male clerks who move from early routine clerical jobs to end their occupational careers in administrative and managerial occupations.

Where the focus of analysis has been women's employment, an important issue has been the significance of domestic labour and life cycle events on women's participation in and remuneration for paid work. This approach demands longitudinal data for its full exploration. Cross-sectional data will not allow examination of the impact of a break from paid work for childcare, or a shift from full- to part-time work on women's careers. There are pitfalls in the longitudinal approach, however. An analysis restricted to the use of longitudinal data – since it will not reflect structural or labour market changes – might be tempted to explain women's careers in terms of life events such as marriage or children, rather than seeking causes for low pay or fractured career patterns in wider labour market structures. Hence the strengths of longitudinal data are best utilised in conjunction with cross-sectional data.

In looking at labour market change in Lancaster we make use of two types of longitudinal data: the Lancaster Women's Work History Survey (LWWHS), a survey of three hundred women which collected data on work/life histories (among other things – see Appendix); and the OPCS 1% Longitudinal Study, which links the individual records of 4/365 of the population from census to census and with certain NHS Central Register and other Registrar General Data. At one extreme, then, we have aggregate 'stock' data on structural change in Lancaster derived from the Census of Population; census small areas statistics; Census of Employment and unemployment records (accessed through NOMIS – see Appendix), VAT registrations, and so on. At the other extreme we have detailed life and work histories from the key informant interviews. Bridging the gap between these two extremes are the LS data and the survey of the three hundred women.

Economic Activity

We start, though, with an assessment of economic activity, and this involves considering population as a 'base measure', as discussed above. The 1981 census gives the population (persons present) of the Lancaster District as 121,311, a reduction of 1.9 per cent on 1971. This apparently ends a long period of population growth (11.8 per cent, 1951–71; 7.7 per cent, 1961–71), both in absolute terms and relative to other areas. The usually resident population in 1981 was 118,589, a reduction on 1971 of 1.7 per cent. However, subsequent population estimates suggest that this is a hesitation rather than a reversal, with an estimate for 1988 of 128,000. There is also a discrepancy of at least 1500 between 1971 and 1981 as a result of the 1981 census being held outside higher education term time. Of the change in total population, the net effect of births and deaths is a reduction of 5.2 per cent, with migration contributing an increase of 3.3 per cent. As Table 4.1 shows, this is a distinctive combination compared to other areas, connected to its (now possibly declining) status as a retirement location.

Table 4.1 *Net population change, Lancaster District, Lancashire, North-West region and Great Britain, 1961–81, %*[1]

| | 1961–71 | 1971–81 | | |
	Total	Total	Births & deaths	Migration
Lancaster District	7.66	−1.86	−5.20	3.34
Lancashire	6.63	2.36	−1.50	3.86
N-W region	2.61	−2.77	0.48	−3.25
GB	5.25	0.57	1.15	−0.59

[1]Intercensal net % population change (persons present).

Source: Census of Population 1961, 1971, 1981, calculated from CEN 81 KSLA, Table 1F

The figures for population given in Table 4.2 show that there was a small reduction in the total population between 1971 and 1981; but the population of working age does not appear to have changed at all. Within this, however, married women of working age fell in numbers by about 3 per cent, while single, widowed and divorced women of working age increased by 4 per cent.

The numbers of people of working age in employment in the

Table 4.2 *Population change, Lancaster District, 1971–81*

	1971[1]	1981[2]	Change 1971–81 %[3]
Men	58,295	56,236	−1.1
Women	65,320	62,353	−2.2
Total	**123,615**	**118,589**	**−1.7**
Men, w.a.[4]	*36,105*	*34,800*	*−1.2*
Women, w.a., married	22,800	21,600	−2.9
Women, w.a., s.w.d.[5]	10,050	10,200	4.0
Women, w.a., total	*32,850*	*31,800*	*−0.7*
Total, w.a.	**68,955**	**66,600**	**−0.1**

[1]Persons present.
[2]Usual residents.
[3]% change calculated by estimating a conversion from 'persons present' to 'usual residents'.
[4]Working age.
[5]Single, widowed or divorced.

Sources: Censuses of Population 1971, 1981

Table 4.3   *Employment (working age) change, Lancaster District, 1971, 1981*

	1971	1981	Change 1971–81 %
Men, full-time		26,340	
Men, part-time	420		
Men, total	*28,560*	*26,760*	*−6.3*
Women, married, f.-t.		5,560	
Women, married, p.-t.		6,690	
Women, married, all	10,730	12,250	14.2
Women, s.w.d., f.-t.		4,920	
Women, s.w.d., p.-t.		990	
Women, s.w.d., all	5,540	5,910	6.7
Women, all, f.-t.	10,680[1]	10,480	−1.9[1]
Women, all, p.-t.	5,590[1]	7,680	37.4[1]
Women, total	*16,270*	*18,160*	*11.6*
All	**44,830**	**44,920**	**0.2**

[1]1971 f.-t./p.-t. split for women (and hence 1971–81 changes) estimated from converted 1971 Census of Employment proportions.

Sources: Censuses of Population 1971, 1981; Census of Employment 1971

Lancaster District for 1971 and 1981 are shown in Table 4.3. This table has been drawn from Census of Population data in order more effectively to calculate 'activity rates' below. It is interesting to compare this to an equivalent table from Census of Employment data – there are some substantial differences. There are notorious problems with the Census of Employment; but there may also be a significant real effect resulting from confining attention to employed of 'working age' in the Census of Population data. This table includes a measure of 'full-time equivalent' employment, on the basis of two part-time for one full-time job. The appropriateness of such a measure is debatable, but it does at least give some indication of the quantity of work as distinct from the number of jobs. On this basis, as Table 4.4 shows, Lancaster District contained hardly any more paid work in 1981 than in 1971, distributed in about 4 per cent more jobs.

The relationship between employment and unemployment is increasingly problematic when we are considering economic activity. It has for some time been argued that official unemployment rates are a poor guide to the labour market position of women. This can now also be maintained for men, since the same factors, such as the numbers of 'discouraged workers', the effects

Table 4.4   *Full-time, part-time and full-time equivalent employment change, Lancaster TTWA, 1971, 1981*

	1971	1981	Change 1971–81 %
Men, full-time	24,286	23,142	−4.7
Men, part-time	1,193	1,681	40.9
Men, total	25,479	24,823	−2.6
Men, f.-t.e.[1]	*24,883*	*23,983*	*−3.6*
Women, all, f.-t.	10,607	10,343	−2.5
Women, all, p.-t.	6,518	9,105	39.7
Women, total	17,125	19,448	13.6
Women, f.-t.e.	*13,886*	*14,896*	*7.3*
All	**42,604**	**44,271**	**3.9**
All, f.-t.e.	*38,769*	*38,879*	*0.3*
p.-t. as % } men	4.7	6.8	44.7
of total } women	38.1	46.8	22.8

[1]Full-time equivalent.

Sources: Censuses of Employment 1971, 1981

Table 4.5   *Modified activity rates, Lancaster District, 1971–81, %*[1]

	1971	1981	Change 1971–81 %
Men, full-time		75.7	
Men, part-time		1.2	
Men, total	*77.5*	*76.9*	*−0.8*
Women, married, f.-t.		25.7	
Women, married, p.-t.		31.0	
Women, married, total	47.1	56.7	20.4
Women, s.w.d., f.-t.		48.2	
Women, s.w.d., p.-t.		9.7	
Women, s.w.d., total	51.3	57.9	12.6
Women, all, f.-t.	31.8	33.0	3.8
Women, all, p.-t.	16.6	24.2	45.8
Women, all	*48.4*	*57.1*	*18.0*
All	**63.6**	**67.5**	**6.1**

[1]This table is constructed using various correction factors in order to arrive at a 'best estimate' of population and employment at these dates. However, our main conclusions are equally supported in the uncorrected data.

Sources: Censuses of Population 1971, 1981; Census of Employment 1971

of exclusion from eligibility for benefit, and other forms of disguised unemployment, apply to them. In much of what follows we therefore place emphasis on the 'participation rate' of the corresponding group of the working-age population. This involves the assumption that the general preparedness to participate in paid work stays relatively constant, and that changes in participation therefore reflect changes in the labour market more reliably than changes in corresponding rates of unemployment. Table 4.5 looks at activity rates, taking employment as a percentage of the corresponding group of working age. It shows that activity rates for men between 1971 and 1981 hardly changed, while those for married women and, especially, for part-time women workers increased dramatically. However, since there is also a small increase for full-time women workers, this is not a *substitution* of part-time for full-time women's work.

Sectoral Mobility

To examine sectoral mobility we use a very simple twofold distinction between 'production industry' – including primary and extractive, manufacturing and construction industries and gas, electricity and water – and service industries. The decade 1971–81 saw a continuation of the strong structural shift in the economy from production to services, and this is shown in Table 4.6. For men nationally, over the decade, there was a switch from production to service industries equivalent to some 6 per cent of men in employment, so that by 1981 men were equally divided between the sectors. Less than one third of women were in production industry in 1971, and those numbers fell by a further third from 1971 to 1981, leaving less than one quarter of women in production industry. As we saw in earlier chapters, Lancaster's deindustrialisation came sooner and bit deeper than the national average, so that Lancaster had a location quotient for men in manufacturing industry of 0.91 in 1971, while the equivalent for women was 0.68. If Lancaster's continued switch from production to services was slightly slower than the national average, then this is because the shift had already occurred.

These data summarise the *net structural* changes in Britain and in Lancaster, but the circulation and recomposition of the population depend crucially on the *'flows'* of people which resolve into these structural changes. We can explore these processes with data from the 1% Longitudinal Study. However, we cannot make a direct comparison of this data with the structural data from the censuses, because there will be a 'cohort effect' as the sample ages ten years.

Table 4.6 *Industrial sector, Great Britain and Lancaster District, 1971, 1981, %*[1]

	1971 GB	LD	LQ²	1981 GB	LD	LQ	1971–81 GB	LD
Men & Women								
Production	47.5	39.9		39.3	34.3		−17.3	−13.9
			0.84			0.87		
Services	52.5	60.1		60.7	65.7		15.7	9.2
			1.15			1.08		
Men								
Production	56.8	51.6		50.7	48.3		−10.8	−6.3
			0.91			0.95		
Services	43.2	48.9		49.3	51.7		14.2	5.6
			1.13			1.05		
Women								
Production	31.3	21.4		22.1	15.5		−29.3	−27.9
			0.68			0.70		
Services	68.6	78.6		77.8	84.5		13.4	7.6
			1.15			1.09		

[1]Sectoral distribution and change, 1971–81, GB and Lancaster District, persons in employment.
²Location quotient.

Sources: Censuses of Population 1971, 1981

Table 4.7 *Sectoral destination, England and Wales, 1981, %*[1]

1971	1981 Production	Services	Unemployed, retired, permanently sick	Total
Men & Women				
Production	67.0	21.4	11.7	100
Services	14.2	78.2	7.7	100
Unempl., retd., perm. sick	23.7	29.7	46.6	100
Total	40.3	48.2	11.5	100
Men				
Production	69.7	17.9	12.4	100
Services	16.4	74.5	9.1	100
Unempl., retd., perm. sick	27.2	22.6	50.2	100
Total	46.5	40.6	12.9	100
Women				
Production	53.9	38.1	8.0	100
Services	10.6	84.1	5.3	100
Unempl., retd., perm. sick	14.4	48.6	37.1	100
Total	24.0	68.3	7.7	100

[1]Population of working age in 1971 and 1981.

Source: OPCS 1% Longitudinal Study

We have selected a population of working age in both 1971 and 1981: for men, 15–55 in 1971 and 25–65 in 1981; for women, 15–50 in 1971 and 25–60 in 1981. We have also departed from usual census table practice in separating those out of employment rather than classifying them by their last job. This is because we regard knowledge of 'unemployment' as destination to be more important than knowledge of the class location of the last job. For men nationally the switch from production to services is quite modest, despite the contraction of the sector, with a proportionately almost equal reverse flow from services to production. For women the picture is different, with 38.1 per cent switching from production to services and 10.6 per cent switching back. Though the latter is a small proportion, it is nevertheless quite a large absolute number, given the already unequal size of the sectors for women.

Table 4.8 *Sectoral destination, Lancaster District, 1981, %*[1]

1971	1981			
	Production	Services	Unemployed, retired, permanently sick	Total
Men & Women				
Production	58.0	22.7	19.3	100
Services	13.0	77.0	9.9	100
Unempl., retd., perm. sick	11.1	29.6	59.3	100
Total	30.3	51.8	17.9	100
Men				
Production	60.0	17.0	23.0	100
Services	18.4	66.7	14.9	100
Unempl., retd., perm. sick	9.5	33.3	57.1	100
Total	37.5	39.4	23.1	100
Women				
Production	47.4	52.6	0.0	100
Services	6.8	89.2	4.1	100
Unempl., retd., perm. sick	16.7	16.7	66.7	100
Total	15.2	77.8	7.1	100

[1]Population of working age in 1971 and 1981 and resident in Lancaster District in 1971.

Source: OPCS 1% Longitudinal Study

Table 4.8 shows the equivalent sectoral destinations for Lancaster District, and Table 4.9 brings together the local data and that for England and Wales for comparison. For men the outflow from production in Lancaster is more pronounced, but it is notable that this extra flow goes not to services but to the unemployed, retired and permanently sick category – the fate of fully 23 per cent of this group. For women, the flow out of production is stronger in Lancaster than nationally, with services, rather than the category of unemployed et al., the destination.

Table 4.9   *Sectoral destination, England & Wales and Lancaster District, 1981, %*[1]

1971		1981		
		Production	Services	Unemployed, retired, permanently sick
Men				
Production	E & W	70	18	12
	Lancaster	60	17	23
Services	E & W	16	75	9
	Lancaster	18	67	15
Women				
Production	E & W	54	38	8
	Lancaster	47	53	0
Services	E & W	11	84	5
	Lancaster	7	89	4

[1]Population of working age in 1971 and 1981; for 'Lancaster' rows, resident in Lancaster District in 1971.

Source: OPCS 1% Longitudinal Study

The Lancaster Women's Work History Survey sheds further light on sectoral mobility and confirms the findings from the Longitudinal Study. Table 4.10 uses data from the survey to look at job movement between sectors and shows that, within the sample, 75 per cent of job changes were within a sector and only 25 per cent of the sample experienced sectoral change. Of the 25 per cent of women who did experience sectoral change, while more shifts were from manufacturing to services, confirming the LS picture, the number is small. Overall, 41 per cent of moves were from services to production, as compared with 59 per cent from production to services. There is a more marked shift from manufacturing to services when all working life is taken into consideration, suggesting that the pattern which Dex describes whereby 'women reflect the process of deindustrialisation in their individual experiences' (1987: 102), may have changed over the 1970s.

Women's typical break out of the labour force is now known to have a detrimental effect on their position in it, and a Department

Table 4.10   *Women's job movement by sector*

| | 1960–80 | | All working life | |
	No.	%	No.	%
Production to service	36	15	188	24
Service to production	25	10	121	16
Service to service	123	51	278	36
Production to production	57	24	186	24
Total	241	100	773	100

Source: LWWHS

of Employment/OPCS survey of 6000 women showed that they were likely to re-enter the labour force at a lower occupational level than that at which they had left (Martin and Roberts, 1984). In sectoral terms the fact that much part-time work is in the service sector and that many women returning to the labour market after having had children seek this part-time work would suggest that we might expect women re-entrants to the labour market to return to the service sector, even if their previous job had been in manufacturing. However, Table 4.11 shows that this is not the case in Lancaster. Here the majority of women returners took employment in the same sector that they left; most changes between sectors involve job-to-job changes. The employment break was of little significance in understanding the shift of women into the service sector in the Lancaster sample, although it is the case that women were more likely to return part-time than full-time.

Table 4.11   *Women re-entrants and job change*

| | Number of job changes | |
	Job-to-job	Re-entrant
Production to service	65	33
Service to production	64	11
Service to service	79	199
Production to production	70	116

Source: LWWHS

Where a sector is declining, as with production in Lancaster, then the age of those who are expelled from it could make a critical difference to the area's 'recomposition'. Where there is contraction short of total closure, firms could seek to retain their younger workers through redundancy settlements, or established workers could retain the remaining places at the expense of younger ones. Older and younger expelled workers might in turn experience quite different possibilities of recruitment into expanding sectors. Table 4.12 shows sectoral mobility for Lancaster District for men and for

Table 4.12   *Sectoral destination by age, Lancaster District, 1981, %*[1]

1971		1981			
		Production	Services	Unemployed, retired, permanently sick	Total
Men					
Production	16–30	68	18	15	100
	Over 30	56	17	27	100
Services	16–30	33	63	4	100
	Over 30	14	74	12	100
Women					
Production	16–30	50	50	0	100
	Over 30	44	56	0	100
Services	16–30	5	95	0	100
	Over 30	8	87	6	100

[1]Population of working age in 1971 and 1981, resident in Lancaster District in 1971.

Source: OPCS 1% Longitudinal Study

women, with a twofold age split of 16–30 or over 30 in 1971 (but still of working age in 1971 and 1981), so averaging an age split at age 35 across the decade. For men, it is clearly the older group who are disproportionately expelled from production, and again it is clear that the destination of this extra flow is unemployment, retirement or permanent sickness rather than service industry. It is unexpected, too, that one third of men in the younger age group and in services in 1971 have moved to production in 1981. For women, too, it is the older age group who leave production in larger proportions, but this time with a service industry destination.

Using the interviews with key informants we can begin to tease out the way in which such sectoral moves are perceived by individuals experiencing them. Qualitative data show how complex the experiences of individuals are. The way in which sectoral change was perceived varied by gender, by household income and by age at which the sectoral change took place, to name but a few variations.

We interviewed only people who were in employment at the time of the interviews (1987); hence we have no insight into the experiences of those men whose destination on leaving manufacturing was the unemployed, retired or permanently sick category. However, the experience of those males who had moved into services following a spell of unemployment (that is to say, they had not made the move voluntarily), after working in manufacturing for some considerable time, suggests that such a move entailed a considerable downward shift in terms of both pay and the perceived status of the job (the exception was one respondent who had changed from manufacturing to services very early in his career, aged twenty-two, and who had remained in the same occupational group).

One man had been made redundant from Lansils after thirty years as a maintenance fitter. When interviewed he was working as a hotel porter, a job he got through family connections, after spending twelve months unemployed. As a hotel porter he was earning about £1.80 per hour: 'We are very low paid you know . . . this job isn't well paid . . . it doesn't suit anybody, the money's a lot to do with it you see. At the end of the day if you are not getting money to pay your way you may look for something better' (KI21: 9). He personally felt, though, that it wasn't worth his while looking for another job because of his age (fifty-eight).

Another 54-year-old man had worked as a paint sprayer and spot welder in a local manufacturing company and was employed as a hospital porter when interviewed. He earned just under £2 per hour, a rate of pay he described as 'terrible'. His wife, who worked part-time as a nurse, said: 'We just sort of manage. We are sort of living . . . you are scrimping if you want your holiday . . . We are just holding our own. We haven't had a holiday for a bit. What we spend we spend on the house. When [the children] were babies we were better off than we are now' (KI15: 19). This husband and wife (who had two children, one in full-time work) felt that they were considerably worse off than they had ever been. They had both given up going out in an attempt to economise and felt very bitter about their situation. Both husband and wife agreed on this:

> *Wife*: It wouldn't be so bad if they sort of gave you a good wage to live off. But unless he gets [overtime], somebody is off sick and you are working all the time, you are making nothing . . . And my wage stays in the bank and it pays the mortgage, rates, the water rate, the gas bill, the electric bill, and we never have anything left.
> *Husband*: And we are getting by on mine you see. And I struggle to run my car really.
> *Wife*: We just get through, just about. And we had either to give up the car or give up going out. So we gave up going out . . .
> *Husband*: . . . I suppose the only pleasure we have is the car really . . . I don't think we are living good really. (KI15: 26–7)

For this particular individual deindustrialisation had cut across an early work pattern which had seen him make a number of job moves within manufacturing: 'At one stage [in Lancaster] you could finish off one job one weekend and start on Monday morning at another place, no problem' (KI15: 27). Although the respondent was not unemployed, and recognised that he was 'better off' than some, his move into the service sector had seen a diminution in his own and his household's living standards.

These examples highlight one of the problems of identifying the meaning of sectoral change for individuals. For individuals do not directly experience the vagaries of economic change; rather, that change is mediated by the household. The standard of living of men varied, depending on the earnings of other members of the household; and the ability of unemployed males to take a job at rates of pay of £1.80 to £2 per hour must also vary, depending on the income of spouses and/or adult children living in the household. The inflexibility of the benefit system and the low pay of unskilled jobs on offer in services mean that a choice between unemployment and work is circumscribed where there is no other substantial earner in the household. Similarly, there were varied experiences for women in the service class. Life for those women supporting a household, such as the full-time hospital sister supporting a disabled husband and two unemployed sons, or the divorced teacher with two children, was very different from that of women with high-earning partners.

One male key informant had moved, aged twenty-two, from manufacturing to services in 1967, having just completed a six-year engineering apprenticeship. He described how he took the decision to leave:

> that was about the time . . . the take-over was [Nairns took over Williamsons] . . . The factory was split up into maintenance gangs and . . . they took two or three lads off each gang to more or less go around every machine with an 'x', like when you go through a forest, every tree with an 'x' on, you cut it down, and that's what we were doing, literally, we were stripping the machines down, loading [them] on to wagons, and they were taking them to . . . Kirkcaldy . . . So every machine that went, the process people they were made redundant right away. It was just a matter of time before they would have made me redundant. (KI19: 3)

This respondent had taken a drop in pay and moved into the National Health Service as a maintenance engineer in 1967, remaining there over the next twenty years. When he was interviewed, his wages were good (about £175 per week without overtime) and he had good prospects of promotion.

Men who had moved from manufacturing to services perceived this as a step down in terms of status as well as pay (although the work itself was not necessarily seen as unskilled). As a hotel porter put it, 'Me being an engineer, this type of job is like you being a doctor and ending up being a bus driver isn't it . . . I think this sort of work is lowering myself. Which I shouldn't do really' (KI21: 4, 12).

Women who had moved from manufacturing to services, although some were as poorly paid as the men, didn't see the move in the same way. Their view of sectoral change was less straightforward, fragmented and fractured by the compelling and multi-faceted demands of home and family. For many, manufacturing work had been done full-time before domestic commitments (usually children) had forced them to seek more flexible hours. However, interestingly, and in line with the evidence from the LWWHS, none had straightforwardly given up a full-time manufacturing job on the birth of a first child and then moved back into part-time service occupations after a spell of full-time child-rearing. Of those whom we interviewed who had made a move from manufacturing to services, all had continued to work full-time in manufacturing after the births of first and (sometimes) second children. For instance, one of the sample of three hundred women, re-interviewed in 1987, was working as a school welfare officer. This woman had returned to full-time work in manufacturing after the births of three children. She had worked as a machinist, but said that she wouldn't like to go back to it – 'too much like hard work' – although she had enjoyed working with the other girls (KI18: 1).

Similarly, another woman, working as a hospital cleaner in 1987, had gone into manufacturing (a shoe manufacturers) when she left school at fourteen:

> Straight to work. In a shoe factory. That was the in thing at the time here . . . It's gone down now I think . . . but it was the in thing, the best money. Actually I did go in to be a nurse, the very first months, but the wages was 30 shillings and you had to give 10 shillings of it back, for the uniform and things. And then the girls I went about with they were on £2 3s 0d a week which was a bit more so I didn't go into nursing. [I went to] K Shoes. I was there till I was married, when my first child was born, and then I went back after she was born. I was there about eighteen years in all I think. (KI25: 2)

This woman had worked full-time in manufacturing after the birth of her first two children, and had then moved to work as a nursing auxiliary in the evenings, 'so there was somebody to look after the children'. After leaving her full-time manufacturing work she had held a variety of jobs in the service sector. Asked about the reasons for job changes, she said:

> Children. Always children. I used to do a lot of shifts which didn't work in at home, so I went on to nights . . . That got difficult and so I went to school dinners, and I was alright then doing dinners because the

youngest was at . . . the school I was cooking at . . . And then I'd to have a hysterectomy so I couldn't go back to that because it's quite heavy work . . . that was out. I had to pack that in and go. (KI25: 4–5)

These female respondents had taken manufacturing jobs because they paid well, and had subsequently sacrificed better pay for flexibility. They had not given up manufacturing work, or indeed work of any kind, when children were born. Rather, as the demands of family became more pressing, they found it necessary to seek different types of work. The hospital cleaner quoted above, for instance, had not had any time when she was not working – 'none whatsoever since fourteen . . . I cannot sit at home. It bores me at home. I'll clean, I'll polish and that's it' (KI25: 3–4).

In a similar vein, a woman who had moved to Lancaster from Rochdale described a shift from a clerical job in distribution (typist in a mail order factory) to assembly work and then back to private services.

Then I went to . . . which was part of Philips which was making components for televisions and stuff like that. Well I went there because it was better money than what I was on . . . it was assembly work . . . it wasn't a dirty job or anything like that. Then I moved here and . . . I worked in an arcade as a cashier and then . . . I got married and I got the job at the hotel and then I found out I was pregnant, I had my little girl and I went back to the hotel mainly because it fitted in with having her as well, and I do a part-time job at a night club two nights. (KI17: 4)

Several respondents saw the opportunity for manufacturing work and for women to earn 'good money' as having disappeared from Lancaster. We could hypothesise that for this reason women were less likely to drop out of manufacturing work as a result of the births of children than is the case in the service sector. At the same time, the prevalence of part-time opportunities in service work may encourage women in that sector to give up full-time and return to part-time work in that sector. Indeed, there may be pressure on them to do so. Deindustrialisation in Lancaster, and indeed nationally, could hence be hypothesised as reducing women's choices. This issue is discussed more fully on pages 124–30.

Class Mobility 1971–81

The decade 1971–81 was one of major structural change in class location. We shall consider this first using the class distribution of the population as a whole. As is well known, the question of the means of deriving a measure of social class from official statistics is problematic and controversial. The census variable 'Social Class' is particularly unsuitable for most sociological purposes, since it contains an amorphous 'Intermediate' category, and does not distinguish manual from non-manual in semi-skilled and unskilled work. For the census data, we shall be using a measure of class derived from the census variable 'Socio-Economic Group' (SEG) because it allows a sociologically more pertinent (though by no means perfect) scheme to be drawn up, and also because it permits comparison with some other recent examinations of these issues (Fielding and Savage, 1987; Savage and Fielding, 1989). We distinguish five class groups, as follows:

1 Service class
    SEG 1   Employers and managers – large establishments
    SEG 2.2   Managers – small establishments
    SEG 3   Professional workers – self-employed
    SEG 4   Professional workers – employees
    SEG 5.1   Ancillary workers and artists
2 Petite bourgeoisie
    SEG 2.1   Employers – small establishments
    SEG 12   Own account workers (other than professional)
    SEG 13   Farmers – employers and managers
    SEG 14   Farmers – own account
3 Intermediate non-manual
    SEG 5.2   Foremen and supervisors – non-manual
    SEG 6   Junior non-manual workers
    SEG 7   Personal service workers
4 Upper working class
    SEG 8   Foremen and supervisors – manual
    SEG 9   Skilled manual workers
5 Lower working class
    SEG 10   Semi-skilled manual workers
    SEG 11   Unskilled manual workers
    SEG 15   Agricultural workers

The change in the class structure for men and women between 1971 and 1981 on this measure is shown in Table 4.13. The most striking change for Great Britain as a whole is a 28.9 per cent increase in the proportionate size of the service class, balanced by a fall in the size of the working class: 14.4 per cent for the 'upper' and 9.2 per cent for the 'lower' working class. In both the classes where the rate of change for Lancaster differs markedly – the service class and the lower working class – this denotes a return to the national average in 1981 from a distinctive difference in 1971. When the changes for men and women are considered separately (Tables 4.14 and 4.15), then some differences between them

Table 4.13   *Social classes, Great Britain and Lancaster District, 1971, 1981, %*[1]

Men and women	1971			1981			1971–81	
	GB	*LD*	LQ[2]	GB	*LD*	LQ	GB	*LD*
1 Service class	18	*20*	1.09	23	*23*	1.01	28.9	*18.8*
2 Petite bourgeoisie	7	*11*	1.58	7	*11*	1.58	−0.6	*−0.6*
3 Intermediate non-manual	28	*26*	0.96	28	*27*	0.95	1.8	*1.2*
4 Upper working class	25	*21*	0.87	21	*19*	0.88	−14.4	*−12.9*
5 Lower working class	23	*21*	0.94	20	*20*	0.98	−9.2	*−5.3*

[1]Economically active (GB 1971 includes retired); Armed Forces and inadequately described excluded.
[2]Location quotient.

Sources: Censuses of Population 1971, 1981 (10%)

emerge. For the petite bourgeoisie, for example, a static condition overall conceals a 6.4 per cent increase for men and a 14.2 per cent decrease for women. Table 4.16 allows this comparison to be made more easily. This table also shows a class 'segregation' ratio, in which a value of 0 would indicate a class entirely populated by women, and a value of 1 a class entirely populated by men. The upper working class shows the most extreme male domination, increasing slightly as the class contracts. In the intermediate non-manual class the concentration of women has increased from 67 per cent in 1971 to 74 per cent in 1981.

Table 4.14 allows a comparison of class changes 1971–81 between Great Britain and Lancaster District to be made for men. From a similar starting point in 1971 (a location quotient of 0.99), Lancaster's service class expanded much more slowly: 19.7 per cent compared to 30.4 per cent nationally. Lancaster's most distinctive feature is the size of its petite bourgeoisie, maintaining its 1.5:1 differential across the decade. Lancaster men are relatively under-

Table 4.14 *Men's social classes, Great Britain and Lancaster District, 1971, 1981, %*[1]

	1971 GB	LD	LQ	1981 GB	LD	LQ	1971–81 GB	LD
1 Service class	19	19	0.99	25	23	0.91	30.4	19.7
2 Petite bourgeoisie	9	14	1.51	10	15	1.52	6.4	7.2
3 Intermediate non-manual	14	13	0.90	12	11	0.91	−15.2	−14.4
4 Upper working class	34	30	0.87	32	28	0.90	−8.1	−4.7
5 Lower working class	23	25	1.06	22	23	1.07	−6.4	−6.1

[1]Economically active (GB 1971 includes retired); Armed Forces and inadequately described excluded.

Sources: Censuses of Population 1971, 1981 (10%)

Table 4.15 *Women's social classes, Great Britain and Lancaster District, 1971, 1981, %*[1]

	1971 GB	LD	LQ	1981 GB	LD	LQ	1971–81 GB	LD
1 Service class	16	21	1.31	20	24	1.19	28.6	16.7
2 Petite bourgeoisie	4	8	1.92	4	7	1.93	−14.2	−13.7
3 Intermediate non-manual	52	49	0.95	53	49	0.93	2.4	0.3
4 Upper working class	7	7	1.04	5	5	0.97	−32.6	−36.9
5 Lower working class	21	15	0.71	18	15	0.83	−13.1	1.8

[1]Economically active (GB 1971 includes retired); Armed Forces and inadequately described excluded.

Sources: Censuses of Population 1971, 1981 (10%)

Table 4.16   *Men's and women's class change and segregation,
Great Britain, 1971–81, %*[1]

		1971	1981	1971–81
1	Total	17.9	23.1	28.9
Service	Men	19.1	25.0	30.4
class	Women	15.7	20.2	28.6
	Segregation	0.69	0.66	−4.4
2	Total	7.3	7.2	−0.6
Petite	Men	9.0	9.6	6.4
bourgeoisie	Women	4.1	3.5	−14.2
	Segregation	0.80	0.81	1.3
3	Total	27.6	28.0	1.8
Intermediate	Men	14.2	12.1	−15.2
non-manual	Women	51.7	53.0	2.4
	Segregation	0.33	0.26	21.2
4	Total	24.7	21.1	−14.4
Upper working	Men	34.3	31.6	−8.1
class	Women	7.2	4.8	−32.6
	Segregation	0.90	0.91	1.6
5	Total	22.5	20.5	−9.2
Lower working	Men	23.3	21.8	−6.4
class	Women	21.3	18.5	−13.1
	Segregation	0.66	0.65	−2.6

[1]From tables 4.14 and 4.15

Sources: Censuses of Population 1971, 1981

represented in the intermediate non-manual and upper working classes, moving slightly closer to the national average in the latter, through a slower decline.

For women, Table 4.15 shows that there is also a slower expansion of the service class for Lancaster than nationally: 16.7 per cent compared to 28.6 per cent. Here, though, the decline is not from parity, as for men, but from a location quotient of 1.31 in 1971 to 1.19 in 1981. Women in Lancaster figure even more prominently in the petite bourgeoisie than men, at nearly double the national rate in both 1971 and 1981, reflecting the catering and accommodation activities in Morecambe. Women in Lancaster were heavily under-represented in the lower working class in 1971 – a location quotient of 0.71 – but this class actually increased slightly by 1981, by contrast with a national decrease of 13.1 per cent.

These data summarise the *structural* changes on this measure of social class in Great Britain and in Lancaster, and we can again explore the circulation and recomposition of the population with data from the 1% Longitudinal Study. Table 4.17 is constructed

Table 4.17   *Class destination, England and Wales, 1981, %*[1]

1971	1981						
	1 Service class	2 Pte. bourg.	3 Intermed. n.-m.	4 Upper working class	5 Lower working class	6 Unempl., retd., perm. sick	Total
Men and women							
1 Service cl.	63	6	12	6	4	9	15
2 Pte. bourg.	9	58	7	10	7	9	7
3 Intermed. n.-m.	15	4	60	4	9	7	24
4 Upper w. cl.	7	6	5	55	15	12	29
5 Lower w. cl.	3	4	10	19	48	15	20
6 Unempl., retd., perm. sick	5	6	12	12	16	49	5
Total	17	9	21	23	18	12	100
Men							
1 Service cl.	67	6	9	7	4	8	18
2 Pte. bourg.	9	60	3	11	7	9	8
3 Intermed. n.-m.	27	5	42	7	9	9	13
4 Upper w. cl.	7	6	4	57	14	12	36
5 Lower w. cl.	4	5	4	23	47	17	20
6 Unempl., retd., perm. sick	5	7	4	16	17	51	5
Total	20	10	10	29	18	14	100
Women							
1 Service cl.	40	6	34	3	7	11	8
2 Pte. bourg.	8	44	30	2	9	6	3
3 Intermed. n.-m.	7	3	73	2	9	6	55
4 Upper w. cl.	3	3	23	32	31	9	7
5 Lower w. cl.	2	2	26	9	52	9	21
6 Unempl., retd., perm. sick	4	3	35	3	14	41	5
Total	8	4	53	6	20	9	100

[1]Population of working age in 1971 and 1981.

Source: OPCS 1% Longitudinal Study

from the LS on a similar basis to Table 4.7, and similar observations apply. It shows, for England and Wales, the intra-generational class 'destinations' in 1981 of the population in each class 'origin' in 1971: men, women, and both together. For men and women together, the average 'immobility' (that is, the likelihood of remaining in the same class, weighted by the size of the class in 1971) is 58.4 per cent. Mobility does, therefore, reflect the structural 'fate' of the class, with 63.2 per cent remaining in the expanding service class and 48.2 per cent remaining in the reducing lower working class. When the sexes are separated, men's mobility follows the general pattern, but with particularly marked movement out of intermediate non-manual, 27.1 per cent of whose destination is the service class, confirming again the gendered character of these occupational positions as a career staging post for men but a ceiling for women. It is also of some interest that, despite its structural expansion, there is considerable long-range downward mobility for men from the service class, with 8.6 per cent of destinations in intermediate non-manual and 10 per cent in the manual working class over one decade. The 'weighted average immobility' for men is 52 per cent.

Table 4.18   *Class destinations, England and Wales, 1981, %*[1]

1971		1981					
		1 Service class	2 Pte. bourg.	3 Intermed. non-manual	4 Upper w. cl.	5 Lower w. cl.	6 Unempl., ret., perm. sick
1 Service class	Men	67	6	9	7	4	8
	Women	40	6	34	3	7	11
2 Petite bourgeoisie	Men	9	60	3	11	7	9
	Women	9	44	31	2	9	6
3 Intermediate non-manual	Men	27	6	42	7	9	9
	Women	7	3	73	2	9	6
4 Upper working class	Men	7	6	4	57	14	12
	Women	3	3	23	32	31	9
5 Lower working class	Men	4	5	4	23	47	18
	Women	2	2	26	9	52	9

[1]Population of working age in 1971 and 1981.

Source: OPCS 1% Longitudinal Study

The intermediate non-manual class dominates the table for women's mobility, and dominates the 'weighted average immobility' at 58.3 per cent. There is a particularly strong contrast with men of service class origin, and also in women's movement out of the working class. These contrasts, for England and Wales, are more conveniently presented in Table 4.18. These figures relate, of course, to those in one or other of the class positions at both censuses – for women, just roughly one third of the age group. Table 4.19 shows the differences between men and women when other statuses of economic activity are included. These normally excluded statuses should be borne in mind when assessing all the longitudinal data.

Table 4.19 *Class and economic activity destinations, England and Wales, 1981, %*[1]

1971		1981				
	Classes 1–5	Unempl., retired, permanently sick	Other inactive	Dead	Other & missing	Total
Men						
Classes 1–5	71	9	0	4	16	87
Unempl., retd., perm. sick	34	36	1	9	20	5
Other inactive	50	6	1	1	41	5
Inmigrant to E & W	70	6	0	0	24	0
Other & missing	45	7	0	2	46	2
Total	67	11	0	4	18	100
Women						
Classes 1–5	50	4	25	2	19	53
Unempl., retd., perm. sick	26	18	31	5	21	3
Other inactive	36	3	42	2	18	43
Inmigrant to E & W	37	10	32	0	22	0
Other & missing	37	4	32	1	25	1
Total	43	4	33	2	19	100

[1]Population of working age in 1971 and 1981.

Source: OPCS 1% Longitudinal Study

Table 4.20 shows the intra-generational class destinations for those who were present in Lancaster District in 1971 (though not necessarily in 1981) – the local equivalent to the data for England and Wales in Table 4.17. Table 4.21 re-presents the data from Tables 4.17 and 4.20 so that the comparison between Lancaster and England and Wales can be more easily made. Men in Lancaster were considerably less successful at remaining in the service class. They were, by contrast, more successful at surviving in the petite bourgeoisie, though also at the expense of less upward mobility into the service class. Men in all classes had nearly double the chance of becoming unemployed, retired or permanently sick, but this is most dramatically the case for the lower working class, 40 per cent of whom end up in this category. There is more than twice the movement of men from the upper working class to the petite bourgeoisie locally than there is in England and Wales (see Table 4.21).

Table 4.20 *1981 class destinations of those resident in Lancaster District in 1971, %*[1]

1971	1981						
	1 Service class	2 Pte. bourg.	3 Intermed. n.-m.	4 Upper working class	5 Lower working class	6 Unempl., retd., perm. sick	Total
Men and women							
1 Service cl.	56	11	11	8	–	14	100
2 Pte. bourg.	6	66	6	6	6	11	100
3 Intermed. n.-m.	7	5	65	1	11	11	100
4 Upper w. cl.	6	13	7	47	9	18	100
5 Lower w. cl.	–	–	18	9	42	30	100
6 Unempl., retd., perm. sick	–	12	4	12	8	64	100
Total	11.4	15.9	24.4	16.2	11.8	20.3	100
Men							
1 Service cl.	53	13	10	10	0	13	100
2 Pte. bourg.	0	72	0	8	4	16	100
3 Intermed. n.-m.	13	7	50	3	7	20	100
4 Upper w. cl.	6	15	5	47	8	19	100
5 Lower w. cl.	0	0	8	8	44	40	100
6 Unempl., retd., perm. sick	0	16	0	16	5	63	100
Total	12.6	18.8	12.0	20.9	10.5	25.1	100
Women							
1 Service cl.	67	0	17	0	0	17	100
2 Pte. bourg.	20	50	20	0	10	0	100
3 Intermed. n.-m.	2	5	75	0	14	5	100
4 Upper w. cl.	0	0	33	50	17	0	100
5 Lower w. cl.	0	0	50	13	38	0	100
6 Unempl., retd., perm. sick	0	0	17	0	17	67	100
Total	8.8	8.8	53.8	5.0	15.0	8.8	100

[1]Population of working age in 1971 and 1981.

Source: OPCS 1% Longitudinal Study

Women in Lancaster in 1971 were, by contrast, more successful in remaining in the service class, and *both* in surviving in the petite bourgeoisie *and* in upward mobility from the petite bourgeoisie to the service class (see Table 4.21). They are also more successful in the very small upper working class category, and in upward

Table 4.21 *Class destinations, England & Wales and Lancaster District, 1981, %*[1]

1971		1981					
		1 Service class	2 Petite bourg.	3 Intermed. n.-m.	4 Upper w. cl.	5 Lower w. cl.	6 Unem., ret., perm., sick
Men							
Service class	E & W	67	6	9	7	4	8
	Lancaster District	53	13	10	10	–	13
Petite bourgeoisie	E & W	9	60	3	11	7	9
	Lancaster District	–	72	–	8	4	16
Intermediate non-manual	E & W	27	6	42	7	9	9
	Lancaster District	13	7	50	3	7	20
Upper working class	E & W	7	6	4	57	14	12
	Lancaster District	6	15	5	47	8	19
Lower working class	E & W	4	5	4	23	47	18
	Lancaster District	–	–	8	8	44	40
Women							
Service class	E & W	40	6	34	3	7	11
	Lancaster District	66	–	17	–	–	17
Petite bourgeoisie	E & W	9	44	31	2	9	6
	Lancaster District	20	50	20	–	10	–
Intermediate non-manual	E & W	7	3	73	2	9	6
	Lancaster District	2	5	75	–	14	5
Upper working class	E & W	3	3	23	32	31	9
	Lancaster District	–	–	33	50	17	–
Lower working class	E & W	2	2	26	9	52	9
	Lancaster District	–	–	50	13	38	–

[1]Population of working age in 1971 and 1981. 'Lancaster' rows, resident in Lancaster District in 1971.

Source: OPCS 1% Longitudinal Study

mobility from the lower working class. Overall in terms of class mobility destinations, then, Lancaster appears to be a place in which men are relatively unsuccessful and women are relatively successful by comparison with the average for England and Wales.

However, we need to consider carefully what is meant here by 'success'. Below the level of the service class, as manufacturing work for women has disappeared, women in Lancaster have been 'successful' at remaining in jobs which are not very remunerative. Interviews with key informants showed that such work was reasonably well paid only for those in secretarial or higher-level clerical occupations (with the university an important employer here). Moreover, those holding such jobs did not, on the whole, expect any significant career progression, even when they were quite young.

Women in the service class in Lancaster were better off. But even here there were significant differences in terms of pay, status and career trajectories between men's occupations and those of women. As we discussed earlier, women in service occupations are caught in a cleft stick. In Lancaster most women in the service class were teachers or nurses, both occupations where there are opportunities for part-time work. However, going part-time in Lancaster appeared to preclude women from promotion and from opportunities for in-service training, and effectively pushed them off a career ladder (interestingly, one part-time nurse who did get effective in-service training was in the private sector). Even young single women were affected by a negative approach to women's careers in the area. One young woman said, of Lancaster District Health Authority:

> Women are creeping up a little bit now but it's mainly men. Men seem to have come into it from the psychiatry angle, and a lot of them were psychiatric trained first . . . I think they think males are more prestigious at the moment. They certainly give different posts and [more] qualifying training to a young male staff nurse than they do to a young female one. They structure it much more . . . They give them a sort of plan of how they see his career developing whereas I've heard of very few young girl students they've done that to. It's more a case of we'll put you there and after that it's really up to you. (KI5)

Traditionally nursing was a young woman's career. Girls moved in straight from school and left on marriage. In the post-Second World War period more opportunities developed for women to return to nursing, but as one nurse put it, 'Nursing has been its own worst enemy because it has been seen as a second job. Something you could take time out of and just go back for some extra money' (KI5). However, the NHS in particular does not appear to have adapted well to the changed career expectations of women, nor to the tight labour market for service class occupations that has developed over the last ten years. In spite of the development of a 'bank' system in Lancaster, employer practices continue severely to restrict the full and effective deployment of available skilled and trained people and to restrict the pool of talent from which managerial promotions are made. The rather greater numbers of male nurses in Lancaster, due to the existence of a large psychiatric and mental health sector, appears to encourage discriminatory practices.

Teaching is a slightly different case, and in the past has offered more opportunities for career development to women. But even here, where severe shortages have developed nationally, women's careers are restricted by employer practices. In particular, an apparent inability to make full use of the talents and skills of part-time and temporary staff gives rise to a clustering of female teachers in Scale One posts, and hence restricts women's promotion to senior management. The effects of such practices on individual women are discussed more fully below.

Spatial Mobility

Table 4.22 *1981 destinations of those resident in Lancaster District in 1971, %*[1]

1971	1981			
	Lancaster	North of England	Midlands & Wales	South of England
Men	84	12	2	2
Women	83	12	1	4

[1]Population of working age in 1971 and 1981.
Source: OPCS 1% Longitudinal Study

Table 4.23 *1981 destinations by 1971 sector of those resident in Lancaster District in 1971, %*[1]

Sector 1971	Location 1981			
	Lancaster	North of England	Midlands & Wales	South of England
Men				
Production	90	9	1	0
Services	83	11	3	2
Women				
Production	93	4	0	4
Services	82	13	2	3

[1]Population of working age in 1971 and 1981.
Source: OPCS 1% Longitudinal Study

Lancaster	Lancaster District
North	Rest of Lancashire, Cheshire, Cleveland, Durham, Humberside, Merseyside, North Yorkshire, Northumberland, South Yorkshire, Tyne & Wear, West Yorkshire
Midlands and Wales	All Welsh Counties, Cambridgeshire, Derbyshire, Gloucestershire, Hereford & Worcester, Leicestershire, Lincolnshire, Norfolk, Northamptonshire, Nottinghamshire, Shropshire, Staffordshire, Suffolk, Warwickshire, West Midlands
South	Avon, Bedfordshire, Berkshire, Buckinghamshire, Cornwall, Devon, Dorset, East Sussex, Essex, Hampshire, Hertfordshire, Isle of Wight, Kent, London, Oxfordshire, Somerset, Surrey, West Sussex, Wiltshire

Figure 4.2 *Spatial Locations, England and Wales*

We have so far considered class and sectoral mobility without taking account of migration. Table 4.22 shows the location in 1981 of those who were present in Lancaster District in 1971, and of working age in 1971 and 1981, in four broad spatial categories. No location will be known for those no longer resident in England and Wales at the 1981 census. It is notable that there is relatively little migration over the decade, that there is no difference between men and women, and that by far the most preponderant destination is elsewhere in the north of England. The south of England, with the most job opportunities, is the destination for only 2.5 per cent of the whole sample and 12 per cent of those who move. When migration is broken down by industrial sector (Table 4.23), then migration is associated more with expanding services than with declining production, indicating that migration is associated with 'opportunity' rather than with 'need'. This is confirmed when sectoral destination is considered together with migration, as Table 4.24 demonstrates. For men, movers and stayers have almost identical patterns of switching between sectors. For women there is an apparent difference between movers and stayers with production industry origins, but the absolute numbers are too small for significance. Overall, therefore, migration is not used as a route for switching industrial sector in a context of deindustrialisation. One could infer that the problems of access to housing, of information and support networks, and uncertainties about access to a social security 'safety net', together outweigh hypothetically greater job opportunities elsewhere.

Table 4.24   *Migration and sectoral change of those resident in Lancaster District in 1971, %*[1]

Men	Movers	Stayers
Production to production	70	74
Production to service	30	26
Service to service	76	76
Service to production	24	24
Women		
Production to production	67	47
Production to service	33	53
Service to service	92	92
Service to production	8	8

[1]Population of working age in 1971 and 1981.

Source: OPCS 1% Longitudinal Study

This raises the crucial question of *resources* for migration, which one could expect to be inversely related to the 'need' resulting from local job loss. One would therefore suppose on this basis alone that migration would be positively associated with class. Added to this, the service class and some other skilled occupations have, at least potentially, a supra-local (regional or national) labour market. Table 4.25 shows the relationship of class to migration for those of

Table 4.25 *Location 1981 by social class 1971 of those resident in Lancaster District in 1971, %*[1]

Social class 1971	Location 1981			
	Lancaster	North of England	Midlands & Wales	South of England
Men and women				
1 Service class	83	13	3	2
2 Petite bourgeoisie	86	14	0	0
3 Intermediate non-manual	79	16	3	2
4 Upper working class	93	3	1	3
5 Lower working class	93	5	0	3
6 Unempl., retd., perm. sick	84	16	0	0
Men				
1 Service class	79	16	5	0
2 Petite bourgeoisie	88	12	0	0
3 Intermediate non-manual	75	19	3	3
4 Upper working class	94	3	2	2
5 Lower working class	96	4	0	0
6 Unempl., retd., perm. sick	88	12	0	0
Women				
1 Service class	90	5	0	5
2 Petite bourgeoisie	82	18	0	0
3 Intermediate non-manual	81	14	3	1
4 Upper working class	86	0	0	14
5 Lower working class	87	7	0	7
6 Unempl., retd., perm. sick	75	25	0	0

[1]Population of working age in 1971 and 1981.

Source: OPCS 1% Longitudinal Study

working age in Lancaster in 1971. For men the association is confirmed, with 22 per cent of professionals moving, followed by skilled non-manual and intermediate workers; and only 4 per cent of the semi-skilled, with no unskilled migration in the sample at all. Even for professionals, though, there is little sign of a *national* job market. For women with male partners, it is likely that their migration associates more closely with their partners' occupational class than with their own.

Occupational Change

We can seek to put some of these different dimensions together in order to explore the fate of members of specific local occupational and industrial groups – their 'trajectories' through the structural changes of the decade. Using LS data we can examine two examples, one from a declining manufacturing sector and one from an expanding service sector. The 'Chemicals' sector, historically important for male employment in Lancaster, declined in numbers by 69 per cent, from 1242 to 385 men, between 1971 and 1981. It changed, correspondingly, from employing 3.5 to 1.1 per cent of men of working age in Lancaster. Accordingly, the Population Census shows the number of men who were chemical production process workers to have declined from 130 (10 per cent sample) in 1971 to 21 (10 per cent sample) in 1981. From this we know the structural decline, but not the fate of these particular workers. The LS shows that of those 1971 male chemical workers who were under sixty-five in 1981, about 85 per cent are still in Lancaster – much the same as for men in general. Of the total, fully two thirds were either unemployed or permanently sick. Perhaps surprisingly, all of the younger age group (aged 16–30 in 1971 and accounting for about one third of the sample) were still in Lancaster and were unemployed. Of the older age group (aged 31–54 in 1971), about two thirds were in employment, dividing roughly evenly between those who had moved up and those who had moved down from their 'firm-specific skills' in terms of occupational status. None were still chemical workers.

By contrast, health sector employment increased by 41 per cent from 3942 in 1971 to 5551 in 1981. Women account for 73 per cent of the 1981 total, with 47 per cent of these women's jobs being part-time. Women in the health sector increased by 47 per cent, from 2759 in 1971 to 4065 in 1981, and this changed correspondingly from employing 8.6 per cent of women of working age in 1971 to 12.8 per cent in 1981. Accordingly, the number of women employed as nurses increased from 152 (10 per cent sample) in 1971 to 226 (10 per cent sample) in 1981. The LS shows that about 80 per cent of nurses aged under sixty in 1981 were in Lancaster in 1971, while 7 per cent came from the adjacent regions and 13 per cent from further afield. That 80 per cent compares with 72 per cent for all economically active women under sixty, showing, perhaps surprisingly, that nurses are more likely than the average to be locally recruited – or again, that women's migration is at the least heavily 'contaminated' by association with their partners' migration. Occupationally, 27 per cent were also nurses in 1971, while about 15 per cent had a diversity of other occupations. The remaining roughly 58 per cent were economically inactive in 1971, made up of an estimated 26 per cent inactive of working age and an estimated 32 per cent below working age. Down at the level of individual occupations, however, it needs to be borne in mind that, at 1 per cent, the absolute sample size is small.

Occupational location is usually considered to be more important than sector in determining the nature of a person's work experience. We need to ask whether those people who change industrial sector also significantly change their occupation. Using data from the LWWHS, we can look at the effect of sectoral change on the occupations of the women in the survey.

The grouping of women's occupations is a highly contentious issue. The conventional grouping of occupations is designed to capture significant differences between men's occupations, though these are themselves controversial. One route through these issues is to ask what are the empirical boundaries to groupings of women's jobs: that is, to empirically investigate the clustering of women's jobs. We did this with the aid of Goodman's technique, the theory underlying which is that movement between jobs is more frequent for jobs that are similar. The application of this method to the job movements of the three hundred women produces an eightfold classification: professional, intermediate, clerical, skilled manual, factory manual, service workers, sales and unskilled. This classification is similar to that produced by Dex (1987) in her analysis of a national sample of six thousand women. It differs from classifications of men's occupations, first, in its separation of factory from service workers (both otherwise subsumed under semi-skilled or scattered), which reflects the distinctiveness of the service sector niche, especially for part-time women workers; and secondly, in its separation of sales from clerical workers, a now widely commented-upon differentiation, where sales workers have worse rates of pay and conditions than clerical workers, more akin to manual workers than white-collar ones.

The most interesting group here is those who changed between production and service sector. Table 4.26 shows the occupational destinations of those women moving from production to services. The largest number of movers are semi-skilled manual factory workers, followed by skilled manual workers, then clerical workers. While the clerical workers tend to stay with clerical work while crossing the industrial divide, the other two groups do not (indeed, logically this would be difficult). They have a tendency to downward mobility, but there is, interestingly, quite a wide spread of destination occupations.

Table 4.26 *Women's occupational change*

From production	To service									
	Professional	Intermediate	Clerical	Skilled	Manual	Services	Sales	Unskilled	Unknown	Total
Professional	2	2	0	0	0	0	1	0	0	5
Intermediate	0	0	3	0	0	0	1	1	0	5
Clerical	1	6	20	0	0	1	1	0	0	29
Skilled	3	5	5	1	1	7	12	10	0	44
Manual	8	9	11	0	1	6	23	19	0	77
Services	0	0	0	0	0	0	1	0	0	1
Sales	1	1	1	0	0	1	2	2	0	8
Unskilled	0	0	3	0	0	2	4	7	0	16
Unknown	0	0	1	0	0	1	0	1	0	3

Source: LWWHS

Table 4.27 *Women's occupational change*

From service	To production									
	Professional	Intermediate	Clerical	Skilled	Manual	Services	Sales	Unskilled	Unknown	Total
Professional	2	0	0	1	3	0	0	0	0	6
Intermediate	1	0	5	2	1	0	0	0	0	9
Clerical	0	2	13	2	4	0	1	2	0	24
Skilled	1	0	0	0	0	0	0	0	0	1
Manual	0	0	1	3	2	0	0	0	0	3
Services	0	0	1	6	8	0	2	4	0	18
Sales	2	4	2	2	13	0	1	4	0	32
Unskilled	0	1	1	2	12	0	3	7	1	27
Unknown	0	0	0	0	0	0	1	0	0	1

Source: LWWHS

In the reverse sectoral movements, from services to production, among the three hundred women we find most of the movement involving women previously in sales, unskilled service occupations and clerical occupations. Table 4.27 shows that the majority of clerical workers moving away from services remained as clerical workers, though to a lesser extent than in the move away from production (see Table 4.26). Both sales and service workers in the sample moved primarily to manual factory work, with other destinations clearly in an upward direction. For female sales and unskilled service workers, the movement from services to production correlates with upward occupational mobility.

Looking at occupational destinations for movers within sectors, clerical workers constitute one of the largest sets of movement from service to service sector occupations, and again just over half stayed in the same occupational group, though with a wide spread of other occupational destinations among those who changed (see Table 4.28). The largest set of movements involved sales workers, of whom just over half stayed in sales, the others being widely spread. Few professional movers left professional occupations here.

Movements within the production sector for women involved less movement between occupational categories than other moves within or between sectors, as Table 4.29 shows. The biggest set of movements involved manual factory workers, of whom 71 per cent moved within the same occupational category. Skilled manual workers were the next largest set of movers, with movement out of this category primarily downwards to the category of manual factory worker. This downward mobility was not associated with taking a break from paid work, since 33 per cent of job-to-job movers suffered in this way as compared to 24 per cent of re-entrants. Clerical workers in production, to an even greater extent than in other sectors, remained in clerical occupations when they changed jobs within the production sector.

The LWWHS shows, then, that in Lancaster most women who moved between sectors did so without changing their occupation. This occupational continuity is especially striking for clerical workers moving away from production to services. We have also seen that the movement from production to services tends to be associated with downward mobility, and from services to production with upward mobility. Movement within the service sector did not particularly correlate with upward or downward mobility, and movements within the production sector involved the least mobility across occupational boundaries.

Table 4.28 *Women's occupational change*

From service	To service									
	Professional	Intermediate	Clerical	Skilled	Manual	Services	Sales	Unskilled	Unknown	Total
Professional	88	2	8	0	0	1	4	1	1	105
Intermediate	0	22	9	0	2	6	11	4	1	55
Clerical	16	9	69	1	1	7	21	5	2	131
Skilled	0	1	0	2	0	1	4	0	0	8
Manual	0	2	1	0	1	0	2	2	1	9
Services	4	2	3	0	0	21	6	8	1	45
Sales	6	20	16	2	4	8	80	26	1	163
Unskilled	1	5	2	0	0	5	17	75	2	107
Unknown	1	1	0	0	0	1	1	0	2	6

Source: LWWHS

Table 4.29 *Women's occupational change*

From production	To production									
	Professional	Intermediate	Clerical	Skilled	Manual	Services	Sales	Unskilled	Unknown	Total
Professional	3	0	1	1	0	0	1	0	0	6
Intermediate	0	1	2	0	3	0	0	0	0	6
Clerical	0	0	28	1	5	0	0	0	0	34
Skilled	1	0	0	36	16	1	0	3	1	58
Manual	2	1	3	16	78	1	2	7	0	110
Services	0	0	0	0	1	0	0	0	0	1
Sales	0	0	1	0	0	0	0	0	0	1
Unskilled	0	0	1	1	11	0	0	8	0	21
Unknown	0	0	0	0	0	0	0	0	2	2

Source: LWWHS

Part-time and Full-time Work

To discuss the issue of working hours is primarily to discuss the structural position of women in the workplace. The change in the European labour market, which has seen an enormous growth in part-time employment, has been most marked in the UK. Between 1951 and 1981 there was a fall in the number of full-time employees of 2.3 million, with part-time employees rising by 3.7 million. By far the majority of these part-time workers are female, with women accounting for over 80 per cent of part-time employees (Robinson, 1988).

In *Patriarchy at Work* (Walby, 1986b) the author demonstrates that patriarchal and capitalist structures must be seen as mutually reinforcing and yet in a condition of constant tension. It is in the interests of employers to bring women into the workplace because of their low levels of remuneration. It is in the interests of men to seek to exclude women from paid work, both to maintain their own wage levels and to retain first call on women's unpaid household labour. The mechanisms through which these tensions have been resolved in the UK in the second half of the twentieth century have been occupational segregation by gender and the development of part-time working for women (Walby, 1985; 1988). Both these mechanisms have ensured that, in spite of the widespread movement of women into paid work, their primary affiliation can still be regarded culturally and politically as the domestic sphere. The main political site on which such practices have been maintained has been the workplace organisation of male workers. The current 'liberalisation' of the labour market, as exemplified in the recent White Paper *Employment in the 1990s*, has, arguably, been partly brought about by an attack on trade union restrictive practices, threatening the uneasy truce between capitalism and patriarchy. Labour market liberalisation, set alongside shortages of key skilled workers and fears about the decline in numbers of young people entering the labour market in the 1990s, could potentially improve the labour market position of women in terms of occupational segregation. However, forecasts suggest that part-time work will continue to be the main growth area for women. Moreover, culturally the 1980s have seen a backlash against working mothers and the development of a rhetoric of 'parental responsibilty' (for which read 'women's responsibility') in a number of spheres. While most working women at any one time do not have dependent children, the break that women take out of paid work 'infects' the careers of both childless women and older married women returners. This typical break out of the labour market is now widely recognised as having a detrimental effect on the careers of individual women and on the overall position of women in the labour force. The effect is exacerbated if a woman returns to work part-time rather than full-time. Many women slowly regain their original occupational level (a process that obviously sets them well behind their male peers in terms of upward occupational mobility), but some never do. Few women returners will ever better their original labour market positions (Dex, 1987; Martin and Roberts, 1984).

Table 4.3 showed that, in the Lancaster District, married women's employment grew by about 1500 between 1971 and 1981, while men's employment declined by a similar number. All this growth was accounted for by a growth of part-time work, which increased by 37.4 per cent, with full-time employment for women declining slightly, by −1.9 per cent.

Table 4.30   *Women's full-time to part-time changes*

	Full-timers moving to part-time	
	Job-to-job	Returners
Production to service	17	48
Service to production	4	31
Service to service	8	24
Production to production	5	5

Source: LWWHS

Using the LWWHS data, we examined the impact of time out of the labour force on women's working hours. This confirmed the hypothesis that women are more likely to return part-time than full-time. Table 4.30 shows that returners were more likely than those making job-to-job changes to move from full-time to part-time work. This tendency is to be found least in production-to-production job changes, and most among those returners who changed from the production to service sector on re-entry, reflecting the lower availability of part-time work in the production sector in Lancaster.

A further question is whether women re-entrants changed their industrial as well as occupational niche on their return. Existing evidence would suggest that they would have done, because most part-time work is in the service sector, and it is to this part-time work that many women initially return and which is generally held to be responsible for their subsequent occupational trajectories.

The LWWHS shows, curiously, that two thirds of the job changes from production to services were job-to-job changes, and only one third involved re-entrants (examining data over the whole work histories of the women). Table 4.11 (page 101) shows that, typically, re-entrance was to the industrial sector in which women were previously employed. The majority of women returners took employment in the same sector that they left; most changes between sectors involved job-to-job changes. That is, the employment break was of little significance in understanding the shift of women into the service sector.

Conventionally, women's work experiences are considered to be primarily mediated by their domestic and familial arrangements. They are considered less attached to the labour market than men, and their labour market involvement is seen as structured around domestic responsibilities. Men's labour market experience, on the other hand, is rarely considered to be structured by their position as fathers or husbands. Hence we have a gender model for explaining women's labour force movements, and a work model for men.

The LWWHS shows that there are correlations between life events and whether women work full-time or part-time, but those life events do not explain change in the industrial sector. Returners are more likely to make a transfer from full-time to part-time working than those making job-to-job changes. But returners are also more likely to take a job in their previous sector of employment than job-to-job changers.

Interviews with key informants in Lancaster show how contradictory the movement between full-time and part-time working is for individual women. In the absence of non-domestic childcare arrangements such as nurseries or crèches, part-time work is often the only way in which women can continue to work at all. For women in the service class, particularly, many appreciate the opportunities that part-time work offers, yet are also keenly aware of the disadvantages in terms of cash and careers.

Such issues began to emerge in our earlier discussion of sectoral change, where we focused on the dilemma faced by women who worked in manufacturing, with both full-time jobs and children. For these women, going part-time was often seen as a once-and-for-all shift from a reasonably well paid job in manufacturing to a low-paid part-time non-manual occupation in services. One woman who had worked as a full-time weaver at Williamsons for sixteen years, moving to work as a part-time night nurse for the social services on the birth of her first child, said:

> I enjoyed every minute I was there, but things come to an end don't they . . . You see it was set hours at Williamsons. I think it was half past seven to half past five, so I had to find a job that would fit in with [son] so that's when I went to work nights, and I used to put him to bed

before going to work and then come home the next morning and wake him up and he never knew I'd been. (KI97)

Similarly, lower-level workers in services often saw the move to part-time work as one-way. Such a move, however, could often not be made when desired because of low levels of household income. One clerical worker explained:

> when my son was born we'd just bought the house and I really couldn't afford to give up work . . . eventually my husband got a better job and we could afford me just to work part-time so that's why I went into part-time work, because obviously I wanted to spend more time at home . . . we'd worked so hard to get the house . . . so we decided that I would carry on full-time and then I would finish completely. And it's never happened and I'm still working part-time . . . I don't think I would ever go back to work full-time. (KI11)

For women in the service class the part-time option was more attractive, offering them the flexibility to cope with increased domestic commitments and the chance to retain skills. Rates of pay for part-time teachers and nurses are on the same scale as those of their full-time colleagues (although eligibility to benefits and to job security are lost). At the same time they feel part-time work offers them the option of 'keeping their hand in' and a wider variety of job experience than they might have working full-time. One teacher commented, 'It suited me to do the part-time just for the extra money . . . It worked both ways. It earned me a bit of money and also I could keep my hand in with the teaching, you know, I could keep up with what was going on' (KI12). This respondent felt that part-time temporary teaching work required more skill than a full-time permanent job 'because you are working in so many different groups and different ages, different subjects'.

Similarly, a staff nurse explained that working on the 'bank' gave her control over the number of hours and the times at which she worked, while the transfer from ward to ward meant that she was getting a lot of different experience and improving her professional skills. Yet both these women also recognised the professional price they had to pay for working part-time. Both missed the continuity of 'having your own class' or running your own ward: 'On the bank you just do what you're told,' the nurse said (KI3). While both these women were paid the same rate as full-time workers, both were excluded from promotion – the teacher restricted to a Scale One post and the nurse to a staff nurse position. As a sister in the NHS said, explaining her switch from part to full-time work as one carried out for 'cash'. 'You can't work part-time in this district as a Sister' (KI86). Women in service class occupations who worked part-time also felt they missed out on in-service training courses.

It is ironic that part-time work, which appeared to widen their skills and competences, also excluded them from training, often aimed precisely at broadening the skills of employees.

Conclusion

We have found that, even for so 'coherent' a locality as Lancaster, the processes of circulation and recomposition for the people within it are varied and complex. Lancaster has shared in the general shift to part-time working (still almost exclusively for women), which has meant that – on a crude measure of full-time equivalent jobs and in relation to the population of working age – Lancaster has experienced no increase in the amount of work, but it has been distributed in 4 per cent more jobs. Economic activity for men is virtually unchanged, while that for women has increased by 12 per cent – dramatically for married women, and massively for part-time work.

These shifts are clearly bound up with the changing structure of the economy from production to service industry. For men, nationally, the proportion employed in production fell by 17 per cent, producing a net switch from production to services equivalent to 6 per cent of men in employment in 1971. By 1981, men were evenly divided between production and services. Only one third of women were in production in 1971, and there was a proportionate net loss of a further third of that by 1981. Lancaster mirrors these trends, but more slowly, because it was already ahead in its deindustrialisation: its location quotient for production industry for men and women in 1971 was 0.84, and for women alone it was 0.68. Using the Longitudinal Study to look at sectoral mobility, we see that for men nationally the switch of individuals from production to services was relatively small and – more importantly – was almost equally balanced by a reverse shift from services to production. For Lancaster, more individual men were expelled from production than nationally, and the destination of this extra flow was to unemployment, early retirement or permanent sickness – the fate of nearly one quarter of the group – rather than to services. This must be connected, too, with the fact that it was older workers who were disproportionately expelled. For women there was also more outflow from production in Lancaster than nationally, and it was also concentrated in the older age group, but with services as their destination.

These shifts are also reflected in occupational changes, producing major structural shifts in social class. Nationally, and in round terms, the service class increased proportionately in size by 30 per cent over the decade, while the upper working class shrank by 15 per cent and the lower working class by 10 per cent. The gender segregation of the service class fell back very slightly, from 69 per cent men to 66, while in the intermediate non-manual class the concentration of women increased from two thirds to three quarters. The proportion of women with upper-working-class jobs – already tiny – slumped by a further third. The structural changes in Lancaster, by contrast, show a significantly slower expansion of the service class – for men, 20 per cent compared to 30 per cent nationally – a location quotient in 1981 of 1.2. The petite bourgeoisie is another local peculiarity, with a location quotient for men consistently over 1.5, reflecting tourism in Morecambe and the shut-down of major manufacturing enterprises. The former applies also to women, with a location quotient of 2 in 1981.

The results from the Longitudinal Study show that, nationally, class mobility destinations reflect the structural fate of different classes, but nevertheless with significant long-range downward mobility for men from the service class – 10 per cent of destinations in the manual working class. For women, the most striking contrasts with men's mobility are their expulsion from the service class, and from the petite bourgeoisie, to intermediate non-manual – presumably associated with life-cycle employment breaks; and also the stark inequality of upward mobility from intermediate non-manual to the service class. For Lancaster, the fate of the service class is rather different. There is more downward mobility for men, and no upward mobility into the service class from the petite bourgeoisie. But there is also twice the national rate of mobility from the upper working class to the petite bourgeoisie. Both of these reflect, again, the total closures of major manufacturing enterprises. Men from all classes have double the national chance of a destination among the unemployed, prematurely retired or permanently sick, but this is especially so for the lower working class, 40 per cent of whom met this fate. For women, by contrast, their chances of surviving in the service class and in the petite bourgeoisie, and of upward mobility from the petite bourgeoisie to the service class, are better than the national average. This applies, too, to their chances of upward mobility from the lower working class.

There was relatively little migration out of Lancaster across the decade, with no overall difference between men and women. What migration there was showed the rest of the north of England to be by far the most preponderant destination. Migration was more strongly associated with service industry origins than with production, indicating that migration is not a means that is practically open to those attempting to cope with expulsion from production industry. Migration is associated with class for men, as one might expect, but even here there is no strong evidence of a *national* labour market for the service class. Overall, recomposition has massively outweighed circulation in the form that the effects of restructuring have taken in Lancaster. But finally, in focusing in detail on very particular occupational groups in particular industries, we can see clearly the grim fate that accompanies deindustrialisation. Of 1971 Lancaster chemical workers, two thirds – and all of the younger age group – were unemployed, retired or sick in 1981.

It is, then, not really a matter of a north-south divide, nor even of 'coarse' and 'fine' spatial scales – the distinctiveness of a place like Lancaster *vis-à-vis* 'the north' in general. It is rather – as indeed we would expect – that divisions and distinctions reach into the heart of the locality. Gender emerges as a crucial, if not *the* crucial, dimension to what is *distinctive* about Lancaster. On almost every measure, Lancaster offers worse prospects for men but better prospects for women. This is relative, of course, to their respective national averages, not to each other, and we have shown that these 'better prospects' for women revealed by aggregate employment data are, in reality, highly circumscribed. Although the social, political and cultural changes which we discuss in Chapters 5 and 6 obviously cannot be directly 'read off' from these shifts, it is nevertheless clear that they are 'informed' by them.

5

Culture, Civil Society and Urban Form

Social Relations 'Outside Production'

Those engaged in writing on restructuring have, from the start, conceived it as a political as much as an analytical project, intended to grasp in the round the constraints and possibilities faced by various social groups in a changing world (Massey and Meegan, 1985). Yet we have also seen, in Chapters 2 and 3, the strong pull towards economic restructuring and class relations in the labour process that has marked much of this work. A key issue facing restructuring theory, therefore, is the need for a systematic means of analysing social relations which lie in some sense 'outside production'. Initially, such matters were treated through the extension of class relations rooted in production, 'spilling over' into other spheres such as local politics. This is still an appropriate and important component, but it is increasingly clear that it is incomplete. For example, gender relations and ethnic relations are equally present and significant in production within the formal economy, but here it is even clearer that they cannot be reduced purely to the nature of capitalist production relations, while local (and non-local) social movements operate almost entirely outside this sphere. If class, gender, race and other relations possess an effectivity outside production, then the problem becomes one of the *contrast* between accounts of changing forms of production and production relations, for which there exists a powerful and relatively coherent set of concepts and putative material processes, and a much more vaguely conceived collection of extra-production relations (see Dickens, 1988, for much relevant discussion).

Various attempts have been made to cover this gap. For example, in *Spatial Divisions of Labour* Doreen Massey seeks to uncover the links between production relations and the 'wider social relations of society', paying attention to the manner in which these wider relations not only form a context for, say, location decisions, but also influence the internal structure of production itself (1984). However, the term that she applies to these relations is 'the *ideological*', arguing that the ideological and the economic are integral to the construction of each other (1984: 43). There will certainly be a role for ideology, properly conceived, as an aspect of both production and non-production relations, but Massey's usage highlights precisely the problem of the contrast between an elaborated theory for economic/production relations and a residual terminology for the rest.

Her usage has implications for the manner in which socio-spatial changes can be analysed. Massey uses the example of Mandel's account of differentiation between Flanders and Wallonia in Belgium, based on their different class histories (Mandel, 1963), and the example will serve to illustrate the problems of the approach. Mandel argues that one of the reasons for Belgium's very low wage levels was regional differentiation, since Belgium was only half-industrialised, with Flanders remaining essentially agricultural. Moreover, the specific nature of social relations in Flanders was produced by an alliance between a still omnipotent clergy and a particular class of employers who would together ensure that it was *Catholic* trade unionism that was promoted. The spread of socialist trade unions was further blocked by the internal spatial structuring of the region, as Catholic governments sought to prevent the urban concentration of the proletariat through a system of extremely cheap railway season tickets and by facilitating the purchase of village smallholdings. The result was that the mass of Flemish workers continued to live in the country, travelling many hours per day to work, thereby blocking the possibility of organisation around production relations. A more recent manifestation of the differentiation is interregional and linguistic conflict – now, ironically, impeding effective state control and the formation of national government (Massey, 1984: 60–2).

'Here, then' (says Massey) 'we have it all.' Yet, despite the recognition given to some non-production aspects of the social, it should be clear that we do *not* have it all. The account of the imposition, conspiracy-style, of the clergy–capital–state programme is relayed without any consideration of *struggle*. And this should remind us that the usual account is of the forcible clearance, ejection and urbanisation of a rural peasantry, not of their forcible retention. The situation described sounds very much like the articulation of desires that one would expect to emanate from a peasantry itself, and hence to reflect its strength not its weakness. The real puzzle may be what the local configurations of agricultural production relations and organisation within civil society were, such as to produce this strength (cf. Shapiro, 1985a). And even if this in particular were not the case, an account of a methodologically similar kind would be required to explain these localised differences in the form of transition from agricultural to industrial production.

The inadequacies of the account have arisen, first, from its 'downward' character – the imposition of dominant class interests – and secondly, from the absence of systematic concepts and categories for extra-economic relations. These two are closely related, since without concepts for the organisation of 'civil society' it is hard to build its active determination into any account. Of course, Massey's point that the *spatial organisation* of households in Flanders impedes organisation around industrial class relations is certainly important.

Various other accounts have been developed which, though they may also have other objectives, do attempt to theorise social relations outside production. Prominent amongst these are various discussions of 'collective consumption', the work of many authors on the 'reproduction of labour power', and a growing recent attention to 'local cultures'. The validity of each of these may be subject to debate in its own terms; but they suffer from two *additional* problems from the perspective of the restructuring of social relations. First, they view those social relations from a particular, one-sided perpsective. This does not necessarily mean that they consider only a restricted set of such relations, but that they consider them in ways which remain blind to much of their causal potential. For example, the 'reproduction of labour power' may be conceived quite narrowly (for instance, as bare physical survival) or quite broadly (for instance, as entertainment, spiritual refreshment, satisfaction) in terms of the kinds of activities and relations that fall within its ambit. But in either case the term refers strictly to the *evaluation* of those activities from the point of view of whether they secure (or fail to secure) a supposed functional requirement for the continuation of accumulation. But whether this is fulfilled or not is (with a few exceptions) an *effect* of people's individual and collective struggles to eat, sleep, reproduce and stay sane, and the concept of the 'reproduction of labour power' is, therefore, of limited use in analysing the forms and origins of those struggles. Whether the outcome is problematic for the reproduction of labour power, whether any agents of capital or state perceive it to be problematic and seek to intervene for this purpose, and if so whether such interventions are successful, are all contingent.

The second problem with these terms is that they are often used not in their specific sense but as a 'catch-all' for a whole set of social relations, or even as a 'respectable' (because apparently theoretical) gloss for the entirety of social relations outside production. As a result the contribution that such terms could make to systematic analysis is dissipated.

In the following we shall employ two terms to refer to relations outside production – 'civil society' and the 'state' – each of which is to be viewed as systematically structured in complex ways. We turn first to civil society.

Civil Society

We propose that the analysis of civil society should start from three aspects: first, the processes involved in the constitution and transformation of subjects; secondly, the nature and constitution of material interests and relations of various kinds; and thirdly, the contexts and resources available to subjects individually and collectively for their organisation, communication and struggle around these interests and relations. Given the small scale and immediacy of many of these processes, it is particularly important to consider the spatial scales and configurations within which they operate (see generally here Urry, 1981; Dickens, 1988).

The Constitution of Subjects

First, a key aspect of civil society is the various interpellations and practices through which individual subjectivities are constituted. However, the legacy of the concept of 'interpellation' must be considered in ways which replace the functionalist, pre-given character of such processes with ones that recover their diverse, fragmented, multiple and contradictory aspects. To neglect this leads, as Rustin points out, to an abstracted and asocial individualism in which popular forces are reduced to a shapeless 'mass' (1987: 31). Though infancy may retain a privileged emphasis in the constitution of identity, it is not assumed that such processes terminate there, or that their product is a unified, self-consistent subject. Rather, subjects may be hailed by and deploy a repertoire of discourses according to time and context.

It is arguable, however, that these complex subjectivities will tend to strive to 'locate' themselves in time and space: that is, they will derive or invent a history, and a sense of place – all the more so, since for many that place will have been chosen rather than given (Rustin, 1987: 33). Spatially, at a national scale, subjectivities are constituted through practices and presumptions of citizenship, and through nationally organised practices and symbolic systems such as media, education, sport and especially the monarchy (Nairn, 1988). We would argue that at a *regional* scale few such processes operate, and that the 'region' is a minimal generator of aspects of subjectivity or of identification and 'belonging'. In the *locality* the social environment will be composed of the forms of social relations – traditional industrial, modern, service-oriented patterns of male and female economic activity, and so on – and of the degree of differentiation to be found – for example, highly differentiated housing environments. The rural, urban or conurbational context of a locality and its 'boundedness' with respect to other localities are also significant. A crucial characteristic of locality for subjectivities is the kind of work available and the work contexts or 'workplace regimes' that it contains (Warde, 1988b). An extreme form of this – the 'occupational community', as in the mining or fishing village – has long been recognised, and was placed in sharp focus during the 1984–5 miners' strike. However, these events also underlined how *exceptional* these forms are, given the spatial and occupational restructuring of local civil societies that has taken place.

Moving to the immediate *locale* or neighbourhood, then, the forms and organisation of social relations are again central, in terms of their density; the homogeneity or heterogeneity of class, gender and ethnic relations; housing patterns; the balance of local private and collective provision; and the collective or private character of neighbourhood practices. The *household* is obviously one of the most intense sites of the constitution of subjectivity in terms of its wealth or poverty; its class, gender, ethnic, generational, kin and community relations; the extent of 'privacy' in relations with other household members and with neighbours; and the physical characteristics of the household itself.

The social context of successive waves of migration is also crucially important. Historically, this has often meant rural–urban migration, prompting a series of questions. What are the social relations of the locations of origin: for instance, compliant or 'deferential' rural relations versus rural struggle? Do the circumstances of particular migrations tend to retain together or to disperse migrants? Are they concentrated in distinctive areas in their localities of destination, or dispersed throughout it? Are ties and links with places of origin and with kin and fellow migrants to other destinations maintained or disrupted? What are the features of the encountered local context (labour market, workplace regime, and so on)? Are they broadly comparable with or do they run counter to the context of origin? For example – to put it very crudely – migrants from countryside to town may encounter class relations either of conflict or of 'paternalism'/suppression, both at origin and at destination, producing four basic patterns which will condition the possibilities for subsequent social and political mobilisation (see Figure 5.1).

Long-term and temporary migration both have a current relevance. Migration of members of the service class produces con-

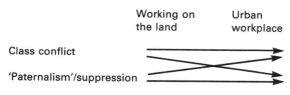

Figure 5.1 *Class struggles in countryside and town*

centrations in some localities, and we argue below that a degree of 'service class hegemony' has overtaken Lancaster in the 1980s (on the south-east, see Dickens, 1988). In Heysham, the effects on local politics of the temporary in-migration of skilled and unionised nuclear power construction workers are discussed in Chapter 6. Besides migration, pertinent aspects of the history of local contexts include the continuity or 'sedimentation' of local practices, housing patterns, workplace regimes and occupational structures.

The Constitution of Material Interests and Relations

A number of the elements listed under the constitution of subjects and of subjectivity are also relevant to the constitution of material interests and of resources. Interests organised around class relations are obviously central, and include the ownership and non-ownership of capital, the possession of credentials, and the performance of management functions for capital and for the state. These interests are organised on a local, national and (primarily for capital) international basis in varying ways: it has, for example, been shown that the size of the labour market or travel-to-work area varies markedly by class and gender (Coombes et al., 1988; Green et al., 1986). Sectoral (industry) and segmental (work-group) divisions of interest also have national, regional and local manifestations which can be contradictory, as in the promotion of 'beggar-your-neighbour' policies. At the local level, class interests will come down to quite specific struggles in particular working environments or 'factory regimes'. Class interests and class relations remain crucial in structuring, but not determining, struggles organised around other interests in civil society and in political formation (Warde, 1988b).

Gender relations are equally pervasive in the constitution of interests both inside and outside the workplace and at all spatial scales (as we tried to show in Murgatroyd et al., 1985). Gender relations in the workplace and the household intersect in the way in which the subordination of women in the household, and the constraints on the level and type of paid work that they have access to, are mutually reinforcing. There are systematic differences in men's and women's interests in the household, the workplace, the local community, and the local and national state. For example, to the extent that women are less geographically mobile, so they are likely to have a proportionately strong 'interest' in their locality (Dickens, 1988: 216). *Generational* conflicts of interest are also manifest at all these levels. As well as immediate interests within households, these connect to the 'youthful' movement towards destruction, play and modernity, and the 'ageful' movement towards preservation, security and amenity. *Ethnic* interests also intersect with class, gender and other dimensions in the community, the workplace, the local and national state, and – sometimes – the household.

There are many outcomes of the interrelation of such class, gender, ethnic and generational processes. Most immediately, these include basic material circumstances such as levels of income, conditions of work and security of employment. These in turn generate a range of interests around the form in which different services can be provided: through the national state, the local state; the market, neighbourhood exchange; voluntary/charitable sources or the individual household (see pages 191–211). Different social groupings clearly have interests in different modes of provision. For example, given the discriminations in access to the 'family' car, public transport has a gender, as well as a class, ethnic and generational aspect. There are also differences of interests of 'spatial' collectivities, besides the straight 'beggar-your-neighbour' competition for development. For instance, in private provision for consumption the interests of an immediate locale are for good quality small-scale distributed suppliers, while the interests of a broader locality or region are for sophisticated shops in concentrated centres.

Complex currents of interest also cluster around the notion of '*amenity*'. At a national scale, this can mean access to seashore and countryside, care of the environment and control of the polluting and despoiling activities of private and state bodies; but also the construction of motorway networks so that access to amenity can be conveniently enjoyed. At another national level it means support for the 'high arts' and/or for a critical and creative popular media. These intersect with interests in '*citizenship*', and *freedoms*, which discriminate both formally and informally by class, ethnicity, age and gender. At a local level, 'amenity' can mean the preservation of a privileged rural or suburban context; or protection against private or public city centre redevelopment and the expulsion of the urban working class to a penal periphery (as in Glasgow or Liverpool). Thus, for different spatial (and other) interests, 'amenity' can mean both the availability of and the preservation from, say, city centre car parks! These aspects of amenity, though they certainly contain an aesthetic element, relate fairly directly to material interests. Other, more purely aesthetic cases also exist, as with the current politicisation of architecture and the intense struggles over the precise styling, as well as the material character and purposes, of changes in the built environment (see Dickens, 1988: 113ff., on how the resultant politics of locality is splitting the Conservative vote in the south-east).

Interests in *use values* that are relatively independent of both commodity relations and the state also constitute material interests. Spaces for self-provisioning and autonomous organisation – allotments, community halls and so forth – serve as resources for particular groups, in whose interest it is to defend them against the encroachments of state, capital and contrary local interests (see Ward and Crouch, 1988, on the allotment). A Lancaster example concerned the closure of a youth centre in 1983 in order to construct a large retail store on the site. Similarly, community forms of mutual support – which imply trust, a rough homogeneity of condition and a lack of privacy – are unlikely to survive much geographical or social mobility, or the 'gentrification' of local areas.

We might also identify a related set of interests around *'security'*, referring to the capacity to defend and perpetuate a desired or familiar set of conditions, or ward off a threatening one. A struggle for security may incorporate a collection of other disparate struggles, which are then experienced as a unity. The desire for new jobs to replace those that disappear through processes of restructuring is both a struggle to secure and expand the material conditions of life and a struggle to secure a given context. But interests around security apply equally to resisting having a home for the mentally handicapped, a council estate development or a toxic waste plant as a neighbour. At a national level, environmental or 'green' politics and the peace movement may combine such elements of 'security' within an articulated political position. We consider below one such local issue, the building of a city centre relief road, in this context.

A key set of interests concerns *housing*. There is a close relationship between labour market and housing market position: in a depressed region there is both less chance of employment and fewer chances of gaining capital through house price inflation. People are locked into particular areas, since the differentials in house prices make it difficult to sell up in a depressed region and purchase in a prosperous one in pursuit of a job. Housing is, therefore, compounding the tendency for localities themselves to become a basis for stratification – but, conversely, much income in prosperous regions 'disappears' in funding giant mortgages. Barlow and Savage also argue that working-class owner–occupiers retain an interest in council house provision for sons and daughters, so that they can either redeem personal amenity or realise capital by 'trading down' (1986).

A key feature of a locality, therefore, especially for the 'service classes', is whether it offers a stock of affordable 'houses of character': that is, old rather than new, of a recognisable style or period, spaciously laid out and with 'craft' standards of fixtures and embellishments. Lancaster has a range of, predominantly, Victorian terrace houses of different sizes, and house prices which were, until the early 1980s, amongst the lowest in the country. It also offers a range of very accessible 'rural' village and country houses, though in a significantly higher price range. Lancaster is therefore potentially a part of the national 'market in meaning' (King, 1987) of period property, and has, for example, featured in magazine articles on 'the cheapest Georgian townhouses in Britain' (O'Reilly, 1987; King, 1987). Not surprisingly, house prices increased by 54 per cent between 1982 and 1986 (figures from the Nationwide Building Society).

Resources for Organisation, Communication and Struggle

The constitution of subjectivities and the identification of sets of material interests indicate the foci of struggle, but the realisation of interests in such struggles depends on the resources available to different groups within civil society. Where there is a pre-existing unity to a group or interest, then organisation and struggle will be facilitated. Hence corporate entities, such as firms or state institutions, have an automatic advantage since they already involve continuous association, a legal identity, an internal structure and hierarchy for reaching decisions and making representations, and resources of money and expertise (Offe, 1985b).

Failing a pre-existing unity, an established institutional base in the form of, for example, a trade union, a political party or a church can provide a means for organisation, communication and funds (Lash, 1984). To a greater degree than with a hierarchically structured corporate entity, this will always involve negotiation and compromise, and will be harder to achieve the further a particular struggle is from the immediate direct interests of that institution. Organisation and communication will also be made easier if there is an existing form of association that brings potential participants together. The central case is the workplace, where common (though normally segmental) interests go together with an automatic form of association. Another example would be a school, in which a, usually, local population has both an interest and a focus.

Struggles will be easier if there is a congruity with other units of organisation or other struggles, so that efforts can be mutually reinforcing – green and peace movements, for example. Conversely, where the struggles and interests of overlapping groups are contradictory – over the preservation of 'amenity' and the desire to attract employment, for example – then struggles will be debilitated. The assets available to groups in struggle are obviously significant, and the larger the spatial scale over which a group attempts to organise, the more it is dependent on substantial funds (see also Pickvance, 1976: 212–13).

A further determinant of the resources available consists of the degree to which a movement can *mobilise* the division between the 'people' and the 'state' (Lash and Urry, 1987: ch. 7). Within civil society there is often a relative continuity over time of popular traditions which can be appropriated or reappropriated by different social groups. One such tradition is of a localist mistrust of and hostility to the central state, or at least to some elements of it (this generally excludes the monarchy and its 'mystique' (Nairn, 1988)) Associated with this also is a mistrust of centralised organisation. Contemporary social movements around gender, the environment and nuclear weapons are often decentralised, and hostility may be expressed at attempts to organise from the centre. The women's movement in Britain illustrates this well. First, its strength now is primarily local through the formation of a multitude of locality-based campaigning and other social groups. Secondly, there is a similarly strong resistance to a central state, seen as violating the rights of women as individual citizens (through, for example, failing to prevent wife-battering, rape, and so on). The national state, once seen by women as necessary to ensure equal rights to education, employment and welfare services, is now often viewed as a cause of rather than as a cure for patriarchal practices, particularly as 'the state, violence and sexuality' have become the most salient issues in the contemporary movement.

The State, Planning and Locality

We have suggested that there are mutual determinations between the spheres of production, civil society and the state, but the question remains of the form and extent of these relations. Recent debates have pursued in a more open and thoroughgoing manner the degree of autonomy of the state, as well as its constraints (for example, Evans et al., 1985). This involves a commitment to the complexity and variety which real state systems are likely to reveal, and starts from this assertion: 'Heuristically, at least, it is fruitful to assume both that states are potentially autonomous and, conversely, that socioeconomic relations influence and limit state structures and activities' (Evans et al., 1986: viii). Skocpol (1985) explores the conditions which will foster the autonomy and capacities of states, emphasising that this variability can be carried through *within* states as well as between them: some *parts* of the state for some *periods* and over some *issues* will be more autonomous than others.

More specifically in relation to planning and development, we have argued that the distinctiveness of the state for planning struggles lies in its imposition both of a particular *form* of struggle that constitutes the participants in specific ways – for example, the public inquiry – and of a particular legally constituted *resolution* or '*moment*' of a given struggle (Shapiro, 1985b: 117–20). However, we have also argued that this state settlement, while embodying certain powers, does not itself finally determine outcomes, which continue to be subject to further struggles in the social practices which realise or modify state resolutions. There is a further nested layer to these issues, in the question of the nature and extent of the autonomy of the local from the national state. In considering these relations in the history of health provision in England, we have shown that the central state undoubtedly has wide powers over the local state, although these vary with the particular form of fiscal regime and are often applied in contradictory fashion (Mark-Lawson, 1988). However, the central state will not always have the knowledge or the interest to exercise its powers, either to compel or to block local action. The capacity of the local state to act (or refrain from acting) will, therefore, continue to be highly dependent on the balance of local forces and interests in local struggles.

Since the character of this 'local relative autonomy' depends in part on the local balance of forces, it follows that whether local struggles will be oriented primarily towards the local or the national state depends on whether the particular interests and struggles concerned fall inside or outside this 'local hegemony'. In examining the place of women's interests in local welfare provision in the period 1918–39 we have shown elsewhere that women's interests were *included* in labour interests in Nelson; were *excluded* from male-dominated definitions of labour interests in Preston; while *both* women's and other labour interests were excluded in capital-dominated Lancaster (Mark-Lawson et al., 1985). This does not dispose of the question, however, since women also campaigned *nationally* on these issues of women's health and welfare (Mark-Lawson, 1988). We could indeed expect that groups waging struggles around particular interests would not be especially concerned with the formal location of responsibility, but would campaign and struggle opportunistically, as and where the chance arose. Hence we could expect groups in struggle to adopt alternative routes: locally, if the balance of forces in the 'local hegemony' is favourable; nationally, if it is not; and both, if possible.

It follows that, contrary to the view of Cawson and Saunders (1983), there is no straightforward *functional* separation between the politics of national and of local state struggles. Indeed, it is arguable that where the national state has powers to direct the balance of local state spending, it can be more easily persuaded to impose local obligations, in so far as it does not have either to meet the cost or to face the consequences of reducing the resources of locally powerful groups. This depends, however, on the capacity of struggles to achieve a national scale of organisation, and on there being a sufficient difference between local and national hegemonies.

To talk, though, of the 'local' requires us to pay some attention to the notion of locality, which has become one of the most used and most troublesome terms in contemporary social science (Duncan, 1986; Savage et al., 1987; Urry, 1988b). As we noted in Chapter 1 (page 9) there is a very wide range of causal elements that impinge on any locality. They comprise a set of substantive entities and social collectivities, each of which possesses its own spatial shape and range, and they include households; housing communities; school catchment areas; ethnic and religious communities; classes at local, regional, national and international scales; political party districts at various scales; factory catchment areas; local labour markets; labour markets for occupations which are non-locally organised; the state at district, county, regional and national scales; firms at all spatial scales and shapes; extra-local patterns of connection between ethnic, religious, class and migratory populations; and voluntary organisations and social movements.

Since all of these overlie each other and can enter into substantive relations where they overlap, social reality is made up of the totality of these significant interrelations over space. We argue in Chapter 1 (pp. 10–11) that a 'locality' is a ring drawn around one set of these interrelations of elements in the formal economy, civil society and the state, impinging on the locality but operating over a whole range of spatial scales. Although such a ring must be somewhat arbitrary, there are many advantages to choosing localities on the scale of the free-standing town or TTWA, in which subjects can pursue relatively well informed struggles.

We shall now consider one set of such struggles, concerned with the local state and planning, in the Lancaster locality – struggles which reveal the processes within civil societies that are concerned with subjectivity, interests and resources, as outlined above.

Reconstruction Struggles

In this we shall be concerned to explore the ways in which economic, social and cultural changes, and struggles in production, civil society and the state, impinge on the ways in which the locality is understood and experienced by various groups within it. There is, for Lancaster, an especially convenient vehicle for this purpose, since in March 1986 a draft local plan for Lancaster was published by the District Council under the Town and Country Planning Acts, followed in February 1987 and in August 1988 with revised versions of the Lancaster Local Plan. These included controversial new road and city centre redevelopment proposals, and unleashed a period of intense mobilisation and widespread resistance – over 1400 individual and institutional formal objections were lodged – and an unparalleled local politicisation of architectural, planning and development issues. A public local inquiry opened in July 1987, and its report was published in February 1988. These events offer a singular opportunity to try to capture the character of the changes that have befallen Lancaster, and of the projects and paths which various of its inhabitants are struggling to forge through those changes.

One way of conceiving these relations is in terms of the 'urban meanings' that are ascribed to particular towns and cities, within a broader context of 'lived meanings' which mediate the straightforward aggregations of material interest: 'Places – specially buildings, but also landscapes, contain and convey meanings, and are impoverished where they do not' (Rustin, 1987: 33). In some ways, and for some people, the prospects for places like Lancaster are looking up. To quote Rustin again:

> Most people cannot live in Manhattan or its like, or even visit it very often, and the undue adulation of the marvels of such centres is a symptom of an unduly stratified, mercenary, and centralised cultural market place . . . We should favour a culture as well as a politics of decentralisation, and have some confidence that ordinary sized towns need not be places where one would only live if one has 'no plans of one's own'. (1986: 494)

In southern England, certainly, small towns are the most 'desirable' places to live, and the most dynamic economic locations, under fierce development pressure (the fate of Europe's small and medium-sized towns has been the subject of a recent colloquy in

Durham, itself a United Nations World Heritage Site (Ardill, 1988)). The perspective of an 'ordinary sized town' as a desirable place to live was confirmed by a number of respondents in the survey of employees in Lancaster:

> Oh, Lancaster is not too big, it's not too small, it's close to the country-side . . . It's just convenient. If I moved somewhere too small I would miss the facilities that Lancaster has, if I moved somewhere too big I'd miss the cosiness of Lancaster . . . It's a nice area . . . We've got Morecambe, we've got the seaside, and we've got the Lake District, it's a nice place to live. (KI: HSC)

But these meanings and the materialities that underlie them are by no means unitary and uncontested. For others, the victims of Lancaster's deindustrialisation, such 'facilities' are a mockery of their personal confinement, since they no longer have the income to explore them.

Indeed, the changes in Lancaster's economic role and fortunes are at the core of the proposals of the Lancaster Plan. What is implied here is that the 'geological metaphor' of the ways in which rounds of economic restructuring overlie and interact with each other in the economic constitution of 'localities', must be supplemented with an 'architectural metaphor' of the reflection of these changes in the built form. Indeed, the built form often very directly reflects not only the function but the spatial relations into which it is inserted: whether this is a castle embodying its adminis-trative relation to a region, the castellated headquarters of a mighty manufacturer, the glass skin of a corporate nerve-centre – or the hutments, barracks and bungalows of a plantation, oriented around the transport which will funnel its produce away. This does not just apply to individual buildings: suburbanisation, involving high rates of home and car ownership and a particular *style* of separate, single-family homes, may be interpreted as being essential for expanding consumption in modern industrial market economies (King, 1983: 245). Yet the built form is not simply given by its functions, and the relations between political economy, culture and aesthetic expression are complex.

Architects clearly play a pivotal role in these relations. The new phase of urbanisation world-wide reflects the shift from manufactur-ing to service employment, conglomerate dominance and the inter-nationalisation of corporate activity which, together with the coun-ter-urbanisation of the 1970s and 1980s, gives the experience of Lancaster a broader relevance. Knox (1987: 355–6) points out that in the US, architecture is now the fastest-growing of the traditional professions, outpacing even law and medicine. Blau (1988) shows that the most distinctive feature of this is the relative growth in the numbers of architects in small and medium-sized cities with an expanding middle class. It falls to architecture, then – as a producer service of the corporate economy and (though decreasingly) of the state – to mediate the failures of and the revulsion against 'modernism', and the increasing adoption of the 'vernacular'; aided by the fact that modernism has never been the *only* design philosophy of the postwar period, merely the dominant one (Knox, 1987: 359).

However, overlying this are broader changes concerned not just with the existence of different social groupings in an area but also with the changing patterns of social activity, and particularly with how the built environment is experienced, is viewed, as a source of pleasure. We will see that the increased importance of the 'touristic' appropriation of buildings has transformed the respective potential of both Lancaster and Morecambe.

Lancaster City's population is approximately 50,000, with the rest of the district's total population of around 128,000 divided between Morecambe, Heysham and the rural hinterland. The city has three distinguishing visual features. First, it is a compact city, surrounded by countryside (except for Morecambe and the Morecambe Bay coast lying to the west), and with generally well defined and agreeable city/country boundaries. Secondly, it occupies a hilly terrain, with city centre hills and scarps, and with the land rising steeply to a ridge of hills to the east. The River Lune winds through the city, forming the north and west boundary of the centre. This lends Lancaster City a panoramic, textured feel, and contributes to its boundedness and clarity. Thirdly, the city has been *relatively* untouched by the ravages of 1960s planning – it has largely escaped 'urbicide' (Berman, 1983). There is an old centre, spread around the castle and the priory on a hill, with surviving open fields stretching down to the River Lune. It has not been flattened for wholesale city centre redevelopment, or slashed by urban motorways and clearways. Some mediaeval and many Georgian and Victorian buildings survive, laid out on a relatively unchanged street plan. Though many individual buildings have been replaced in various periods and styles, there are only three significant 'modernist' outcrops that 'mar' this picture: a small 'Arndale Centre' of shops, offices and government buildings on the south and west perimeter of the market; the St Nicholas Centre, a 'scheme' covering one part of the old centre with two decks of car parking, a pedestrian shopping deck and the only 'high-rise' office block in Lancaster (currently being demolished); and a set of three blocks of tower flats on the north bank of the Lune in Skerton. Even the modernism makes extraordinary concessions for the period: both of the city's car park buildings are stone-faced!

Changes in the built environment involve changes in the use of buildings or spaces, not just their construction and destruction. In Lancaster, St Leonard's House can stand for some of the significant changes. It was initially the Gillows furniture factory; subsequently it became the first site of the university when it was established in 1964; and it then became the 'seedbed' side for new industrial and commercial start-ups, established by a Council which was very early in the game of local development initiatives (Urry, 1990). Similarly, the imposing bulk of the castle was an administrative centre for the county and subsequently a prison, and there are now plans to turn it into a major hotel and international tourist attraction. Down on the quayside many of the buildings have been transformed: the old Customs House into a museum, and the Georgian warehouses into gentrified flats. These changes of use are redolent with meaning, but can also mislead. Thus, Gillows abandoned St Leonard's House through decline, but the university adopted the site through expansion; and when the Prison Department relinquishes the castle, this will certainly not be an indicator of that sector's demise.

Some aspects of the Lancaster Plan were broadly acceptable to most parties and social groups. There was a heavy stress on conservation, with two adjoining conservation areas, and green belt and special landscape areas protecting the city's boundaries. However, there were three particularly contentious proposals. First, it was proposed to create an ambitious 'shopping mall' development linking three areas of the city centre: the market hall site to the south (the Victorian market had been recently destroyed by fire), the site of a former brewery and a Co-operative Society store building in the centre, and the site of the bus station and its surroundings to the north (see Figure 5.2). It was claimed that this would be a 'new-generation' environmentally sensitive development which would preserve nearly all of the city centre buildings and façades, linking them with courts and atria; and, indeed, that some of the disfiguring 1950s and 1960s developments would be replaced as part of the plan. The objective was to produce over 200,000 square feet of gross additional retail floor space in a bid to promote Lancaster to the status of a subregional shopping centre, drawing on a wide hinterland.

Secondly, it was proposed to relocate the market from its current site – which was coveted for the expansion of city centre stores, in particular Marks & Spencer – to the bus station redevelopment, where it was to be perched on top of a two-storey car park. While

Intended Layout

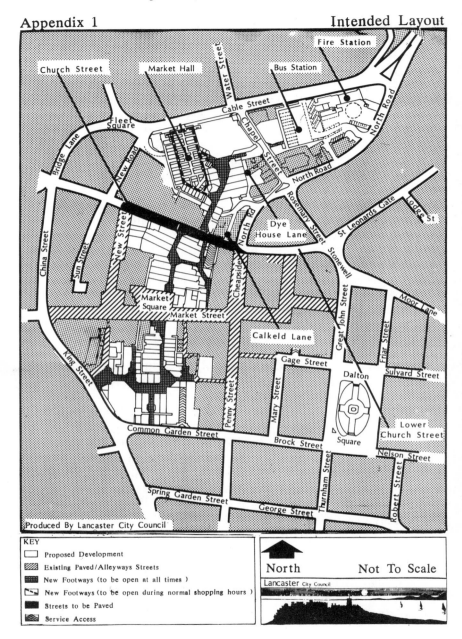

Figure 5.2   *Lancaster city centre retail development proposals*
Reproduced by kind permission of Lancaster City Council

largely part and parcel of the shopping centre plans, the relocation of the market became a separately and very hotly contested issue.

And thirdly, it was proposed to construct a relief road, passing to the east of the city centre and to the west of the Lancaster Canal. This partly resurrected previously rejected plans for an eastern relief road, but on a smaller 'town road' scale. The proposed route was now mostly empty of buildings, as a result of its long-term reservation for this purpose. In connection with both the relief road and the shopping developments, it was also proposed to build some multi-storey car parks.

These proposals unleashed a period of intense mobilisation and resistance, and local politicised debates about the nature, future and built form of the city: debates which spilled over to encompass Morecambe and the surrounding areas too. We shall review these developments, partly in terms of the differing 'modernist' and 'post-modernist' aesthetics with which they are bound up; and partly as struggles on the part of different groups to realise various 'projects': projects of class, of 'race' and of gender, which take distinctive forms through the relations of civil society discussed above.

Although it is pertinent to speak of such groups and 'popular forces' as engaging in struggles over the built form, few are themselves empowered to effect changes directly – unless, perhaps, in the shape of consumer influence over the styles of private housing. Their struggles for control therefore take the form of their seeking to influence 'in their own image' the ways in which others make and remake the built environment. Hence, it is relevant to consider the shifts that have taken place, over time, in who the principal 'agents' of such changes are. This is important in setting both the character of contemporary restructuring and its amenability to different sources of pressure and influence. For the Lancaster District, different principal agents of change in the built environment have been successively dominant since the mid-nineteenth century. Initially it was private capital that built the textile mills, the furniture factories and – later – the Williamsons and Storeys lino and oilcloth factories; and also accompanying tracts of housing of graduated size and status, civic amenities, and self-aggrandising monuments such as the extraordinary 'folly on the hill' that was Williamson's monument to his wife. Later, from the 1930s to the 1950s, the initiative passed to corporate capital, with their advanced factories in artificial fibres, fertilisers, refining and plastics; and also to the local state, this being the period in which most of the major council housing estates were laid out. In the 1960s and 1970s the lead was taken by the national or 'sectoral' state with the establishment of the university, the expansion of health services, and the decisions to site first one and then a second nuclear power station at Heysham. In the 1980s the dominance – though not necessarily all of the initiative – reverted to corporate capital. The Local Plan is explicitly couched in terms of the 'partnership' between local initiative and private finance necessitated by the fiscal incapacity of the local state to act alone; and the constraints that this imposes are acknowledged. Having recognised these shifts, it is, however, not just a question of *who builds?*, but for whose use, under what controls, and with what kind of imperatives?

There are, we think, five kinds of restructuring that are especially significant for what – we argue later – is the current crossroads or choice point that Lancaster has reached. These changes have created a crisis for the self-conception of some groups and interests within the city, and hence for their sense and image of the city itself.

The Restructuring of Manufacturing Capital

The withdrawal of manufacturing capital and the area's far-reaching deindustrialisation were spelled out in Chapter 2. Major industries have abandoned most of their main sites, which could then be transformed for other uses. The scale and distribution of industry have also changed, with the remaining manufacturing employees divided among a much larger number of small firms.

State Restructuring

We have seen that for a period in the 1960s and 1970s the contraction of manufacturing employment in Lancaster was largely 'balanced' by the growth in state services, especially in education and health, and also in state utilities with the construction of the Heysham nuclear power station. In the 1980s, with the contraction in state expenditure on public services, these trends are much less marked. There has been a parallel shift in the relations between the central and the local state, with the imposition from the centre of fiscal restraints and the stripping away of powers and discretion from local authorities. The Local Plan also explicitly acknowledges both the extent of deindustrialisation and the end to the previous public 'service replacement' effects. Meanwhile, state (or ex-state) utilities have remained important, with the construction of the second nuclear power station and the establishment of Heysham as the service base for the Morecambe Bay gas field.

There is a further aspect to the state here, and this concerns the nature of aesthetic control. Following a speech by the new Secretary of State for the Environment in 1979, the Conservatives have generally asserted the superiority of developer 'patronage' as opposed to a democratic system of development control (Punter, 1986–7). The subjectivity of aesthetic judgement has been emphasised, combined with an attempt to protect the interests of gentrified Georgian, Victorian and Edwardian suburbs, and picture-postcard villages. This has been achieved by a two-tier system of strict aesthetic control in the areas to be conserved, and of allowing the developer the 'freedom' to uphold consumer sovereignty in the rest of the country. In a recent example in Lancaster, the attempt by the Council to prevent the establishment of a DIY supermarket close to the city centre (but outside the conservation areas) was overturned by the Secretary of State. Whether these central government priorities are now changing remains to be seen.

The Restructuring of Retail, Finance and Property Capital
If the restructuring of manufacturing capital and of the state defines the nature and scope of the 'problem' for Lancaster, it is the restructuring of retail, finance and property capital which dictates that a shopping centre might be a rational 'solution'. It is widely agreed that the vast expansion of consumer credit has been central in fuelling the boom in consumer spending – in June 1988 consumer credit was running at £24.3 billion. Finance capital has developed the new products, and the corresponding new techniques for evaluating and controlling credit risk. Retailers have both adapted to these products as a vehicle for increased sales and entered the field themselves, turning the supply of tied credit into one of their most profitable lines.

Retailing has, on the one hand, concentrated into larger units of capital and groups of stores; but, on the other, has fragmented into different, more specialised outlets, each seeking to project a differentiated image for a 'niche' market segment. One consequence – together with associated cultural and aesthetic changes discussed below – is a spatial hierarchy of different kinds of shopping location, offering a graduated 'experience' of consumption. This has, in turn, affected the property values of different kinds of retailing location. As the earning power per square foot of the more sophisticated retailers grows, so the value of just the right kinds of retail property soars, and the less sophisticated are squeezed out. A recent survey has estimated that shop rents in Lancaster city centre rose 15- or 16-fold between 1973 and 1988 compared to a national average of 5-fold (*LG*, 20.5.88). The Co-op, for example, has been forced to leave the city centre after its main location was purchased by the Sun Alliance Group, to be integrated into a development scheme with neighbouring properties which they had also purchased.

'Cultural' Restructuring

One of the most central aspects of cultural restructuring for the Lancaster District is the set of changes that have overtaken leisure and tourism. This is because of both the decline in the fortunes of Morecambe as a seaside resort (Urry, 1987b) and the development of Lancaster as a centre for 'history and heritage' tourism. The rise of mass holidaymaking at the seaside in the second half of the nineteenth century should be seen as an integrated aspect of industrial society – the 'industrial holiday' for the industrial working class. The seaside resort – with its healthy sea air and sea bathing, its contrived entertainments, its standardised accommodation and its access by mass transport – is the reverse face of the coin of the industrial town or city. Resorts have been part and parcel of the experience of 'modernism': the mass consumption of mass tourism that corresponds to a regime of mass production.

Recently, as part of the development of postmodernism in aesthetics and culture, it has become relevant to contrast these earlier pleasures with the condition and experiences of the 'post-(mass) tourist' (Urry, 1988a). Feifer (1985) identifies a number of features of the 'post-tourist'. First, he or she does not need to leave home in order to see many of the objects of the tourist gaze. Especially with TV and video, such things can now be seen, compared and contextualised, and there is no single authentic view. Secondly, the post-tourist is aware of change, and delights in the multitude of choice. S/he is freed from the tyrannical distinctions of 'high' culture and 'low' pleasures, but can move easily between them. When the miniature Eiffel Tower is purchased, it can be simultaneously enjoyed as a piece of kitsch, as an exercise in geometric formalism and as a socially revealing artefact (Feifer, 1985: 270). Thirdly, and most importantly, the post-tourist knows that s/he *is* a tourist: that tourism is a series of games with multiple texts and no single, authentic tourist experience. S/he knows that one will have to queue time and time again, that there will be 'hassles' over foreign exchange, that the glossy brochure is a piece of pop culture, that the 'authentic' local entertainment is as socially contrived as the 'ethnic' bar and the quaint fishing village preserved in aspic.

These changes in the tourist experience draw on broader trends of 'postmodernism'. It has been argued that in its relationship to cultural products postmodernism is thoroughly *anti-auratic* (Benjamin, 1975; Lash, 1987). It proclaims the demise of an aesthetic aura through undermining the uniqueness of the work of art and disputing the separation of art from life, and the division between 'high' and 'low' culture. Three developments in particular underpin these changes. First, there is a transformed semiotics of everyday life. Baudrillard (1981) has argued that we now consume signs or images rather than products: identities are constructed through the exchange of sign values. All images are accepted in the spirit of 'spectacle', and people refuse to accord them the 'authority' they sometimes claim. In this world of spectacle there is nothing original, no real meaning; everything is a copy or a 'text upon a text'. Secondly, and relatedly, there is a decentring of stable identities. This is partly because spatial and social mobility and the restructuring of economic and social life have extended the range of experiences that many people encounter, but also because the communications media have both diluted and popularised these 'particular cultures'. Hence individuals from all social groupings are exposed to the 'generally available' systems of information, and each grouping can now see some representations of the private spaces of other social groupings. And thirdly, there are increasing numbers of relatively unanchored social groupings to act as the audience and as 'carriers' for these postmodern forms. A central place in this is played by members of the 'service class': that is, credentialled professionals and senior managers located within a set of institutions that 'service' capital, or service the state, although not themselves substantial owners of capital (Lash and Urry, 1987: ch. 6). These have started to impose their framework, and hence their distinctions of taste, across the wider society.

One can, however, identify three distinct strands to the postmodern with regard to the built environment. First, there is '*consumerist postmodernism*', which takes its cue from Venturi's famous cry to 'learn from Las Vegas' (1972). This involves a depthless 'Disneyland' consumerism of theme parks and shopping malls, celebrating commercial vulgarity in which 'art' and 'life' are fused or pastiched in the playful and shameless borrowing of ornamental style. Secondly, there is '*traditional or patrician postmodernism*', in which what is celebrated is the classical form, the architecture of an elite. This finds its highest point in Georgian architecture and in the modern neo-Georgian imitations of Quinlan Terry. Here what is desired is a return to the aura of the fine building. It reflects itself in the British obsession with the country house – 4.2 million visitors a year in 1986 (and see Wright, 1985). Finally, there is '*local vernacular postmodernism*', the main principle of which is 'that the environment works better if the people who live, work and play in it are actively involved in its creation and maintenance' (Wates and Krevitt, 1987: 18). This involves reducing the power of the architect *vis-à-vis* clients, channelling resources to local residents and communities, and restoration – or, where new building is involved, ensuring that it is appropriate to the local context and reflects a scholastically correct local vernacular style. This development derives from two sources. First, groups of people living locally appear very strongly to want buildings which express the particular locality in which they live. Secondly, people are increasingly 'tourists' in their everyday lives, appropriating, as visitors, places as sites of pleasure. And what it is that people like to gaze upon are buildings which distinguish that place from others, which demonstrate difference and appear to express an appropriate urban meaning. A very good example in the north-west is Wigan Pier, which now attracts one million visitors a year.

These developments, and especially the last, favour the chances that Lancaster will develop into an important tourist site. This stems from the extraordinary growth of 'history and heritage' in the public imagination and in its leisure activities. Lancaster is favourably placed to 'construct' itself in this way. It has not only historic *sites* but a potentially – an ironic concept in this context – historic *setting*. As Relph (1987: 253–4) notes, the overriding characteristic of many postmodern townscapes is that of 'quaintness'. This is, above all, a recovery of the 'mediaeval', and involves intricate sequences of enclosures, winding passages, little courtyards, canopies over pavements, a continuity of appearance between the inside and outside of buildings, few straight lines and right angles, and provision for pedestrians, street theatre and the like. All towns and cities have thus become potential objects of 'quaintification' and the tourist gaze, and Lancaster is one of the best-endowed of the British cities that are not already widely celebrated in this way.

The Restructuring of Population

A fundamental consequence of the kinds of shifts that we have been describing is literally to change the inhabitants of the locality. This is partly through in- and out-migration in response to labour market changes, and partly through transforming the conditions and experiences of those who live there. The 1970s and 1980s have seen a sharp rise in the influence or 'local hegemony' of Lancaster's 'service class', at the expense of both the local bourgeoisie and the local industrial working class. This is a national phenomenon; but the depth of deindustrialisation, and key events such as the establishment of the university and the concentration of health care professionals, have served to exaggerate it within Lancaster City and its rural hinterland.

Aesthetic Interests and the Plan

We have argued in the previous section that Lancaster has been brought, by the intersection of a range of restructuring processes, to a critical juncture. Deindustrialisation has destroyed much of its past; state restructuring is weakening its present; but developments in retailing, consumption, aesthetics, leisure and culture hold out a certain prospect, and shifts in the 'local hegemony' increase the likelihood that it will be seized. The Local Plan is therefore extremely timely in crystallising and offering to reify these processes as changes in the city's built form. In doing so, it has unleashed intense struggles over the realisation of this and of alternative 'projects', each of which seeks to engage this context in its own way – a kind of 'style wars' for Lancaster's soul.

It is important to recognise this *conflict* over cultural and aesthetic direction. Much of the discussion of cultural change and of post-modernism has been unsatisfactorily disembodied, in that it is implied that they are immanent processes which are at once 'every-where' and 'nowhere'. Though they are indeed identified with *inter-ests* (frequently those of the development of the next, highest stage of 'capitalism in general' or multinational capital in particular), there is no clear sense of the protagonists, the opponents or the mechanisms of these transformations. However, it is also clear that these cultural and aesthetic forms cannot be *simply* identified with particular social groupings, such as classes or sections of classes. There *is* a sense in which these cultural alternatives are 'in the air' and available to all; and complex, un-unified subjects, deploying a repertoire of discourses, will adopt and adapt fragments of them at different times and in different places, or even simultaneously. Given that a one-to-one relation is not possible, we argue that it is nevertheless useful to approach the social bases of cultural programmes by seeking to identify, in an 'ideal–typical' way, the social interests and positions that could plausibly be generating them.

The Local Plan seeks, particularly in its two proposed conser-vation areas which together cover most of the city centre, to pre-serve at least most of its heritage resources and to *put them to work* in generating tourism. The proposed shopping development is distributed over three separate parts of the city centre, and the plans involve the preservation of frontages, alleyways and 'wynds', the creation of covered courtyards, galleries and fountains, and the use of glassed-over atrium-type structures to link the different parts together. It therefore seeks to create a 'quaint' town, stressing the vernacular, but which also has its share of playful, eclectic and 'pastiched' elements and which is at the same time very much 'open-for-business'. It would therefore seem to qualify as a properly postmodern scheme. For Lancaster, therefore, the question is: What are the significant positions and interests generated around these proposals? We identify a total of six main 'parties'.

Consumer Service Capital

First, then, who are the protagonists of this kind of postmodern redevelopment? Most obviously, they include the sophisticated end of consumer service capital in retailing and distribution, and the professional agents in architecture, design and market research who work for them. For them, such development is primarily an exercise in high-level marketing. Once established, many 'smaller fish', such as up-market antiques, crafts and fashion retailers, latch on. At its extreme, it can almost seem to be 'the place' itself that is being consumed, and the act of purchasing that realises it, as Thrift (1988b) points out about Bath.

Local State Professionals

The professionals in the local state, and especially in the planning department, are inescapably implicated in initiating and elaborating the development proposals. We have argued that in Lancaster circumstances have combined to give the paid officials of the Council considerable autonomy, which they have sometimes used to pursue initiatives that might seem surprising on the part of a Conservative Council (Urry, 1989). In this case, we would argue that planning officials have quite a sophisticated perception of the restructuring of Lancaster, and for them the Plan is a 'technical' solution: it seeks to strike the best pragmatic bargain between development prospects, tourism and conservation. As the introduction to the Draft Plan argues:

> 1.   The context in which this Plan is set is influenced by the policies of many different agencies. The economic context is determined largely by Government Policy. There is little the Plan can do to change this. Its policies and proposals have been tempered by the present financial restraint on the many public sector bodies involved in the development and improvement of Lancaster. This restraint emphasises the importance of encouraging the private sector to become more involved in developing and improving the city.

Noting the impact of economic restructuring on job loss, first in manufacturing and subsequently in public services, the document states that:

> 12.   The Local Plan cannot itself create new jobs. It can, however,

promote improved opportunities for development which are attractive both to traditional industry and to the employment growth sectors of distribution, office employment, tourism and retailing. (*Draft Local Plan*: vii–ix).

The Local Service Class

If we turn from the agents to the 'clients' or 'audience' for the redevelopment, our earlier discussion would suggest that it should be embraced by the local service class. However, the reality is more complicated, and postmodern eclecticism and pastiche are not the service class's only 'style'. There is quite another side to the modern service class, in which the emphasis is not on artifice, contrivance and 'culture', but on wholesomeness, asceticism and 'nature'. This reveals itself in the passion for healthfoods, real ale, real bread, vegetarianism, 'traditional' medicine; wool and cotton rather than man-made fibres; antiques, old houses; cycling, walking and mountaineering rather than organised leisure, and so on. Bourdieu talks of the liking that this class has for 'natural, wild nature' (1984: 220), and this is reflected in the range of 'middle-class' groups concerned with both using and protecting the countryside. For example, between 1971 and 1987 the membership of the National Trust increased from 278,000 to 1,404,181; of the RSPB from 98,000 to 529,000; and of Friends of the Earth from 1000 to 28,500 (Central Statistical Office, 1987, quoted in Thrift, 1988a).

These tendencies sit rather uneasily with some of the core features of postmodernism. Authenticity of artefact and of experience is heightened rather than abandoned, and with it the salience of aura. These practices are, of course, equally constructed and subject to shifts in meaning; but they have a core of practitioners or custodians for whom they are almost scholarly activities, based on a corpus of knowledge and textual authority. Such views are more associated with the state professional sector of the service class – and perhaps especially with the education sector – many of whom will be intellectually dismissive of the casual pleasures of postmodern consumption. This stance will often be associated with 'left–green' politics. For this group a purist distinction between authentic history and the 'heritage industry' remains important, for the historical process represents unfinished business, rather than celebrating a colourful past as merely the antecedent to a comfortable and satisfactory present. They stand, therefore, in a truculent relation to the antics of capital, and will work on the plausible assumption that anything 'big capital' proposes must be bad. This is, therefore, far more an anti-modernist than a postmodernist stance, at least in the terms in which Berman (1983), for instance, understands modernism as the dynamic principle of capitalism.

This group formed the main core of objectors to the Plan, so that the inquiry took on the character of a struggle between different fractions of the service class. Aesthetically, it is logical that the 'arts and crafts' vernacular would be particularly celebrated, and the proposed demolition of some such buildings was the subject of many of the objections to the shopping development (see Figure 5.6).

The objections turned, essentially, on the question of: Whose town? – Lancaster for local people rather than roads and car parks for out-of-towners; solid local shops rather than 'glitzy' stores; and the market (capitalism on a human scale) in its 'traditional' place. This view can, of course, be interpreted either as a genuine reflection of the interests and wishes of 'the local people', or as a patronising misrepresentation. This connects, too, to the 'spatial' interests of inhabitants of different areas or 'neighbourhood enclaves' of the town. The objection to the relief road was partly that it would just bring more cars into the town ('roads generate traffic'), but mainly that it would sever the areas to the east of the road from the city centre. These areas, climbing steeply up the hill to the Williamson memorial, contain the Catholic cathedral, the grammar school and large areas of Victorian terraced housing. The houses are graduated into sub-areas, and vary in size and building quality from simple two-up two-downs to substantial residences. The area therefore has a very mixed (though reasonably harmonious) character of long-established working-class 'communities' with relatively stable membership – including a large Catholic community in the area of the cathedral – and gentrified enclaves of mostly in-migrant service class professionals. This compounds the complexities, since many of the service class objectors live in that area: they are clearly representing their own perspective on the Plan; there are clearly working-class 'communities-to-be-represented' there; but the relation of objectors to that community is less certain.

This section of the service class is, then, to be distinguished from the consumerist service class who are so central to the 'different country' that Britain has become since the 1970s. If the previous type was state service sector workers in education, then the corresponding type here would be the private sector managers, with the younger members fuelling the more postmodern and 'stylish' elements. One might coin the term 'yucoms', or 'young consumption-oriented managers'. These are the purchasers of 'lifestyle' that the sophisticated retailers service and nurture; the agents of what Thrift has tagged the 'Barbourisation of British culture' (1988a: 15). This group has a ghostly presence in the debates about the Plan: no representatives register either as objectors or in sup-

Figure 5.3 *Lancaster Castle and Priory with government offices below*

Figure 5.4   *Looking east over Lancaster from Castle Hill*

Figure 5.5 *Market Square: a 'genteel' space often taken over by 'alternative' users*

Figure 5.6 *Local vernacular architecture: the Odana Café
scheduled for demolition*

Figure 5.7 *Canalside mills converted to accommodation*

Figure 5.8 *Art déco: the Midland Hotel, Morecambe, designed by Oliver Hill and completed in 1933*

port of its proposals. They figure only in the market projections, property deals and jockeying for position on the part of retail capital.

This does not exhaust the service class/middle class positions, however, since a third, 'liberal/conventional', stance of the service class is also significant. This position is perhaps most close articulated by the Lancaster Civic Society, which lodged several objections and presented detailed evidence to the inquiry. The Civic Society had played an important oppositional role in previous redevelopment contests, but on this occasion they expressed broad agreement with the Plan. Surprisingly, perhaps, they accepted the relief road proposals; they accepted 'well designed' city centre car parks and even proposed some additional ones; and they accepted the proposal to move the market from its current site, but were sceptical of the additional shopping floor area projections and proposed a different new site for the market.

As well as the differences between the various service class/middle class positions or 'projects', there are also some similarities. They all, for example, participate in the gentrification of 'characterful' areas. The main impetus for this came with the development of the university and affected the Victorian terrace areas; it has recently entered a new phase with the 'rediscovery' of many of the city centre and Luneside Georgian buildings, and with a new emphasis on the city centre as a place of residence as well as commerce. Many members of the service classes will be migrants to Lancaster and so – at least to some degree – will have chosen to live there. But for many the prospects of moving elsewhere may have contracted. This is for two reasons (Dickens, 1988: 212–17). First, there has been generally 'declining spatial mobility' for the various middle-class groups in the population between the 1960s and the 1980s. And secondly, the rates of mobility in general decline once people have reached their late twenties. They become established in a given locality, and hence 'the history and relative success of a locality or region are becoming a shared concern for the influential middle classes' (Dickens, 1988: 216). They invest identity in the place – they 'invent' it as a community – and strive to emphasise the features that they 'chose' and to 'perfect' the lacks and lapses. For the Lancaster case this can mean *either* the intensification of a rugged and 'authentic' northern independence, *or* 'rounding out' the city with a touch of the missing metropolitan and cosmopolitan verve. Powerful *nationally* constructed forms of identity such as those derived from the mass media will pull towards the latter.

We should, however, recall that these separate projects or pos-

itions are 'ideal–typical' in derivation, and it is *not* proposed that
there is a direct, literal congruence between these class locations
and the 'corresponding' cultural and aesthetic practices. Rather,
individuals will 'negotiate' and 'inhabit' a mixture of varying proportions of these – and other – perspectives, practices and discourses; and these elements are themselves subject to continual
change. An endearing example of this *mélange* is to be found in
The Official New Georgian Handbook (Artley and Robinson,
1985), which manages, in a slim volume of eclectic pastiche, to
serve as a work of fiction, a biting satire, a self-parody, a text in
aesthetic history, a 'social movement' primer in militant conserv-
ationism and a genuine handbook on restoration.

Industrial Labour

An influential position on the city centre redevelopment can best
be identified with Lancaster's (ex-) industrial labour interest, and
was articulated with considerable energy by the local Labour Party.
From this perspective Lancaster was still (at least potentially) a
manufacturing town; and this resonated with Labour's 1987 national
election platform of the continuing centrality of manufacturing to
Britain and the need to secure its revival. As we have seen, Lancaster was dominated into the late 1970s by a handful of manufacturing
employers. Their importance to the whole character and image of
the place, and not only for their direct employees, was reinforced
by the fact that these were mostly still *city centre* industries: but
nevertheless picturesque, precisely on account of their outdated
buildings. As one nurse put it:

> When we first came and lived around here, when you went out early in
> the morning you saw the workers going to the Storey's factory and them
> coming out in the evening, and then suddenly they were gone. It just
> closed, and it seemed a bit like a dream. And so [Lancaster] has changed
> a lot. I suppose in some senses for the worse and for the better – I'm
> not one of the workers from Storey's!

The stance of the Labour Party involved a mixture of elements,
but reduced in essentials to a traditional 'modernism' of industrial
recovery and of public housing, with little patience for any other
perspective or head of expenditure. The Labour Party and the
Lancaster Plan Action Group succeeded together in forging a quite
substantial local coalition or hegemony of interests opposed to
the redevelopment and defined 'against' the interests of outside
speculators, conglomerates and shoppers. The effects of this on
local politics are considered in Chapter 6.

These sets of class positions are cross-cut by interests of gender.
Women took quite a prominent place in the campaign against the

shopping centre, and of those appearances scheduled in the inquiry programme that are identified with individuals 105 were by women and 197 by men. The issues most explicitly linked to gender in the inquiry were, first, the severance of neighbourhoods from the centre by the relief road, making shopping trips by women on foot, especially if accompanied by children, more difficult and dangerous; and the inappropriateness of the kinds of retailers whom the redevelopment would encourage by contrast with the 'honest local shops' which would be driven out by high rents. Two competing 'positive' images are implicitly juxtaposed here: the housewife shopping for wholesome (local) produce, and the group of girls out shopping on a Saturday afternoon for fashionable gear to wear in the evening. There are, then, intersections of interests of gender, generation and class, and also of representations or misrepresentations of those interests.

Local Capital

With respect to the Plan, local capital can be divided into two principal categories. First, there is the retail sector of predominantly small capital: the local *petite bourgeoisie*. These have been largely bewildered and divided: in favour of 'opportunities' and 'development', but threatened by the inexorable penetration of big capital. This is typified by the stance of the market traders. At first they were vehemently opposed to the relocation of the market and encouraged the very successful petition campaign against it. In this period they participated in a strong 'territorial coalition' with Labour interests and organised under the Plan Action Group. However, they were subsequently persuaded to see some virtues in the proposal, and now accept a revised relocation proposal. Secondly, there is local larger capital, for whom the Chamber of Commerce forms a partial voice. Here, with few directly contrary interests, the 'developmental logic' of the Plan was largely endorsed, though with the strong differences of perspective of Lancaster and Morecambe (see below and Chapter 6) finding some reflection.

'Extra-territorial' Coalitions

Finally, we can identify groups outside the Lancaster locality whose interests may be affected by the Plan. First, there are those who are negatively affected in the 'hinterland', which would be vulnerable to a successful subregional shopping centre. Most obviously, the Plan engages the traditional and developing rivalry between Morecambe and Lancaster. It threatens to complete a shift from Morecambe as the location of 'modern' shopping in the 1960s and early 1970s (the resort had one of the first covered Arndale (shopping) Centres, a food 'superstore' and discount stores). Now Lancaster rather than Morecambe has the local Sainsbury's, Asda, Comet and B&Q. This affects Morecambe residents as consumers and as small shop-keepers; it also affects employment prospects, though perhaps less significantly since Morecambe and Lancaster are already substantially unified as a labour market area.

Secondly, the proposed development similarly threatens interests in the wider hinterland, especially to the north and east, save that here labour/employment interests would be unequivocally affected, and opposition can find representation through the local state since they fall outside both the district and the county boundaries. South Lakeland District Council (which includes the town of Kendal) registered as an objector to the Plan, objecting in particular to the policies on large single-store developments and on promoting Lancaster as a subregional shopping centre: that is, as the main retail centre between Preston, some twenty miles to the south, and Carlisle, some sixty miles to the north.

And thirdly, there are the interests of residents of the subregion in their guise as consumers. For them, 'amenity' means convenient motorised access to a 'tasteful' concentration of competitive and sophisticated retail outlets, in a suitably 'staged' setting.

The outcome of the Local Plan inquiry was interesting and per-haps surprising, since the inspector proved to be largely of the 'authentic' rather than either the modernist or the postmodernist school. This is best illustrated by quotation from the *Report*. On the proposed new city centre car parks the inspector states:

> I appreciate the concern expressed by those who object that the proposed decked car parks would have a detrimental effect on the built form of the City and I am doubtful whether the theoretical parking provision . . . can in fact be accommodated in structures of this kind without intruding into their surroundings . . . The description of its style as 'of classical derivation' belies the fact that it has very little in sympathy with Lancaster's scale and character . . . A great deal of thought will have to be put into the planning briefs for these car parks if they are to 'harmonise with the scale and appearance of their surroundings'. Good design will have to relate more to scale and proportion rather than pastiche if a satisfactory solution to this difficult problem is to be found. (*Report*: 46–7, paras 3.5.7, 3.5.8)

> Lancaster is basically, in my view, a 'street level' town and any develop-ment which sets out to use the natural contours to create large flat 'decks' of development is detracting from the natural and unique character of the city . . . [There is a] need to ensure that the City's pattern of street frontages remains continuous in scale and function, e.g. shops at ground level not multi-storey car parks. *Architectural styles* – I find it difficult, as do most objectors, to reconcile the City's aspiration, as expressed in

the Plan, for Lancaster to be recognised as an historic city of national status with the contrived architectural styles illustrated in the proposals. I seriously question the relevance of the architectural treatment recommended where applied decoration, of doubtful historic origin, is proposed to replace the traditional Lancaster features of simple good proportion and balance of solid to void combined with lasting materials. I suspect, also, that the extensive use of the covered arcade style of development proposed is a concession to current fashion rather than an expression of the City's historical evolution.

My own view is that Lancaster's future development is as an 'historic city in an attractive setting' . . . I can see no alternative but to step back and rethink the present procedure before irreparable damage is done to the character of the city. (*Report*: 88–91, paras 5.4.15–5.4.17)

These (and much else in the same vein) must, in context, be seen as strongly worded criticisms, and a vindication of many of the objections raised. The action group said, somewhat optimistically, that it was 'enough to kill the present scheme stone dead' (*LG*, 19.2.88: 21). This is not at all, however, to guarantee a changed outcome. Two points need especially to be borne in mind. First, the detailed schemes and illustrations which the inspector criticised are not formally part of the Local Plan – just *examples* of how the Council claims they might be realised. Hence, after criticising the illustrations, the inspector for the most part retains the Plan policies intact or with very minor modifications. Secondly, although the inspector is appointed by the Secretary of State, the status of the inquiry is that of a report *to the District Council*. It is advisory, and the Council are not formally bound to accept its recommendations.

In April 1988 the full Council, through the combination of Tory and SLD votes, gave approval in principle to the shopping centre plans, and the city centre subcommittee approved some changes in the light of the inspector's criticisms. These included lowering the bus station site development by 1.5 metres; introducing a new major entrance to the market described as a 'greenery and plant-decorated well of light'; and retaining one street through the site, reducing the car park street frontage. Concerning the market, the subcommittee went through an 'evaluation exercise' in which four alternative schemes for rebuilding the market on its current site were considered and rejected, thus confirming that the market would have to move (*LG*, 22.4.88). On other topics, for example, the Council advanced from having no detailed cycleway network proposal to having an absurd and unworkable one. The relief road, however, was actually increased in scale to four lanes.

Only two weeks were allowed for objections to the modified plans, but some 1200 were lodged by the deadline at the end of

May 1988. Both the Lancaster Plan Action Group and the Civic Society appealed to the Department of the Environment to call in the plans and hold a public inquiry. In June the Council gave itself outline planning permission for the shopping centre proposals, and the action group announced that they would be complaining to the local authority ombudsman that the Council was guilty of maladministration and that the schemes it had approved failed to comply with the provisions of its own Local Plan. In the summer of 1989 a public inquiry into compulsory purchase orders was held, the outcome of which is still awaited at the time of writing.

The Heritage Industry and Contemporary Tourism

We have thus seen how questions of history and heritage have featured centrally in debates around the Local Plan. The issue is how seriously Lancaster intends to 'become' a historic town. As the heritage industry has burgeoned – some 2200 museums in Britain now, half of them opened since 1971, and forty-one 'heritage centres' (Hewison, 1987; Thrift, 1988a) – so too have its critics. Robert Hewison is currently the most celebrated of these, and in publications and broadcasts (for example, Hewison, 1987; 1988) he has condemned the way in which the agenda of the heritage tradition is to promote a mythical English idyll of harmony, community and commonality of interest, and a romanticised and glamourised vision of our industrial and commercial past. The effect of this is systematically to distract attention from the troubles, conflicts and social and material polarisations – the symptoms of decline – which define our real current condition. While our gaze has been fixed on evocations of the past, as at Beamish industrial museum, the reality at Consett has been torn down behind our backs: the 'protection' of the past masks the destruction of the present. In this, the distinction between 'authentic' history (continuing, and therefore dangerous) and heritage (past, dead and safe) is absolute. As many have observed, and as Nairn (1988) has now explored in detail, royalty are given a crucial role in this 'Ukanery'. This is, then, to claim that there are distinct ideological effects of 'living in a museum', of using crass 'invented traditions' to evoke the 'imagined communities' of an 'old country'. Primarily, these work to sustain social and spatial inequalities and to mask a shallow commercialism and consumerism.

This is quite congruent with the critical analyses of the postmodern of, for example, Lyotard (1984) and Jameson (1984). Jameson explores the extraordinary effects of the postmodern as cultural dominant on historicity. What has happened to history, he argues, parallels what has happened to literature, language and social life. Here, the quantum leap and explosion into a host of distinct styles, mannerisms and social codes means that the very possibility of a norm or standard is submerged: a process Jameson (1984: 65) characterises as the eclipse of parody – which is intelligible only through its relation to a norm – by 'pastiche', which is a neutral and promiscuous mimicry. We acquire a voracious appetite for the image, the pseudo-event, the spectacle, the 'simulacrum' – the copy for which no original exists, and whose spatial logic has a momentous effect on what used to be historical time (Jameson, 1984: 66). In nostalgia or '*la mode rétro*', 'real history', especially radical history, is equally submerged in a wash of images and spectacles conveying not representations of the past, but stylistic 'connotations of pastness'. The abandonment of history is thus accompanied not by a loss of interest in 'the past', but by what Jameson redolently terms 'an omnipresent, omnivorous and well-nigh libidinal historicism' (1984: 66). These processes, this 'break-down of the signifying chain', result in a condition akin to Lacanian schizophrenia, in which interlocking syntagmatic sequences of signi-fiers break down into a heap of fragments, of pure material signifi-ers. In this, subjects have lost the capacity to connect themselves across time and to organise their past and future into coherent experience – all now occupies the 'hysterical sublime' of an unre-lated present (Jameson, 1984: 71–7). For Jameson, too, these changes are not free-standing but 'correspond' to the cultural logic of late capitalism. Culture has exploded through the social realm, displacing its former relative autonomy, and the welter of 'unchained' signifiers with which we are bombarded corresponds to the unknowability of the complexity of the economic relations of an elaborated multinational capitalism (see Lash, 1988 on the 'post-modern' as necessarily involving de-differentiation of the many spheres of social life).

These critiques of 'living in a museum' are tempting, while the theoretical accounts of the 'end of history' in the postmodern are exhilarating, and offer to underpin them. But they do have a dis-turbing similarity to an earlier generation of critique of the commer-cial exploitation of debased and ignorant mass taste with ideological effects, to be found in 'mass society' theories (see, for example, the analysis and critique of mass society theories in Giner, 1976; Swingewood, 1977; Morley, 1980). Stauth and Turner (1988: 510) go so far as to suggest that academics may be 'congenitally commit-ted to ontological nostalgia' derived from a pessimistic elitist cri-tique, but this is belied both by the embrace of postmodernism and by nearly two decades of contemporary cultural studies. Hence, the critics of the heritage industry – like the critics of the culture industry before them – imply a number of simplistic and unsustainable assumptions about the nature of the 'messages' and their relationship to their 'audience'. They assume, first, that signs have unitary (and repressive) meanings and can only be read in one way, whereas we should expect that they will be far more complex in their 'encoding' with a range of 'unrecuperated' elements, and will subsequently be 'decoded' and interpreted by a differentiated audience from a wide variety of reading positions (Hall, 1980; Morley, 1980). Secondly, they assume that these messages are dangerous in their effects on a naïve and gullible public (though not, of course, on us), whereas it has never been possible to demonstrate any such simple hypodermic-model media effects, largely because of the complexities of writing and reading just mentioned. Thirdly, they assume that consumption is 'escapist' in allowing us to indulge in a world of fantasy (or even of false, mediated 'engagement'), so distracting us from our real condition and disconnecting us from real struggles; whereas the notion of 'escape' as a useful description of our engagement with popular culture has long been deconstructed (McQuail et al., 1972). Fourthly, they assume that these spectacles are necessarily debased, commercialised, slavishly populist, inauthentic and pandering to the lowest common denominator in taste. But many are in fact 'scholarly' and professional in their design, and so may either be élitist but 'authentic' in their construction, or may relate explicitly to past popular and labour movement struggles; and they will serve a critical audience differentiated by political perspective, education and specialised interests. At Wigan Pier, for example, one is invited to sign a petition supporting women's suffrage. Fifthly, they imply an idealised and fictional 'prior alternative': that is, a golden age before the heritage industry when people were *not* duped and understood their pasts and presents accurately. And there is a sixth common feature, which is the propensity of the critics to indulge, when no one is looking, in the practices that they have condemned: which of us would truly detest a day at Beamish?

One can indeed look upon a Camelot theme park and shudder, though Wigan Pier would seem to bother the historicists more: it is the starting point of Hewison's (1987) critical journey. Yet this is ironical, since the Wigan Pier development exemplifies many of the limitations of the heritage industry critique. It is highly 'educational'; it presents a history of intense popular struggle; it identifies 'the bosses' as in part to blame for mining disasters; and it celebrates a non-élite popular culture. These characteristics are worthy of notice, since they typify at least one wing of the heritage industry. It is organised by 'public enterprise', by a Labour council with ambitious cultural policies (it has a celebrated and innovative music in schools programme), and with an explicit objective of glorifying 'heroic labour' while also recognising women's struggles. The text for such spectacles is written by professionals – social history graduates? – with a commitment to radical and authentic history. It attracts a large local as well as tourist clientele, and invokes a substantially thoughtful and creative engagement from its audience. None of this guarantees perfection – indeed, it arguably reflects a dated and unreflective romance of labour which is insufficiently postmodern – but it is far from uniformly dire and reactionary. Even for the worst uncritical constructions of 'merrie England', however, it is hard not to see that the contrast offered by this idealised past with the lived present must produce *some* critical reverberations.

There remains one key area in which the negative potential of the heritage industry must be taken very seriously, and that concerns those who are likely to find themselves excluded from *all* of the current constructions of the 'national' or 'local' culture. These representations of the past are overwhelmingly likely to be populated by *white* faces and images and so to naturalise racist exclusions from culture and history (cf. Gilroy, 1987). These visible signs of difference can therefore enshrine in an 'obvious' and unconsidered way a qualitative distinction between recent and earlier periods of inward and outward migration on local, regional, national or international scales, and the relations and struggles between cultures and subcultures. In this sense, of course, 'Britain' has *always* been multicultural (Thomas, 1987, quoted in Thrift, 1988a). These are, then, *universal* issues of the ways in which populations have been 'circulated' in historical restructurings, and the ways in which class, gender, ascriptive and ethnic/cultural relations of dominance, subordination, resistance and accommodation have played themselves out. These issues are not beyond the reach of the representations of the heritage industry, and there are grounds for hoping that its sophistication will increase – will be demanded – as it grows. A simplistic and jovial myth is most sustainable in the English south-east, but is already scarcely tenable in any other British region or locality, let alone nation. One must work for the realisation that *everyone* has a history, and that every place has an intricate past of internal and external relations. Perhaps the impact of 'Roots', the American television series about black slave origins, provides a (albeit somewhat disturbing) harbinger.

Meanwhile, Lancaster has been working hard to augment its 'heritage'. In March 1988 the city won a top architectural award –

the Diploma of Merit in the European Year of the Environment awards – for four restoration schemes: the Ashton Memorial, Castle Hill Cottages, St George's Quay and the Palatine Hall (*LG*, 18.3.88: 1). The first of these, the Ashton Memorial, first opened in 1909, was officially reopened in May 1988 after renovation costing £750,000 (*LG*, 6.5.88: 6). It includes an exhibition of working conditions in the linoleum industry of the period, and a multi-screen production of *The Edwardians*. At the same time, the Council announced its new 'Vision for Lancaster' campaign – a three-year £150,000 Tourist Development Action Programme, part of the English Tourist Board's 'Vision for England' strategy – to promote the city's heritage as a major tourist attraction and boost visitors to the area by 25 per cent. In June 1988 the Council announced that it would employ marketing consultants to manage the TDAP, develop a 'corporate image' and coordinate the district's forty-five 'heritage attractions' (*LG*, 10.6.88: 3). In all this it has been ignoring – some might say schizophrenically – the incompatibility between this aim and the city centre retail redevelopments pointed out by the inquiry inspector and the critics of the Local Plan.

We have stressed the way in which competing 'aesthetic interests' struggle to remake aspects of the whole of Lancaster 'in their own image'. What is at stake here is what kind of a place Lancaster is to be. These struggles are intensified by the city's position, balanced on a knife-edge between being just another deindustrialised and 'de-state-servicing' town and becoming a 'Northern Lights' type of success – most of the prerequisites for which are almost in place – along the lines of Chester or York. Faster links to London and to international airports are probably the most significant pieces missing from the jigsaw. While this is at one level an enticing future, the memories of a more rugged productive existence are still fresh enough to make the prospect of Lancaster as an 'outpost of the south' distasteful to many.

Elsewhere we have explored in detail the growth and current malaise of Morecambe as a seaside resort, making a marked contrast with the debates over Lancaster's opportunities (Urry, 1987b). Morecambe is, of course, spatially organised around its seafront, promenade and (now derelict) piers; but the *approach* to Morecambe from any direction, whether by road or rail, involves traversing a sea of bungalows which make up its hinterland and stress its function as a place of residence and retirement as well as a place to visit. Whereas we have found the debates on postmodernism a useful entrée to the urban meanings and built form of Lancaster, we shall – briefly – engage Morecambe via a quite different literature. In his book *The Bungalow* (1984) Tony King uses this particular housing style as a vehicle for exploring a wide-ranging social history of the relations of class and space, and their intersection in the built form. He outlines the origins of the bungalow in India and its subsequent adoption as an imperial residential and administrative design, becoming a world-wide adjunct of colonialism. When the bungalow was first brought to Britain around the 1880s, it was as a distinctly modernist innovation. It was adopted primarily by the expanding professional middle classes, often as second homes. Its functions and connotations were of simplicity, convenience, efficiency in domestic economy, 'naturalism', freedom from excessive dependence on servants (there was already a 'servant problem'), and consequent privacy. Indeed, the bungalow quickly became associated with 'loose living' and took on a distinctly Bohemian aura.

Later, from around the 1920s, the ease of construction of the bungalow – either by large or small commercial builders, or in kit form as system-build units in a range of sizes and specifications – meant that it played a major part in the rapid, and state-subsidised, expansion of housing in this period. Before the spread of planning legislation, commercial estates, but also very large numbers of self-build bungalows, began to sprout everywhere (especially throughout the south-east) as a means to a degree of independence and freedom for progressively lower strata of the middle and even working classes. This is the origin of the quite extraordinarily intense vilification of the bungalow and of 'bungaloid growth'. Indeed, the bungalow represents perhaps the starkest instance of contrary aesthetic evaluations in the built environment. On the one hand it is a significant vehicle for the aspirations, self-expression and self-determination of the lower middle class; on the other hand – no doubt relatedly – it is loathed and detested by virtually every other class. For the latter it represents all the worst suburban petite bourgeois values of cosy privacy, complacency, decency, family, narrow individualism, insularity, kitsch and ignorance. Yet for the former, blithely ignoring these attributes of 'habitus', the bungalow is desired and even adored.

Morecambe not only contains bungalows in large numbers, but there is a symbolic sense in which Morecambe *is* the bungalow: it is the suburb made town. Its lower-middle-class character is reflected in the Census data on population structure, occupation and education, and can be grasped also in terms of its primary functions as a holiday and retirement location. Although much of the clientele for the 'industrial holiday' are members of the industrial working class, these holidays are primarily *serviced* by members of the lower middle class, many of whom may indeed be recently 'mobile' from the working class. The lower middle class could, then, be said to have carved out a significant 'space for action' in Morecambe, both materially – petite bourgeois commercial – and aesthetically residential bungaloid. It is significant as a site of resistance to the relentless spread of service class hegemony. Little wonder, then, that Morecambe's rivalry with Lancaster is growing and that its political dependence on the larger unit of the district is particularly resented (as discussed in Chapter 6). These relations can be sampled through a little ongoing squabble between city officers and Morecambe guest-house owners. In the Tourist Development Action Plan referred to above, the resort's accommodation was criticised as substandard in various respects, particularly the dearth of rooms with *en suite* facilities. It transpires that, by contrast with other resorts, there had been virtually no applications to the North West Tourist Board for grants to carry out this sort of conversion. The response of the Morecambe Hotels and Caterers' Association was angrily to reject the criticisms and issue a challenge to the city architect to come and 'see how nice a place can be without en-suite' (*LG*, 11.3.88: 6). To the proprietors, this is typical of 'toffy-nosed' interference from city officials; to the professionals it underlines the hopeless and irredeemable character of the Morecambe petite bourgeoisie and their incapacity to move 'up-market'. Later the tourist information office pointedly released figures showing that two thirds of those inquiring about accommodation in Morecambe wanted private bathrooms (*LG*, 25.3.88: 1).

'What to do about Morecambe' has become an increasingly pressing problem as it has found itself the bewildered victim of a relentless decline. For a while the construction of the nuclear power stations at Heysham gave a respite – at its peak during the construction of Heysham 2 some 6500 people were employed – but this has now virtually ended. There is still some growth in private nursing homes and homes for the elderly. But for the leisure industry, all the features that once made Morecambe extra-ordinary – smoke-free air, continuous entertainment, modern amusements – are now commonplace; worse, in the new system of 'distinctions' they have come to stand for the vulgar, common and low. As they are, they offer no attractions for what we have termed earlier the 'post-tourist'. Rather than attempts to postmodernise there have been some half-hearted attempts at modernising the existing environment. Thus the fun-fair has been incongruously retitled 'Frontierland', with unconvincing 'Wild West' hoardings applied to the frontage. The result – a 'modernised high modern' – is more a poignant exaggeration than a remedy. There would seem only to be two possibilities for the resort. Either it could pursue a 'heritage' route and seek to re-embody its own past as a living and working Edwardian 'museum of the seaside', reinforced by its proximity to the 'genteel' Lake District and by its spectacular views of the mountains across Morecambe Bay; or it could resign itself to a future as a second-rate Blackpool overspill, dependent entirely on the fate of that style of holiday and on that place.

There remains one jewel in Morecambe's crown, and that is the Midland Hotel, designed by Oliver Hill (1887–1962) and completed in July 1933 (see Figure 5.8). Hill moved in both society and avant-garde circles, and had been much influenced by the 1925 Paris Exposition des Arts Décoratifs, one of the key founding moments of art deco. In designing the hotel (for the LMS railway, and with a brief to build it within the estimated cost for an equivalent conventional hotel), Hill employed a 'pure' sweeping curve following the shore line, set off by a circular café at one end and an oval spiral staircase with a glass outer wall piercing the skin of the building at the centre of the curve. He collaborated with many of the most striking and original British art deco designers and artists of the time. Eric Gill's contributions included a large bas-relief symbolising hospitality filling one lounge wall (the original design, entitled 'High Jinks in Paradise', was considered too daring for Morecambe); a medallion in the ceiling above the spiral staircase; a large incised pictorial map mural of the north-west coast; and a pair of giant seahorses perched high above the entrancē. Eric and Tirzah Ravilious did some dramatic interior paintings, especially the depictions of 'Night and Day' around the walls of the circular café, though sadly these murals were structurally unstable and disintegrated within a few years. Marion Dorn produced superb hand-tufted Wilton rugs and other textiles for the hotel, and Edward Bawden a fresco for the children's room. Equally important, however, was the craftwork and technical detail of the design in the polished cement and carborundum surfaces, the iron, aluminium, glass and rubber work, and the furniture, fittings, plumbings and services. In this it is an important example of industrial art, and *Country Life* (18.11.33) said of its use here that 'Industrial Art is emerging as an aesthetic category in which the technical and artistic processes are successfully combined, instead of "applied" art unrelated to technical composition.' Indeed, the hotel was greatly celebrated, when it opened, as the most advanced in design in Britain, if not the world. *Country Life* went on to say that it was 'the latest thing in construction, materials and decoration. It is exquisite, with nothing in the least cheap or shoddy about it. It is of the best.' And Lord Clonmore in the *Architectural Review* (September 1933) spoke of it as 'something quite new as far as this country is concerned, with . . . extreme simplicity of design . . . The new hotel at Morecambe Bay is in complete harmony with its natural surrounding.'

In the 1980s, layers of surface decoration and modernisation depart significantly from the original vision of the Midland. Almost everything about the furnishing and style of the hotel is 'wrong'; but the structure and the setting are completely – perhaps uniquely – intact, and the possibilities for a full art deco recreation are stupendous. There are signs that, after long neglect, the new management may be becoming aware of this potential: they have researched and mounted an exhibition about the opening of the hotel to mark the fifty-fifth anniversary. If such a recreation were effected, it would provide a veritable orgy of rétrochic and place the Midland firmly on the international architectural tourist itinerary. But would the rest of Morecambe wish to follow such a lead?

Conclusion

In delineating 'aesthetic interests' we have focused considerable attention on class relations in civil society and on how conflicts can be analysed in terms of subjects, interests and resources. But in conclusion we will briefly clarify how relations of ethnicity and gender are also crucial to the analysis. The data from Chapter 4 showed that Lancaster has had anomalously low 'ethnic minority' populations, which should probably be related to the recruitment practices of the major manufacturing industries which dominated employment in Lancaster in the 1950s and 1960s. Most of these are now closed, but in them Asian workers were concentrated in the worst (male) jobs, and particularly in the night shifts of these plants. At that time several parts of the city had concentrations of Asian households, but this has now shrunk back to one main enclave around Blade Street. As elsewhere, this has had the effect of changing these into 'non-spaces' or 'devalued spaces'. It is noticeable, for example, that the adjoining Dallas Road is in the city centre conservation area, but the plan kinks to avoid Blade Street, which lies alongside it and is comparable in style and period.

Retirement resorts often have strong links with particular catchment areas – in Morecambe's case, with Bradford and other parts of West Yorkshire. It can be argued that such movements in retirement have in recent decades become imbued with additional meanings of 'racist escape' from manufacturing towns and cities. And yet, in the new Lancaster that is being forged, its monocultural drabness is a key liability, and contrasts with the celebration – and touristic exploitation – of cultural vibrancy in Bradford. Also, we have discussed above the ways in which the 'heritage' movement is concerned with constructing 'our' unified past in ways that have strong exclusionary tendencies and so can very easily work in racist ways.

Turning to gender, we have seen above that several of the aspects of the Local Plan engaged interests of gender, and were variously represented as doing so. Thus, the interests of working-class women, and other women denied access to the 'family car', were argued to be for small shops in residential localities rather than the further concentration of shopping in the centre. By contrast, the reassertion of the importance of traditional manufacturing industry and 'real jobs' would seem to be the most clearly 'male' of the various 'projects'. Gender interests are also fundamentally engaged in the form of housing provision in the locality, and the patterns of 'household' that it presumes. Lancaster has always shown remarkably high levels of owner occupation in housing, and this has intensified with the national increases in recent years. 'Family houses' predominate in the small local authority sector, and the main forms of new private building are *either* estates of detached brick houses with neo-Georgian appliqué for the middle-class market, or terraces of 'cottages' on tiny plots, with a nod to vernacular styles and scales. All the pressure in housing provision is, therefore, towards the heterosexual nuclear family, with little space for other household forms, or means, for example, for women and children to escape male violence in the home. This is, perhaps, surprising in view of the strength and independence of the women's movement in Lancaster, and the imperviousness of the local state to such pressures is discussed in Chapter 6.

Thinking of Morecambe one thinks inevitably of the seaside landlady. This disparaged figure of fun should in fact serve as a reminder that the seaside resort has also been a place in which lower-middle-class, petite bourgeois *women* could pursue their own projects. This must be related to the very limited means that exist for women – and especially for non-credentialled women – to make a better place in the labour market. Morecambe is, then, in part a domain of largely self-created women's opportunity. Morecambe is also a place for pursuing socio-sexual projects. The seaside holiday is used very visibly both for homo-social activity in groups or 'gangs' of older and younger men and women, and for sexual encounters. Indeed, both were striking features of the seaside holiday when the Mass Observation studies decamped to Blackpool in the late 1930s. Both very obviously persist, but the *form* of the Morecambe holiday is no longer very enticing for either of these youthful projects, with accommodation fragmented into small guest-houses under the landlady's panopticon, by comparison with the facilities and lack of regulation of a 'Club Med'.

Subjectivities, interests and resources are thus crucial to the formation, maintenance and effectiveness of different projects pursued by various social groupings within civil society. In this chapter we have examined some of these projects in relationship to cultural change and the built environment. In the next chapter we shall go on to analyse some of the main features of local political change, and in particular how it is to be analysed, once we recognise that neither politics nor culture simply reflect the processes of *economic* restructuring.

6
Social Restructuring and Political Mobilisation

In previous chapters we have discussed economic and social restructuring in terms of manufacturing and services, occupational change and issues concerned with civil society. This chapter looks at local politics and changes in what we define as 'local political environments', and relates political change to the processes already discussed. We would not, however, wish the order in which these issues have been presented to be seen as reflecting our understanding of the patterns of causality. Throughout the book we have argued that social restructuring is a complex interaction between a number of different factors, and that there are no predictably defined outcomes. The local, we have argued, is a convenient site on which to examine these processes – at once an arbitrary cut-off point and a focus (particularly in the case of civil society) for identity and mobilisation. The case of politics is slightly different. For one thing, the locality *is* a defined unit of political life; for another, local politics could never be national politics in microcosm – it is structurally and institutionally different.

The fact that local political environments cannot be compared, even hypothetically, with 'the national', forces us to take a longer view in this chapter than we have done in the rest of the book. In order to identify the significant elements of the political environment, it must be compared with something: to both provide this comparison and demonstrate how the restructuring of a political environment can be identified and described, we have used the case study of Lancaster to show changing political environments in the twentieth century. Our aim has not been to describe an unfamiliar terrain upon which familiar and aspatial institutions, such as political parties, act. Instead we place stress upon the complexity of interactions between various factors within the political environment.

Territoriality and the Spatial

While changing occupational structure and changing patterns of work will affect the transformation of a local political environment, none of the recent changes in political behaviour, whether in electoral or popular mobilisation, can be attributed directly or solely to industrial change. Curtice and Steed (1982), for instance, convincingly demonstrate that in itself this is quite insufficient to explain new territorial aspects of electoral behaviour. What matters besides is unclear. One proposition canvassed in recent literature has been the increased importance of the local with respect to political life. Evidence for this comes from a variety of sources. Perhaps the most general is from voting behaviour, inspired by observation about new tendencies and trends in terms of the end of the 'nationalisation' of politics. The American literature is now divided about the issue of whether there is increasing regional variation in voting behaviour (Agnew, 1987). The British literature acknowledges a tendency for greater spatial variation, though there is no widely accepted explanation of that process.

There are other localising trends in evidence, too. Local government has become an important focus of struggle in recent times, perhaps as a result of Conservative dominance in national electoral terms, so that issues of local socialism, municipal economic strategies, local environmental and anti-nuclear policies become sites for radical aspiration (Wainwright, 1987; Massey, 1987). This has raised interesting issues in the analysis of the politics of place concerning distinctive local political cultures (Johnston, 1986a), sources of local differentiation in mobilisation (Agnew, 1987) and renewed inquiry into the functions of local government (Duncan et al., 1988). These last usefully observe that the local state in capitalist society performs a dual role:

> Because social relations are unevenly developed there is, on the one hand, a need for different policies in different places and, on the other hand, a need for local state institutions to formulate and implement these variable policies. Local state institutions are rooted in the heterogeneity of local social relations, where central states have difficulty in dealing with this differentiation. But . . . this development of local states is a double-edged sword – for locally constituted groups can then use these institutions to further their own interests, perhaps even in opposition to centrally dominant interests'. (Duncan et al., 1988: 114)

The local state then becomes both a means by which central government deals with the problematic effects of uneven development and a mode of representation of interest groups potentially opposed to the centre. From this potentially contradictory nexus comes the dynamics of local political variation.

But why should place matter to political actors? At least four explanations are apparent. First, in a system of local jurisdictions where there is a local state, especially where it provides certain sorts of predominantly collective services – housing, education, leisure facilities, public transport and so on – the local is a focus of mobilisation around these services. Secondly, in an electoral system based on territorial units, the influence of the territorial will always be felt. There is a fundamental difference between a territorial logic of representation and a functional (that is, class or other interest cleavage) logic of representation. If electorates were organised as occupational colleges, say, rather than as geographical populations, the stakes in politics would be much more closely related to class differences. Thirdly, where local or regional economic policy is in operation, material benefits and local prosperity depend partly on demonstrating to central planning agencies that the particular nature of the place and its component population deserve resources. Finally, as we argued in Chapter 5, locality is a source of identity: neighbours and neighbourhoods, estates and accents, churches and football clubs, architecture – all are part of urban meaning, where identities are formed and where subjects are constituted. They are at once a resource for organisation and the terrain on which political identity can be formed.

Changes in the character of politics are closely related to the process of industrial restructuring. But there is a danger in assuming a direct connection between restructuring and political response. Writers over-impressed by the growth of services, for instance, are frequently unable to specify empirically parallel political transformations (Bell, 1974; Gershuny, 1978). There is no direct correlation because there is no unmediated causation between industrial structure and political action. The last chapter showed that local civil societies vary as between places and that they constitute the terrain upon which the processes of economic restructuring occur, but also that those processes were themselves changed by local civil societies. The same is true of local political environments. While those environments will be shaped by the process of restructuring (a process described empirically for Lancaster in the second half of this chapter), previous events set the agenda for change, shaping the issues that will be pursued, the groups involved in local political struggles and the resources available to them. This is not to make a claim for the autonomy of politics; rather, it is an appeal for a more sophisticated account of the mediations between economic change and political activity.

Restructuring Politics: Towards Conceptualisation

Previous authors who have developed and used the 'restructuring thesis' have considered its effects on political action, although on the whole this has not been the main focus of concern. They have considered the effects of industrial change on spatial variation in political action, and accounted for the strength of Labour movements locally (Massey, 1984: 234–96; Cooke, 1984; 1985). Massey showed that industrial restructuring had largely contrary political effects on coalmining areas in South Wales when compared with agricultural Cornwall. The industrial restructuring thesis, connecting as it does sectoral change in industry (often with international origins) to local outcomes, is in some ways well suited to providing a basis for explanations of shifts in local political behaviour. The character of a local labour market is a residue of the previous history of employment of an area – the geological deposit of previous rounds of restructuring. In the composition of the labour force, moulded by the shaping of resident industries and their changing occupational structures, can be found the class and gender composition of that locality. That local social structure is the terrain upon which political behaviour is developed, and the restructuring thesis offers a link between international restructuring and local political mobilisation. But the nature of the link remains obscure (Warde, 1985b).

In previous chapters we have identified a number of problems encountered in using the restructuring thesis. Such problems are equally apparent when an attempt is made to describe the political effects of restructuring. We have argued, for instance, that accounts of restructuring have tended to be unacceptably economistic. Not only does this make it difficult to extrapolate to political behaviour, but it also pre-empts understanding of the way in which local political environments themselves need to be taken into account in describing rounds of restructuring. The organisation of labour in any particular area, for instance, is not only an economic but also a political phenomenon.

We have argued, also, that insufficient attention is paid to those non-class aspects of local social structure which affect political behaviour. We have demonstrated in previous chapters that social restructuring also has a gendered aspect, and in this chapter we will build on this to discuss gender politics and to show the links between the social restructuring of gender relations and political behaviour. Moreover, it is necessary to examine aspects other than the economic in the 'layering' of a locality at any point in time, both in order to overcome the unacceptable aspects of economism and to deal with the difficult analytic problem of the relationship between structure and action in political mobilisation.

Third, we have stated that almost no attention is paid to services and service occupations in the restructuring thesis. Those writers who have looked at the political effects of restructuring have been almost entirely concerned with extractive and manufacturing industry. Yet the steady growth of employment in service industries and occupations is itself an important aspect of restructuring. Lancaster is an instructive example in this respect.

An additional problem with the geological metaphor, not discussed in previous chapters but relating particularly to political restructuring, is that it is difficult to specify conceptually the character of the social configurations that comprise the current surface at any point in time, because 'that surface will be irregular, since it is the effect of several previous forces . . . it is then necessary to determine the rules of combination between various class (and other) residues in any place, since different combinations will produce different political effects' (Warde, 1985b: 198–9).

The sociology of politics faces a perpetual problem in separating out the underlying structural conditions of action from the innovative contributions of actors in choosing strategies, inventing new practices, mobilising pressure and modifying structural constraints. Abstractly, when not just offering a narrative account, one can do little other than postulate a somewhat arbitrary cut-off point between structure and strategy, directing attention towards conceptions of structure that can helpfully delineate the background conditions, or the environment, of action. In order adequately to describe the effects of restructuring on politics, and to shift debate away from static notions of politics such as 'political tradition' or 'political culture', we have developed a concept of local political environment (see also Mark-Lawson and Warde, 1987: 3).

A local political environment may be defined as the sum of the structural preconditions of action of all potential collective actors within a localised political arena. The structural preconditions would include both economic and institutionalised political practices. Those preconditions amount to a local configuration of constraints: economic ones like factory regimes, occupational structure and labour market characteristics (including forms of segmentation); political ones including the embodied material consequences of previous political action (for example, council housing, the built environment), the vitality of local political associations (measured by party strength and activity), local political ritual and political socialisation (including distinctive political histories). What this amounts to is a mix of material structures, institutions of mobilisation and aspects of collective consciousness.

A distinction can be drawn between social bases, resources and organisations as the essential preconditions of action. Bases are ways of identifying interests, or potential collective actors.

Resources refer to the material, political and cultural capacities of different potential actors. Organisation refers to the institutionalised practices that some or all of these potential collective actors have established in the course of time. These three together comprise the political environment. We can separate out the material (strictly economic) from other, non-economic, institutionalised background preconditions of action. Yet none of these concepts presupposes any particular course of action: environment constrains the mode, but not the course, of action. We can see all these elements of the environment as having been developed over time: they are the sediment of previous rounds of accumulation and struggle. They may be fragmented, sometimes contradictory, and sometimes relatively weak constraints upon action, while at other times heavily determining – for the sphere of innovative action is wider in some environments than others. The environment is thus conceived of as an unevenly layered composite of preconditions of action.

Service Occupations and Local Politics

While the occupational and labour process effects of recent economic change are relatively well understood, there are few satisfactory accounts of the effects of the expansion of service industries on political behaviour. There is very little empirical study of the issue, and studies of the politics of particular occupational groups are still predominantly those of the manufacturing sector. Where authors like Massey (1984) have paid attention to the impact of service employment on regional politics, the conclusions tend to be fairly thin, limited to observations about the potential impact on the Labour Party. Most accounts of the impact of services have tended to concentrate on the implications of service employment for class relations, and these have frequently been oversimplified. Perhaps the most critical mistake is to talk of services as if they were homogeneous, to make services a real object of sociological analysis – what Andrew Sayer (1984) calls a 'chaotic conception'. As we have seen in earlier chapters, there are many kinds of service industries; service occupations are not necessarily any different from those of manufacturing industries; and, as Chapters 2 and 3 showed, strategies of restructuring in services may not always differ significantly from those in manufacturing.

Examining Lancaster as a case study of the political effects of restructuring demands a more detailed approach to the politics of service workers, particularly as Lancaster has moved from being a predominantly Conservative manufacturing town to being a service-dominated local economy that has shifted towards Labour. Even these party-political shifts, which in themselves are nothing more than surface phenomena of a local political environment, defy simple explanations. In order to develop our understanding of the politics of service occupations, and before we move on to look at gender politics, we shall briefly examine the occupational consequences of the development of services. However, as we have argued in earlier chapters, the heterogeneity of services must be borne in mind.

The rise of new industries, the changing distribution of industries across space, and changing patterns of employment within those industries all impact upon the occupational structure of localities. In turn, we would expect the presence or absence of different kinds of workers to have important consequences for local politics. But it is not enough to refer simply to the disappearance of manufacturing jobs and the growth in service occupations. There are significant differences in the socio-economic position of, for instance, state employees *vis-à-vis* private sector workers, and the new welfare professionals *vis-à-vis* the old professional class and the petite bourgeoisie. Within the private sector there may be very significant differences between the experiences of employees of multinational companies and those of smaller ones.

Furthermore, the proletarianisation of service occupations and the professionalisation of manufacturing jobs should be taken into account. The former is a movement that has a very long time scale, with the de-skilling of shop-workers and clerical workers beginning in the late nineteenth century. The paradox of employment in services can be illustrated by looking at the fastest-growing service industries in recent years: banking and finance employs a high proportion of professionals, leisure and tourism a high proportion of lower-level employees. Technological change in service industries is often seen as creating a polarisation between hybrid professional/managerial staff on the one hand and lower-level employees on the other, and we would expect these service employees to hold different political positions. At the same time, a 'professionalis-ation' of manufacturing industry has taken place during the last period of restructuring, with manual and craft occupations declining while the proportion of professionals increases.

It is probably not so much a matter of being employed in service industries, as the nature of the labour processes and relations in which workers are involved – as well as issues of autonomy and pay – that affect their political actions. However, the possibilities of collective action in a particular locality are constrained by the alliances available and by the mix of occupations existing in any given place. In this scenario, class is no more significant an occupational divide than gender or ethnicity. This differentiation within the service sector becomes apparent in the field of industrial relations. As we discussed in Chapter 3, there are fewer strikes in service industries than in manufacturing. However, there are very significant variations within services. Public sector services have become much more strike-prone, while private services seem to lack the bases for concerted mobilisation.

Modes of service provision (see Chapter 3) constitute a further set of influences on political behaviour, with changing patterns of state provision having especially significant impacts. As the literature on urban movements, consumption cleavages, struggles over welfare and so on suggest, both in terms of the kinds of workers who deliver the services and of the discontents of the people to whom those services are administered, service provision affects local class relations. The delivery of public services (collective consumption) and the patterns of consumption of services have been recognised as having significant political effects in the new urban sociology, and the range of effects ascribed to consumption practices is very considerable. For example, Manuel Castells and followers have seen enormous radical potential in urban social movements concerned with the allocation of collective consumption facilities. At the same time, recent changes in British electoral behaviour have been attributed to consumption cleavages (around the private ownership as opposed to the public provision of housing, transport and so on). In a similar vein, the political behaviour of the service class/new middle classes has been ascribed to the different situations of publicly employed professionals *vis-à-vis* their private sector equivalents.

The second half of this chapter uses the concept of local political environment to examine these issues. However, throughout this book we have argued against economic determinism, and we would not wish to suggest that political environment simply reflects the occupational structure of a locality. The politics of different kinds of service workers are spatially variable precisely because changes in the occupational structure of local labour markets occur within, and are constrained by, the previous political environment. This previous environment provides the bases, the language and the relations of local political life. Thus it would appear that workers in some service industries are influenced strongly by the character of the local environment into which they are inserted: in the heartlands of the Labour movement, the public sector professionals, the petite bourgeois and white-collar workers appear more favourable to the Labour Party in elections than is the case, for instance, in the south-east and south-west. The critical difference may be related back to the historic form of the local political environment and new patterns of local class formation.

Gender, Social Movements and Women's Politics

Recent feminist work has revised previous accepted, though often contradictory, propositions about women's political behaviour. No longer can it be said that women are more conservative than men (sometimes meaning more likely to support Conservative/traditional parties, sometimes meaning more likely to support an incumbent party which could be socialist) or that they tend slavishly to follow their husbands' or fathers' political choices. Neither can it be maintained that women vote less often than men or that when they do their choices are made for naïve reasons – the personality of the candidate rather than the political manifesto. Instead, the feminist revision suggests that once women become economically active there is no significant difference between male and female political behaviour. We question an implicit assumption underlying much of the 'revisionist' work on women and politics: that once women become politically active they behave in the same way as men. Instead we suggest that, given the differences in the social position of men and women, it is likely that they will pursue different political 'stakes', and draw on different resources for mobilisation and different associational forms.

The assumption that once women become politically active they behave in the same way as men has more frequently arisen from studies of workplace politics. Examining the issue of women's workplace politics, Purcell (1979), Taylor (1978) and Watt (1980) all concluded that differential rates of female workplace militancy could be explained by reference to differences in occupational position. Militancy and non-militancy for both men and women, it was argued, arises as a result of the place individuals fill in the occupational structure rather than as a result of the attributes of the persons filling those places. In this vein Purcell, for instance, argues that 'women's militancy and acquiescence, both at work and at home, can be argued to be a function of their experience as workers rather than as women' (1979: 130). Although she recognises that women's labour market situation is often restricted by gender, Purcell argues that men similarly situated in the labour market will behave politically in the same way. It is the case currently that gender differences are not apparent in voting behaviour, at least in Britain. Thus, in an analysis of the 1987 general election, survey data was unable to distinguish any difference between male and female voters (Massey, 1987). If there have been in the past any gender differences in electoral behaviour – and some writers have argued that Conservatives attracted slightly more female support only because women lived longer and the most elderly cohorts in the electorate were disproportionately Tory (Butler and Stokes, 1987) – there are none now.

In its attempt to correct the excesses of earlier political sociology's approach to women this revision may perhaps have gone too far. Such an approach ignores what we already know about the roots of political consciousness. As Lovenduski has recently argued, 'Just as differences in men's political roles reflect differences in their overall social and economic positions, so do those of women' (1986: 1). And the social and economic position of women is almost invariably different from that of men. Even where women are in the same structural position in the workplace, their position in other institutions, such as the family, is still prescribed by gender. What is overlooked in revisionist arguments is the complexity of the institutional sites in which women find themselves, a complexity we began to describe in Chapter 4. We need an approach to women's politics sensitive enough to recognise that the capacities and the bases for the political organisation of women, given their real social position, are almost always going to differ from those of men.

Examination of these differences is revealing. Women, it is worth remembering, are able to draw on channels other than paid work for political mobilisation. Women's informal association through neighbourhood networks, for instance, has been well documented (Ross, 1983; Roberts, 1984; Cameron, 1985), and it has been used as a basis for mobilisation. Castells (1983) has described the way in which neighbourhood networks engendered the powerful and rapid grassroots movement that developed into the Glasgow rent strike in 1915. In MacIntyre's *Little Moscows*, women were an essential element in the radicalism of the three areas he examined, preventing evictions and identifying and carrying out punitive action against blacklegs during strikes (MacIntyre, 1980). Ardis Cameron has identified the importance of neighbourhood activity during the 1912 'bread and roses' strike of textile workers in Lawrence, Massachusetts. She argues:

> The bonds which nourished female friendships and alliances (often identified as characteristic of pre-industrial cultures) also helped to sustain neighbourhood networks in an industrial setting. Ties between women provided a necessary organisational base for collective efforts and helped to maintain strike discipline and promote class consciousness. (1985: 44–5)

Themes of 'community' and the significance of networks of various kinds are echoed in contemporary women's politics. Neighbourhood, community and friendship networks may offer an alternative base to that of the workplace for political mobilisation. Women may draw on different 'capacities' (Savage, 1987a), using their experience of the work/household divide and the community to both prioritise different issues and adopt distinctive political practices. In particular, women's experience, spanning as it does the divide between 'work' and 'home', means that the cost of basic household essentials – foodstuffs, rent, medical care and so on – is of as much concern as the usual object of struggle, the wage packet. However, to recognise sites other than the workplace or the polling station as significant for political mobilisation should not be to overstress their importance. The success of women in Glasgow in 1915 was based on the links between the neighbourhood and the workplace: links made possible by women's widespread involvement in paid work under wartime conditions. A similar strike in 1922, after the expulsion of women from paid work in that area, was unsuccessful (Castells, 1983; Melling, 1980). Only under particular sets of conditions have women been able to use the alternative bases of the neighbourhood and the community as sites for political mobilisation. Such conditions tend to relate to gender differences in terms of economic position.

We have shown elsewhere that women have a tendency to organise in order to pursue particular sets of material interests. These interests, reflecting differences between men's and women's gendered material position in both the workplace and the household, will be different from the interests of men. In the past one issue involving these interests has been the transfer of responsibility for service provision from the household, the private market and mutual and charitable institutions to the state (Mark-Lawson et al., 1985).

One reason why women's politics can appear indistinctive lies in the practical–political difficulty of turning a gendered material interest into political organisation. The women's liberation movement has had some success in this respect both recently and in earlier periods, but attempts to set up in Britain a women's party and women-only trade unions were short-lived. A shared material base does not of itself generate high levels of political solidarity. Perhaps this could be analysed in terms of powerlessness (Gaventa, 1980), or in terms of lack of access to political (and cultural) resources. Alternatively, it might be argued that women use different channels of political expression when they do engage in politics, such as campaigns and movements. In the last two decades the WLM has had a considerable level of support from and made a major impact upon politics in the Western world. It is a movement with distinctive cultural and organisational features – non-hierarchical, fluid in composition, unorthodox in its political socialisation procedures, polyvalent in the issues to which it addresses itself and a carrier of counter-hegemonic values. It has provided a vehicle for mobilisation that suggests (as does participation through neighbourhoods) that there is a distinctiveness to the conditions under which women enter the political arena over issues of gender. The intervention locally of the women's movement has become a critical aspect of local political environments.

Much of the literature just review raises a number of interesting problems regarding the relationship between industrial restructuring and political behaviour, which can conveniently be illuminated by a case study of a locality. Among the issues that can be examined are the impact of deindustrialisation and the growth of service employment; changing class structure and class relations; the role of territory in mobilisation, with respect to political identification and class solidarity; the functions of the local state in conditions of uneven development; consumption politics as a source of mobilisation and its relationship to class politics; the involvement of women in political activities at a time of changing employment patterns and new political opportunities; and the role of social movements as alternative modes of representing political interests. Lancaster and Morecambe have seen rapid and early deindustrialisation, a changing class structure, new forms of local identity as the local state has been reorganised, a very large proportion of the population employed in providing collective consumption facilities, and the flourishing of 'new' social movements. What the case study illustrates is the mutual interaction of these elements in the transformation of a local political environment.

Lancaster and Morecambe – a Case Study

In this part of the chapter we show how industrial change leads to complex political effects locally. Here we describe a shift in Lancaster City from an anti-Labour environment expressing the hegemony of local employers, to an environment less determined by a single power bloc but more fragmented as new groups with different resources and modes of organisation develop. The distinctive contemporary feature of Lancaster is, of course, the dominance of public sector services. The overall pattern of fragmentation is enhanced by the changes occurring in Morecambe, for since local government reorganisation in 1974 Lancaster and Morecambe and

Heysham have been part of the same district authority. With the collapse of the tourist industry and the impact of the energy sector in the area, a conservative petite bourgeois dominance in the seaside resort is eroding. One of the most distinctive recent features of Lancaster's politics has been the regular calls for secession from the new district authority by the Morecambe Bay Independents. We first examine the character of the distinctive local political environment established and sustained in Lancaster City during the first part of the twentieth century. We then deal with a variety of changes occurring, in terms of the changing occupational structure, territorial issues, urban politics and social movements.

The Old Political Environment of Lancaster

It is in the light of the class composition of Lancaster that its political history appears distinctive. Only once between 1923 and 1987 did it return any but a Conservative MP. Piepe et al. (1969), using aggregate data analysis to isolate places which deviated from the class–party model of voting, showed that in 1955 the Conservatives took 11 per cent more of the vote than would have been predicted on the basis of the class composition of the city, making it the most deviant, pro-Conservative constituency in Britain. Lancaster also appeared conservative in many other respects. There was virtually no industrial conflict in the town before the late 1960s, and Labour institutions were weakly developed.

Politics in Lancaster City in the twentieth century have passed through four distinct phases. First, the years to 1911 saw a nascent socialist movement mount an unsuccessful challenge to a rather idiosyncratic Liberalism sponsored by the town's principal employer, Lord Ashton. Secondly, the years 1911–35 saw a Labour movement that scarcely stirred in the context of a non-partisan, almost apolitical climate that served to entrench the established system of dominance and social order. Thirdly, between 1935 and the 1960s partisan electoral politics developed, though Labour support remained at unexpectedly low levels and industrial conflict continued to be conspicuous by its absence. Finally, the mid-1960s to the present have seen the local political environment transformed by the severe erosion of Conservative support, the growth of more combative workplace politics and the extension of sympathies for 'new' social movements. It has also been affected by the amalgamation with Morecambe and Heysham in 1974, with the development of territorial issues and new types of conservatism.

The second phase of Lancaster politics, which saw the local political environment become dominated by conservatism, started with a decisive political victory for the local employers in 1911. At that point Lord Ashton made a determined effort to extinguish the challenge of Labour. In Skerton Ward, where many of his employees lived, the most prominent militant in the Independent Labour Party (ILP), Patrick Wall, a railwayman, secured the same number of votes as a candidate publicly supported by Ashton. Ashton reacted strongly. He dismissed known supporters of the ILP at his works. He posted notices at the works saying that he was no longer prepared to consider a prospective advance in wages. He announced his intention to cease retaining workers during trade recessions. And he engineered splits within the Trades Council and the ILP. (For a full account see Todd, 1976.) His victory was enormous and decisive. Organised opposition crumbled. But ironically Ashton himself immediately withdrew from any involvement in politics or civic affairs in Lancaster, taking his charity elsewhere as a final response to the 'ingratitude' of Lancastrians.

This defeat of Labour was followed by twenty-five years of immobilisation. The Labour Party made a very poor showing in general elections and, more significantly, scarcely contested local elections. The local Council was controlled by non-aligned Independents and was petite bourgeois in social composition. Its policies were directed towards infrastructure building projects and its expenditure on social welfare measures was niggardly (Mark-Lawson et al., 1985).

The basis of working-class quiescence in this and the subsequent period was the development of a political hegemony founded on and sustained by the economic dependence of labour. Lancaster was a dominated labour market; in 1921 about 35 per cent of the employed population were engaged in linoleum production, the vast majority either at Williamsons or Storeys (Warde, 1989). It was also a relatively isolated, self-contained labour market, with the nearest large towns, Preston and Kendal, some twenty miles distant. These conditions increased the power of employers in the local labour market and restricted the opportunities available to people seeking work. The employers took great advantage of these circumstances, adopting various collaborative practices including the prohibition of general unions, agreement on wage levels and the operation of exclusive internal labour markets (for an extended discussion see Warde, 1988a).

The economic power of the big firms *vis-à-vis* the local workforce was thus very considerable. Obedience or migration was the basic choice for the factory worker. This situation was reflected in industrial politics. There were scarcely any strikes, and none of much size or duration in any of the Lancaster factories between 1900 and 1967. The General Strike obtained support locally only from railwaymen and woodworkers, and the extensive introduction of scientific management techniques into Lancaster firms in the early 1930s saw very limited resistance – only one half-day stoppage. Industrial action in the 1950s was confined to public servants of various sorts; local engineers even refused to take part in national engineering disputes. Capital was well in control in the sphere of industrial relations.

Hegemony was reinforced by another important set of practices, those concerned with the provision of services. This is a vital but often neglected sphere in which employers, and work practices, are frequently implicated (Warde, 1988b). Much of Lancaster's welfare provision was in the voluntary sector throughout the first half of the twentieth century. The civic benevolence of the large employers was especially important in the early years, giving them yet another source of power, not to mention legitimacy, within the town. This, together with fairly well developed voluntary services, appeared to render local state intervention unnecessary. The local authority provided very little – much less, in fact, than many other local authorities (Mark-Lawson et al., 1985). Service provision in Lancaster was not seen as a political issue, which precluded political mobilisation on the issues of urban politics. It was, however, in this sphere that Labour finally was sparked into action, for it was welfare issues, especially housing, which provided the *raison d'etre* for Labour organisation and representation after 1935.

A particular form of Labour politics grew out of these conditions of dependence. The politics of the interwar period were largely non-partisan: the bulk of councillors were Independents who formed an anti-socialist front once Labour began to make an impact in the late 1930s. After the war, expressing regret, many local Independents began to campaign under the auspices of the Conservative Party, but there were still Independents standing for the local Council who were unopposed by Conservatives as late as 1969. Employer hegemony inculcated sentiments of anti-socialism or anti-Labourism, sentiments firmly based on the material reality of the powerless position of the industrial proletariat in the area. This kind of political environment was still largely intact in the early 1960s, so that it was no accident that the political alignment up to the end of that decade was 'anti-Socialists' versus Labour.

The Passing of Political Quiescence
The order established under the hegemony of the manufacturing employers was transformed during the 1960s. Industrial restructuring, deindustrialisation and the growth of public sector service employment brought changes in the class structure and an increased

proportion of councillors who were welfare professionals. Unionis-
ation in the industrial sector saw the development of a more militant
workplace culture. An increased female participation rate began to
change the nature of gender relations in the town. At the same
time the peace movement and the women's movement grew locally,
while new left student political activism emerged and urban protest
movements occurred, all part of a complex changing local
environment.

The shifts in political allegiance in Lancaster in recent times are
illustrated by changes in electoral behaviour. At the beginning of
the 1960s, Labour took up its customary minority position in local
elections with support at around 40 per cent. The level rose between
1963 and 1966, slumped in the period of unpopularity of the Wilson
government at the close of the 1960s, then increased very sharply
in 1971. These trends probably indicate three developments. First,
Lancaster responded more directly to national partisan movement
than in the past. Secondly, and also in line with national trends,
there was considerable volatility of support. Finally, there was a
significant break in the pattern of anti-Labourism in Lancaster: the
electorate was no longer so blatantly dismissive of that party. These
changes coincided with industrial restructuring in the town and with
significant changes in the ethos of the parties locally.

In the late 1960s the anti-Labour environment began to disappear. Both Conservative and Labour politics underwent change.
The Lancaster Division Conservative Association, for instance,
experienced a high peak in membership in 1968 (*LG*, 25.3.70). By
1972 the local Conservative Party was making remarkably strong
calls for political action. Tories needed to 'wake up and fight',
claimed the Tory agent, because Labour in Lancaster had undergone a metamorphosis from a reasonable and safe democratic
organisation to a militant, intellectual left-wing extremism:

> With the left-wing intellectuals now taking over the local Labour Party
> from the more solid and down-to-earth Socialists we are likely to see
> more and more of these irresponsible people serving on our City Council
> . . . that is, unless we Conservatives are prepared to do something about
> it. (*LG*, 21.4.72)

During this period, and as a result of the process of deindustrialisation described in Chapter 2, the social composition of the Labour
Party altered. Workers in education, in particular, made up a significant part of the membership – health service workers seem to
have had less of an impact on the Labour movement. Later in the
period an influx of workers from Heysham power station was to

revitalise Morecambe Labour Party. One Lancaster city councillor, who moved into the area in 1966, felt:

> The bulk of the membership of the Lancaster Labour Party is in effect a white collar membership. An awful lot of intellectual members, an awful lot of people in the teaching professions, a certain number in health and related professions. So we've very few in traditional working-class professions. That's been a gradual change. If you take the situation now and compare it with the situation as it was when I arrived 21 years ago then I think it's a reasonably striking change that a significant chunk of the membership then was made up of manual workers or the wives or families of manual workers. That's a very very small group now of the membership of the [Lancaster] Labour Party. (Interview, Lancaster Labour city councillor)

Another member of the Lancaster Labour Party felt that in the mid-1960s the Lancaster Labour Party was made up of 'two thirds process workers, engineers and such like, with a third others, retired, academics or whatever'. Twenty years later the party had changed considerably, with 'three quarters or even more working in teaching or some allied occupation, and very few people who are working in manufacturing of any description' (Interview, Lancaster Labour county councillor, 16.10.85).

The local organisation of the industrial wing of the Labour movement was also in transition. After more than sixty years of industrial quiescence, Lancaster's factory workers began to engage openly in industrial struggles, with frequent strikes in the manufacturing sector after 1967. These new practices did not have a direct impact on local politics, because, as often happens, industrial militancy, for most workers, did not extend past the factory gates. For instance, the sample of workers made redundant by Williamsons in 1967 and interviewed by Martin and Fryer (1973) were politically moderate, although well disposed to trade unions. While such individuals did not alter their political convictions radically, the experience of structural changes such as employment shifts and job loss in manufacturing nevertheless began to filter through to the labour organisations in the town.

Lancaster Trades Council changed abruptly in the late 1960s and early 1970s, adopting a more overtly political stance. This change stemmed from two causes: first, the influx of different types of workers (those in education seem to have played a particularly significant part); and secondly, the reduced passivity of workers in the traditional industrial base of Lancaster which followed the extension of trade unionism. These two aspects coexisted uneasily, and gave rise to internal strife within the trade union movement in the town. However, a lengthy period of inaction was broken and the Trades Council became a lively, if divided, forum in the early 1970s, involving itself more in local political issues and staging marches and demonstrations against, for instance, the Industrial Relations Bill and the issue of increased council rents.

These changes in the Trades Council and the trade union movement generally in Lancaster were highly circumscribed, and had more to do with a new generation of trade unionists from a different occupational background than with a change of orientation on the part of the traditional union base. Despite the rise in union activity in Lancaster in the late 1960s and early 1970s, the Labour Party appeared to have more success when it organised around service issues. Lancaster Labour Party has never had a strong industrial wing – a situation which continued into the 1980s. In the late 1960s the TGWU was the dominant union on the Trades Council and in the local Labour Party. With deindustrialisation, the membership base of that union has declined and it is now, politically, a relatively minor force. Yet no other union has replaced its influence within the Lancaster Labour Party.

The effect of local government reorganisation in 1974 was that the Lancaster County Borough became part of a much enlarged district authority. As well as taking in Morecambe, the new district included a range of rural areas in the Lune Valley and around Morecambe Bay. Of the sixty seats on the new District Council only twenty-one coincided with the old urban core of Lancaster. Morecambe was staunchly Conservative, having been represented by a Conservative MP continuously since 1906 and having a local Council composed overwhelmingly of Conservatives, Independents and Ratepayers, with very little opposition from Labour. The rural areas were, if anything, even more firmly Conservative than Morecambe. The new District Council then, when it was first constituted by elections held in 1973, surfaced with a very comfortable Conservative majority. And the Conservatives retained an absolute majority on the new District Council in the three subsequent elections (1976, 1979 and 1983). They increased their majority in 1976, but Labour revived in 1979, as did Liberal and Independent candidates. The result in 1983 was similar, but in 1987 the Conservatives were deprived of their absolute majority, losing nine seats overall, Labour gaining six on aggregate, the Alliance three. This result was not widely anticipated. It certainly went against the trend of local elections in 1987 – Lancaster was one of the few places where Conservative control was eradicated as the result of a significant shift to Labour. The results, when examined closely to see what was happening within the boundaries of the old city of Lancaster, are even more interesting in the context of our discussion of a changing political environment.

If we look only at the wards in Lancaster City in the period after reorganisation, we can detect the continuation of the rise of Labour begun in the 1960s. Table 6.1 shows the percentage of the poll obtained by the parties within the old boundaries of Lancaster CB at the five elections since reorganisation. It confirms the proposition that there has been a collapse of Conservative partisanship among the electorate, much of the support going to the Alliance. In the light of the Labour Party's performance nationally in the 1980s, the fact that Labour continued to get a majority of the votes in Lancaster is a sign of its support being very well entrenched now.

Table 6.1 *District Council: total vote and percentage of vote by party in old boundaries of Lancaster CB*

	1973	1976	1979	1983	1987
Conservative	18,111	17,482	24,167	12,524	11,174
	45.1%	46.6%	39.6%	29.3%	24.6%
Labour	21,450	17,918	26,790	19,633	22,321
	53.5%	47.7%	43.9%	46.1%	49.0%
Alliance }	553	2,136	10,021	10,474	12,012
Others }	1.4%	5.7%	16.4%	24.6%	26.4%

In sum, we can see that the effect of a particular pattern of deindustrialisation – public sector service growth, the principal feature of industrial change in Lancaster City – was to transform class alignments in politics. From having been an anomalously pro-Conservative town, Lancaster became unduly pro-Labour by the 1970s, if we take into account in both instances the class composition of the electorate. As the occupational structure shifted from manual working class to professional middle class, the Labour Party gained support. The presence of large numbers of students at the university might be assumed to have had an effect, but the ward in which the university is located returned three SDP candidates in the remarkable 1987 local elections. Almost certainly, Labour is also obtaining firmer support from routine workers, white- and blue-collar, in the health and education sectors than it ever obtained from the process workers in the linoleum and artificial fibres industries. Lancaster thus provides something of a confirming case regarding Dunleavy's hypothesis about the role of sectoral cleavages: being employed in the public sector probably encourages

Labour voting (see Dunleavy, 1980). However, since this does not hold generally, Lancaster must be seen as a case characterised by the presence of particular kinds of public sector workers, primarily unionised welfare service employees. It is not services per se, nor public sector employment, but rather public sector welfare services that matter.

Territorial Matters
Various processes of spatial change in politics can be seen in the district: new identities, local particularities and especially territorial campaigns have become more important than class- and production-based mobilisations since the mid-1970s. The reorganisation of local government in Lancaster redrew political conflict in terms of a territorial divide. As a Morecambe city councillor put it, 'In council you can tell, apart from the divisions between Labour and Conservative, the natural political reaction, you also have divisions . . . between Lancaster and Morecambe' (interview, 29.10.86). Morecambe councillors and officers had been concerned that the amalgamation of Morecambe and Lancaster would give rise to a situation in which Morecambe's particular requirements were given low priority, and they argued against the proposed form of amalgamation and in favour of a 'coastal strip' authority – a campaign that has continued sporadically ever since. The need for infrastructural support for the traditional tourist industry had been a prime factor in Morecambe politics, and it was accurately predicted that local government reorganisation would see competition for scarce resources.

Competing sectoral needs for infrastructural support, with tourism firmly located in Morecambe (although in fact this was already changing in 1976) and manufacturing in Lancaster, gave rise to a territorial fissure in local politics in the area. There was remarkable agreement among Lancaster politicians of all parties and Lancaster trade unionists, that money should be redirected away from tourism towards industry. 'Industry' in this context was seen as providing employment, while aid for tourism – in fact, quite a large employment sector – was regarded as only in the interests of people outside the area. The gender composition of the different sectors may have had something to do with this mistaken assumption. Industry in Lancaster has always been a large male-employing sector, while tourism is a large female-employing sector.

Lancaster Trades Council, for instance, complained about the amount of money being spent in tourism compared to that spent on industry, warning the City Council that, given the ever-growing unemployment, tourists would soon be coming to Lancaster to look at the slums (*LG*, 6.2.76). The Electrical, Electronic, Telecommunication and Plumbing Union representative complained, 'All we ever seem to hear about is the Dukes Playhouse and the tourist season', while the Technical, Administrative and Supervisory Staffs representative said, 'In view of the appalling unemployment situation in this town I think it's obscene that the Council should cater for people from outside the area and neglect the people in the town.' The Labour Group had already adopted a similar position, arguing that since the Council's support of the holiday trade 'benefits only a small minority of the district's population, even a small minority of Morecambe's population . . . the message to the holiday trade from the ratepayers was "Get off our back." The local Conservative Group were in agreement. Councillor John Downey, the Conservative leader of the City Council, argued: 'Morecambe must look to private enterprise for its future development as a holiday resort.' He went on, 'For the last twenty years . . . nearly all the running has been made by the local authority to maintain Morecambe and Heysham's standing as a first-class resort. But now, in view of the public expenditure reduction, the time has come for private enterprise to take up the baton' (*LG*, 12.3.76: 18, col. 1). It was in this context that a Save Lancaster Campaign was mounted in the early 1980s, a campaign directed primarily towards restoring male manufacturing jobs on the increasingly empty industrial sites of the town. A 'spatial coalition' between local employers and the Trades Council, the campaign was one response to deindustrialisation that overrode class differences. Rows in Council over spending between Morecambe and Lancaster became heated, ending with Morecambe councillors walking out.

These territorial divisions have by no means disappeared. Morecambe residents who complain – and most of them do – about the low levels of infrastructural spending in Morecambe still blame amalgamation for the slow but sure decay of the tourist industry in Morecambe (Urry, 1987a). Splits between Morecambe and Lancaster councillors are still very much present as well. One Morecambe ex-Labour county councillor felt: 'Until the age group before the '74 amalgamation has gone you are going to have that division that splits the two up . . . Now this is not just something that's in the Labour Party, this is in the Conservative Group, and it's in the Independents' (interview, 10.2.86). The situation has not been eased, as the old city of Lancaster has itself become more attractive to tourists, selling itself as an historic city at the edge of the Lake District. Morecambe hoteliers, in particular, are bitter about what they see as a redirection of funds towards making Lancaster City more attractive to tourists, an issue that they have hotly contested.

This fissure re-emerged as an important factor in the 1987 local elections. In 1986–7 the major party-political issue was the Lancaster Plan (see Chapter 4). This issue brought together preservationists and environmentalists, Morecambe hoteliers and shopkeepers, and, as Chapter 4 showed, the local Labour Party came out strongly against the Plan. Its opposition was seen as an important factor in explaining the swing to Labour, against the national pattern of the 1987 local elections, together with a sharp reduction in the Conservative vote in Morecambe, where a group fighting as Morecambe Bay Independents obtained considerable support in several wards and took one seat from a Conservative.

These forms of territorial politics provide an instructive instance of 'spatial coalitions', which play an increasingly important part in contemporary British politics. A spatial coalition is 'an alliance which draws support from a variety of social classes and which seeks to promote what it defines as the interests of the area in question' (Pickvance, 1985: 121). The particular form of a coalition will depend, as Pickvance maintains, on, first, the issues at stake and, secondly, the class structure of the area. Working classes are most likely to be involved when employment is at issue. The antagonism expressed in the local Council by representatives of Lancaster and Morecambe is just such an instance on a very localised, micro-spatial level.

In both Lancaster and Morecambe cross-class alliances developed and came to play a central role in local politics from 1974 onwards. The big companies were not much involved, except to the extent that they were sometimes identified as the villains when they announced redundancies. But in such circumstances it is usually only the workers directly affected, and sometimes political representatives, who complain. The notion that there is some systematic connection between multinational firms and local employment opportunities never became an issue of political debate. Industrial restructuring was clearly one precondition of the emergence of territorial politics: in Lancaster the rationalisation of manufacturing industry, in Morecambe the changing demands of the tourist industry, were central. It is to be expected that when, as in the current rounds, spatial relocation is a key feature of restructuring in a recession, that spatial coalitions will be prevalent. It was social groups that were immobile that stood to lose out from restructuring, and one response to the hypermobility of capital was to fight to preserve existing, or attract new, jobs. Yet as Pickvance notes, the pursuit of spatial policies plays a legitimating role because, inter alia, the 'existence of spatial policies discourages the formulation of other, perhaps more radical, kinds' (1985: 131).

Urban Politics and Service Provision

It was around the provision of services, especially housing, that Labour began to make some impact on electoral politics in Lancaster. One of the major issues that contributed towards the shift away from a dominant and particularist local Conservatism in the late 1960s and early 1970s was the classic 'consumption' issue of housing. (This issue was almost certainly implicated in a similar brief shift to Labour in the 1950s.) 1969–70 saw mobilisation of tenants on several of Lancaster's council housing estates, with various actions carried out by the tenants' groups including petitioning, marches through the town and a rather cursory rent strike.

Marsh Tenants' Association, in the course of a protest about rent increases, based their call for mobilisation on the general treatment of council tenants:

> It's about time we stood up and decided we aren't going to be second-class citizens any more . . . We need tenants' committees on every estate. We need to get the Tories out of the council. We need to resist the rent increases. We need to demand the renovation of our houses. (*LG*, 26.6.70)

The view that council house tenants were second-class citizens was contested by other political groups, notably the local Ratepayers' Association, the Independents and the Conservatives. A familiar distinction was drawn between ratepayers who provided council housing and tenants who used it. Tenants' associations had existed in the town from the late 1930s, but the local paper felt that 'the rent issue has succeeded in unifying the city council's tenants for the first time', with tenants from a number of different estates joining a unitary protest in 1970 (*LG*, 24.7.70). The tenants had drawn up a petition signed by three thousand people, and a protest march was planned to demand a better deal for tenants and no rent rises. In July 1970 a crowd of three hundred tenants marched on the town hall and demanded a meeting with the housing committee. There were angry scenes when this was refused, and when the mayor also refused to see them. Fifty people attempted to storm the doors of the town hall and there were a number of arrests.

Council rents were the factor that gave rise to the increased militancy, but a whole range of service issues was later drawn into the campaign, which undoubtedly aided the Labour Party electorally since these dovetailed with its own programme. Up to the late 1960s it was difficult for the Labour Party to gain electoral support – particularly in view of the lack of a strong Labour movement industrial wing. Where Labour did gain support in the town was over non-economistic, non-industrial issues, and housing was one such issue. Mobilisation around housing had been significant in building some kind of base for Labour support in the town in the late 1930s (Warde, 1988a). The same was true of both the 1950s and the early 1970s. This indicates the importance of 'urban politics' in understanding local political environments.

However, while tenants' movements galvanised Labour into action on several occasions, often showing the way towards wider popular political participation and new modes of protest, little political capital was made, in effect, out of these issues in Lancaster. Perhaps, unlike Sheffield in the same period, there was an absence in Lancaster of pre-existing neighbourhood networks with appropriate organisational capacities. The absence of a base for the mobilisation of women within established political parties, and the fact that Lancaster had a strongly patriarchal division of labour in the workplace and in domestic life, may have affected the ability of *any* political party to capitalise on these issues. The fact that Lancaster always had a fairly high proportion of owner-occupied houses also militated against extensive collective pressure for improved public provision. As the town has become more prosperous in the last decade, house prices have increased significantly and the numbers of council house sales have been above average in a locality with relatively few council houses to start with. The effect of housing tenure on political allegiance must, however, be examined in association with class characteristics: there are no grounds for isolating tenure as the principal causal variable in local electoral behaviour (Warde et al., 1988). For instance, in local elections the poorer owner-occupied wards have become increasingly prone to support Labour candidates, suggesting that it is the quality of the environment rather than tenurial status that influences voting choice.

Social Movements

Another significant development in Lancaster politics in the first half of the 1970s was the appearance of social movements. This was, of course, a national phenomenon, but such groups appear to have taken root more firmly in the Lancaster area than in many other places. As with the left-wing socialist groups that developed in the area in the late 1960s and early 1970s, individuals associated with the university, usually students rather than university employees, played an important part in these movements. However, the transient nature of the student population means that local support must have built up within them. Members of such movements interviewed had, on the whole, come to Lancaster as students and had subsequently stayed in the area because it offered wide informal political networks. But such networks shift and change. The local women's movement, in particular, lacking the more structured institutional base of the ecology and peace movements, has waxed and waned as key individuals and households in the networks move off.

Within the national women's liberation movement in the 1970s, Lancaster was well known as a radical centre for women's politics. This almost certainly developed through the university, since wider gender politics in Lancaster in the 1960s and 1970s and in the previous period were fairly patriarchal. A socialist women's group was active in the early 1970s, and after about 1974 there was a marked increase in radical feminist activity in the town. Both radical and socialist feminists were involved initially in the setting-up of a women's refuge in Lancaster in 1974, which came to serve as a focus for radical feminist activity in the area. Subsequent activity produced a rape crisis line, an incest survivors' group, a reproductive rights group, a women in education group, a lesbian line and a *Lancaster Women's Newsletter*, together with various other groups. However, informal women's networks have been more important in the Lancaster women's movement than any institutional bases, and perhaps one of the distinguishing features of Lancaster feminism has been a politics dependent on informal networks and celebrated through the cultural sphere. Lancaster women's conferences have been significant, as have women's discos, feminist book fairs, writing groups and the like. Such phenomena are of course to be found in all large cities, particularly in metropolitan areas, but are more surprising in a town the size of Lancaster, especially since the local Council has given no support to such activities whatsoever.

Socialist feminism working through the channels of the local Labour movement has been less strong. There was a successful campaign about maternity provision in the early 1970s and some involvement in workplace disputes. But socialist and liberal feminism, which might have been expected to produce campaigns around issues of equal opportunity and levels of public service provision – campaigns conducted in other localities – has not been much in evidence in Lancaster. One explanation for this may lie in the absence of women, historically, from political activity in the town. Local political parties and the local authority in Lancaster have proved particularly impermeable to pressure from women's groups. The women's refuge, for instance, unlike refuges in other towns, has had very little help or support from the local Council, and in fact there were several attempts to close it down in the 1970s. Even a demand as apparently innocuous as the setting-up of a well-woman clinic was met only after something of a struggle in Lancaster, while political issues around reproduction, especially abortion, have been highly contentious. A women's section of the Lancaster Labour Party was re-established in 1985, but this seems on the whole to have drawn on women already in the Labour movement, rather than on local feminists outside it.

If the local authority has been more hostile to feminist issues than in some other areas, the peace movement and environmental politics have, by contrast, become thoroughly embedded into the local political scene. A Lancaster branch of the Green Party, for instance, developed more rapidly and earlier than in other areas, putting up candidates in both general and local elections. Concern about the environment, particularly about the local environmental effects of Heysham nuclear power stations and the nearby nuclear reprocessing complex at Windscale, is now expressed by a variety of local institutions – from the health authority to local political parties (although there were apparently no voices raised against the original siting decision in the early 1960s). The local peace movement has had a significant impact on the local Labour Party. One Labour Party councillor felt:

> CND is clearly an important force in Lancaster and within the Labour Party it reflects the concern that I think perhaps wasn't there twenty odd years ago . . . the women's group is . . . the most rapidly growing bit of the Labour movement. It is . . . hard to gauge its political impact as yet, because it is only . . . a year old. CND very easily created a political impact because the bulk of the new membership who have joined the Labour Party in the last few years have been members of CND and that's meant that on that particular issue the Labour Party now has moved to the left . . . Lancaster Labour Party is overwhelmingly pro CND. (Lancaster Labour city councillor, 1985)

Almost certainly the political issues exercising the citizens of Lancaster are more metropolitan today than they were twenty years ago, but there is no evidence that the politics of the social movements represent an alternative to Labour politics. The Labour Party appears to derive considerable support from members of social movements, and there is symbiosis between these movements and the Labour Party. The 1989 Euro-elections saw Green candidates taking 15 per cent of the vote nationally, but in Lancaster such issues were already structuring local politics in the early 1980s. It may be the case that environmental politics were developing in other localities in the early 1980s (although of the other *CURS* localities only Cheltenham demonstrated these tendencies, deriving mainly from a concern with the built environment). Alternatively, early deindustrialisation and the growth of a service class in Lancaster could have created an earlier base for the flourishing of Green issues.

By 1989 the political environment of Lancaster was vastly different from that twenty years earlier. What its transformation shows, above all, is that the relationship between industrial restructuring and political change is a complex, indirect and mediated one.

7

Conclusion

Place matters. But quite what makes the difference between places is not easy to explain. In a certain sense everywhere is different. What we call society is, in a way, just an aggregate of distinctive local sites and experiences. Differences of experience are a matter of degree.

It is a truism of modernisation theory that local differences have a tendency to become less important. There are in modern society institutions with national jurisdiction, having similar effects in all places: central government is an agency regulating localities – the kind of regional political autonomy that characterised the feudal state is no longer. Difference is partly a result of the struggle between central and local government bodies for jurisdiction and powers in an ongoing, irresolvable struggle. The predicament is neatly put by Duncan et al. (1988), who argue that the existence of local government is predicated upon a tension inherent in the uneven development of localities and regions in capitalist societies: central authorities attempt to impose uniform regulation on all places, while people in localities demand, given an unevenly developed economy, that specific, local interests be effectively promoted.

The social scientific analysis of local variation is constantly pulled between competing imperatives: on the one hand, to reduce variation to a few dimensions or factors in order to offer an explanation; and, on the other, to represent adequately the particularities of place. The promise of realism is that it can identify a parsimonious set of mechanisms, the conjoint effects of which will generate a sufficiently subtle matrix of elements as to explain local specificity. Such a mode of inquiry allows one to begin analysis either from consideration of the general mechanisms involved or from a concrete locality. The adequacy of such inquiry depends upon the extent to which findings at these two levels of analysis are shown to be isomorphic. The generating mechanisms and the specific combination of effects should be mutually entailed, with the locality being the compositional effect of the specified mechanisms, and the mechanisms accounting for the presence of elements of the local configuration. Case studies of localities will be an integral part of this approach.

Local configurations are, moreover, the outcomes of mechanisms that operate with different spatial ranges. The industrial restructuring of sectors of production is a process that now occurs at the international level. Studies of the new international division of labour have clearly demonstrated that some capital operates on a global scale. Also, many of the critical political decisions affecting localities are taken at a national level and reflect the priorities of governing parties, though there are also international and local determinants. The impact of both these processes is experienced differently in localities, partly as an effect of accumulated local history and partly because such decisions are filtered through localised norms of everyday life. The politics of the service class and of the feminist movement illustrate the combination of external determinations and local effects.

There can be no doubt about the generative role of economic reorganisation in impelling local social transformations. The difficulty comes in specifying precisely the mediations, demonstrating the chains of causation, between economic change and social life. The principal objective of this book has been to understand more precisely the nature of industrial restructuring, its partly 'non-economic' causes and consequences; and to specify the complex relationships between industrial restructuring and changing social and political practices.

We thus began our analysis from the restructuring thesis, a set of general formulations, a framework of concepts, and a series of hypotheses about the nature of the socio-spatial reorganisation of capitalist production, and of its impact upon local economic and social activity. Judged as a research programme (Lakatos, 1970), it has proved to have certain progressive features. Since it derives from a general critical theory of economic development, two of its virtues are identifying central mechanisms involved in generating the spatial division of labour and directing attention to the compositional effects of that division of labour on local social relations. Understanding of socio-spatial change, at the economic level especially, has advanced – through fresh examination of local economic policy and development, changing class relations and local politics, the diversity of place, and mediations between economic imperatives and civil society – producing insights inaccessible to the empiricism of earlier approaches to industrial location and regional geography. The programme also contains some degenerative tendencies, such as a collapse into descriptivist and parochial case studies, a penchant for economic reductionism, and a difficulty in specifying determinately the effects of the mechanisms of restructuring. That some of its earlier empirical generalisations have proved insupportable, and that it concentrates too heavily upon the labour factor in explaining spatial shifts, are not, however, reasons enough to abandon the research programme. Still superior in its fruitfulness to competing approaches, the further critical elaboration of the central elements of the thesis remains appropriate. That is the main contribution of this book.

In Chapter 2 we offered an analysis of the restructuring approach, paying special attention to empirical arguments concerning a crisis in Fordism and the introduction of post-Fordist flexible production procedures in manufacturing. We concluded that the most appropriate way to understand the processes of restructuring was from the point of view of individual firms set in the context of their environment in different industrial sectors. The strategies available to firms are so varied, however, that it is impossible to predict which strategy a firm will adopt. Indeed, the outcomes of restructuring for individual firms are largely contingent from this point of view, because in situations of uncertainty, with incomplete knowledge, the benefits of choosing one strategy rather than another are often incalculable. At the same time, though, it is possible, by isolating different kinds of strategy, to account retroductively for the decisions that managements have taken, and to show what local effects these will have.

It is a key claim that understanding the processes of restructuring cannot be reduced to a simple logic of capital accumulation. We develop a classificatory scheme that builds upon four general sets of processes of industrial restructuring – technical change, production reorganisation, spatial relocation and product transformation – but we observe that the 'labour factor' that is so central to many strategies of restructuring is not itself explicable in simple economic terms. Workers are conscious agents, located in determinate social positions and institutions, and with biographies, who consequently – contrary to the means by which management calculate their worth – do not arrive in the workplace as pure labour power. Labour brings with it a baggage of attributes acquired as an outcome of the general processes of social reproduction – memories of struggle, skills and expertise, aspirations for autonomy, gendered identities, social obligations, racial identities, political ideologies and organisational capacities. All these attributes are constitutive of the labour factor, conditioning the formulation and implementation of managerial strategies. Restructuring is not simply a process whereby employers make pure, economically rational, unilateral decisions about production, but a complex social process in which a variety of social groups and categories, each with different interests and concerns, interact.

The restructuring thesis and models of post-Fordism either ignore gender relations in employment or treat them as derivative of class processes. Our realist approach presents concrete processes of restructuring as the intersection of class, gender and race relations. Gender relations in employment are forged in local patterns of occupational and industrial segregation by sex, and by social struggles about segregation in the context of capitalist restructuring. As Lancaster deindustrialised, restructuring processes of technical change and rationalisation affected men and women quite differently, a result of local patterns of segregation and of the national legal regulation of women's employment.

The case study of manufacturing industry in Lancaster leads us to doubt whether a new, coherent system of 'flexible' production has been established. Though we find plenty of cases of new policies that might be described as increasing 'flexibility', they are of such variety and occur in such ad hoc ways that more general claims appear exaggerated. Probably the most significant aspect of increasing flexibility in the UK, the 'numerical flexibility' of women's part-time work, cannot anyway be explained in terms of the specific production strategies of enterprises. Rather, the changing employment patterns of women rest upon the social restructuring of mechanisms of patriarchal domination that operate through domestic divisions of labour, occupational segregation, workplace conflicts and state policies.

Moreover, most restructuring theory has been concerned with changes in manufacturing industry. This, though, ignores the largest employment sector in contemporary societies – namely, services. In such industries different factors are important. Although social struggle is vital in determining the mode of provision of services, most versions of the restructuring thesis exaggerate the importance of the labour factor in the restructuring of service industries. Labour costs are but one factor among many affecting the development of service industries. Furthermore, where labour is significant it is in different ways from in manufacturing. This results from the particular form of the service delivery and the complex skills involved in much servicing work. These often involve the production of a particular quality of social interaction. We identify thirteen different strategies of restructuring in these service industries, subsets of the four general processes of restructuring. It should be noted that increasing flexibility is only a feature of two of these thirteen, and the availability of appropriate labour is of central significance in fewer than half.

Another problem in the restructuring thesis has been to ignore the state. This is a major employer of services, and one that has relatively limited options when it comes to restructuring the delivery of these services. The possibilities for implementing technical change, reorganisation, spatial relocation and product transformation are limited. In fact, there are four types of restructuring that the state has tended to adopt most frequently: namely, intensification, commodification, concentration and domestication. The empirical study of the health sector demonstrates the ways in which, in a concrete instance, the British state has attempted to engage in the restructuring of certain public services. Some of the differences as compared with restructuring in private service industry are shown by considering various tourist-related industries, especially those that have been historically concentrated in seaside resorts.

One major effect of industrial restructuring is to alter the occupational structure and the social composition of local areas. Chapter 4 looks in detail at such processes in Lancaster. Such restructuring affects the local occupational structure, either by increasing the circulation of personnel in and out of the area (that is, migration) or by redeploying existing residents. Lancaster exhibits relatively low levels of migration (and that was mostly confined to movement within the north of England, suggesting that the labour market even for the service class is not genuinely national in scope). Instead, Lancaster offers primarily a case study in the local *recomposition* of existing elements. The analysis of the process of recomposition was facilitated by the use of both cross-sectional and longitudinal data. The use of the 1% longitudinal sample from the census, the collection of women's work histories and other interviews with local people, produces a multi-faceted account of the impact of industrial restructuring. The trajectories of individual workers can be captured, showing that for many men, in particular, the effect of the closure of manufacturing plant was long-term unemployment, sickness, or low-paid jobs in service industries. Interview accounts of personal experience uncover what such moves meant to people.

Recomposition had different implications for women. Compared to national averages, service class positions for women in Lancaster expanded rapidly, though the positive effects of that are much modified by the growth of part-time and temporary employment. Sectoral change did not have much effect on women's occupational experience, for they tended to remain within the same occupational grouping despite shifts between industrial sectors. Most of the new recruits to service employment in the 1970s did not have previous experience of manufacturing employment. Detailed analysis underscores the complexity of the process of recomposition within a single labour market.

In Chapter 5, having discussed various aspects of industrial restructuring and the growth of services, and their effects through occupational change upon social composition, we make a series of proposals about the ways in which such restructuring impacts upon extra-economic relations. We elaborate a concept of civil society to generate a systematic set of concepts and categories through which to understand extra-economic relations. We are particularly concerned to understand the parameters of social struggles. There are three critical elements of civil society: the constitution of subjects, the formation of material interests, and the resources available to social groups involved in struggles. We stress that the constitution of subjects is a spatial process, operating at both national and local level, but where the local, and especially households, are particularly important. A variety of competing material interests emanate from the organisation of civil society: class, gender, generation, social provision, amenity, citizenship, use value, security and housing interests are identified. The constitution of subjectivities and the identification of sets of material interests indicate foci of social struggles, but the realisation of interests in such struggles depends additionally on the resources available to different groups. Some find themselves with an already established unity; others try to create unity by means of associations and parties, though in many cases success will depend upon the congruity between the interests and subjectivities of groups who are potential political allies. It is equally important, in analysing the bases of social struggles, to recognise the degree to which the form of the state (whether local or national) circumscribes these struggles – the relative autonomy of the state must be appreciated.

These propositions about the bases of struggle in civil society are illustrated and elaborated in a study of conflicts over the built environment. Built forms and the meanings attached to them provide a way of exploring the nature of local, or urban, meaning. Subjective identity, material interests and resources for mobilisation are all partly constrained by, and partly expressed in, conflict over the built environment. The projects engaged in by different groups trying to influence change in the environment 'in their own image' develop in the context of social recomposition, consequent in part upon industrial restructuring.

A variety of processes of restructuring have impacted upon the sense and image of the Lancaster and Morecambe district. The restructuring of manufacturing capital, of state agencies, of retail, finance and property capital and of the tourist industry have all brought new populations to the city and new aesthetic concerns. A conflict has arisen over aesthetic direction – a struggle that might be conceptualised as being between adherence to the principle of 'historical authenticity', a radical modernism and a playful enterprise-oriented postmodernism. It has been shown that different social groups are potential bearers of distinct environmental and aesthetic projects, with state sector professionals appearing as opponents of the aesthetics of both modernism and postmodernism. A policy directed towards promoting historical authenticity, the other pole of concern in Lancaster, was indicated by a public inquiry, but is likely to have little influence on the ultimate development of the city centre. In the old seaside resort of Morecambe, by contrast, the balance of class forces is such that the dominant collective social project is one of a belated modernism, the expression of petite bourgeois and lower-middle-class subjectivities and interests.

The connections between industrial restructuring, social recomposition and political behaviour are complex and difficult to unravel. Chapter 6 makes a number of general observations.

First, we argue that our elaborated concept of civil society offers a way of understanding aspects of political mobilisation by focusing on the way in which interests and resources, formed in civil society, comprise key elements of a local political environment.

Secondly, we suggest that service classes differ from place to place, and hence that the service class is geographically fractionalised. Our case study both indicated considerable differences in terms of aesthetic preferences within the service class and gave grounds for supporting the idea that public sector professionals are distinctive in their partisan affiliations. The distinctive political trajectory of Lancaster and Morecambe would, otherwise, be incomprehensible. The area experienced rapid and early deindustrialisation, a changing class structure, new forms of local identity as the local state was reorganised, a sharply increased proportion of workers employed in providing public welfare facilities, and the flourishing of feminism and 'new' social movements. What the case study illustrates is the mutual interaction of these elements in the transformation of a local political environment. It also shows that the relationship between industrial restructuring and political change is an indirect, mediated one: Lancaster's experience is a powerful reminder that there is no possibility of reading off political change from an economic base. As a town with a large factory proletariat, Lancaster exhibited anti-Labour sentiment; as it deindustrialised collective sentiment swung away from the Conservatives. The removal of conditions of material dependence, obtaining until the 1960s, made space for the development of the Labour movement in the town. Among the prominent new recruits to that movement were precisely service class personnel engaged in the public sector.

Thirdly, in the realm of formal politics, despite the material inequalities between men and women there were no significant differences in party preference by gender in the 1987 British general election, for instance. However, this does not imply the absence of distinct gendered interests or capacities. Mobilisation in political campaigns is distinctive by gender, and varies locally. The women's movement is instructive regarding the analysis of the spatial levels of political behaviour. The impetus behind feminist politics in Lancaster was national, if not international. It was not local issues, nor was it issues arising from industrial restructuring, that produced a powerful local feminist movement. Nevertheless, Lancaster developed a powerful core of feminist activity. To a significant degree the impact of feminism depends upon the existing balance of political forces: in Lancaster the historical weakness of the Labour movement contributed to a conducive environment for feminism. In the 1970s, because many political demands and activities are necessarily filtered through other political agencies, the relationship to the Labour Party became important as a conduit for feminist interests. The Labour Party thus gained support from the women's movement and other social movements in the town, especially the peace movement, partly because there was no inherited dominance of trade union concerns. There are, therefore, different social bases for Labour mobilisation in different localities.

The shrinking size of the male manual working class, and its less solid support for Labour, though posing immediate problems does not necessarily leave the party with permanent minority status. Studies of local politics increasingly provide evidence of considerable political differences from place to place. For instance, Wainwright's (1987) study of Labour politics in five metropolitan areas showed enormous variation in the social bases, political interests, organisational form and policy programmes. In effect, it would appear that district and constituency Labour Parties are based upon distinctive, local socio-political alliances. It has often been pointed out that the British Labour Party at national level has been a federation of competing political projects (Fabian, ethical socialist, trade unionist, cooperative, and so on). Another way of looking at the Labour Party in the 1980s is in terms of a federation of locally differentiated bands of activists and partisans. In some respects this was always the case (for example, Howell, 1983; Savage, 1987a): there are longstanding local and regional traditions in Labour politics. However, there are severe pressures that operate to reduce local peculiarities. The Labour Party as an organisation has always had centripetal tendencies, not being very content to allows its branches autonomy lest they prove embarrassing to the national executive or the parliamentary party. And when in government, Labour has rarely advocated the decentralisation of the powers of the state.

The last decade has seen the removal of some considerable powers from local authorities to the centre, but an expansion of other local powers – expenditure on local economic policy, for instance. Significant tensions have developed between local authorities seeking to pursue various courses of action in the fields of social and economic policy and a central government primarily concerned to reduce public expenditure. This has generated considerable local–central conflict, and local concerns mobilise people to a greater degree than twenty years ago. The emergence of local social movements, environmental concerns, issues of local and national identity, along with the sharpening of geographical differences in electoral behaviour, suggest that the locality is currently an important base of political mobilisation. In that sense, largely because such concerns almost always require expression and aggregation through political parties, the future prospects of Labour continue to be a function of the varied local alliances in the constituencies. The evidence from Lancaster implies that the processes said to be disrupting the Labour Party as a whole, when looked at as a national aggregate, do not apply locally. Fractions of the local service class have been central in reviving left-wing and social movement politics. The public sector service class is a major pillar of support, something that might be expected to be repeated in other places under similar local circumstances. Local political alignments show no signs of becoming simpler.

Our fourth observation is precisely that place matters, especially as territorial politics become more prominent and as older class cleavages are transmuted into spatial phenomena. The role of spatial coalitions after 1974 indicates the manner in which material bases and particular institutional configurations constrain political practice. Recession and the enhanced mobility of capital render local populations extremely vulnerable to the loss of job opportunities, but simultaneously these seem to have encouraged class cooperation at the local level, a phenomenon even more marked in the USA (Cox and Mair, 1988). In Britain, the degree of spatial polarisation has increased as local authorities pursue different strategies, some concentrating on conservation to make their districts more socially attractive, others trying to provide a less controlled environment for 'market competition'. The reorganisation of local government has further increased the significance of local territorial politics in recent years, as some groups seek to preserve their local identities and protect local interests in the face of their absorption into larger units of administration.

Finally, we draw attention to questions of the significance of deindustrialisation for politics, considering whether the politics of a predominantly service-based economy will lead to new modes of political activity. The case study certainly suggests that issues of access to and distribution of services generate political conflicts along several dimensions – urban–rural, native–in-migrant, Lancaster–Morecambe, modern–postmodern, manufacturing workers–others, home-owners–tenants, ratepayers–local state – as well as between classes, genders and ethnic groups. As these conflicts are aggregated, by political parties or in 'new' social movements, they provide great scope for the formation of fresh alliances and mobilisations.

In sum, we have isolated a number of key causal mechanisms that are too infrequently considered important in the mediation of the effects of restructuring on daily local life: gender relations, the nature of services, the character and mobility of fractions of the service class, the nature of local political alliances, as well as the complex contingent managerial strategies of diverse economic enterprises. Place is the intersection of a multitude of processes, the sedimentations of the past, the social practices of the present and projects for the future.

Appendix: Research Methods

The research reported in this book was conducted under the auspices of the ESRC's *Changing Urban and Regional System of the UK* initiative. This involved studies of seven localities in England (each study received about £40,000 in total), plus funding the collection and the analysis of some national data. A number of initiative meetings were held in order that the research carried out in each locality was cognisant of the research activity of the other teams. However, there was little effort made to ensure strict comparability between the research carried out in the different localities, although there was considerable agreement on the main topics to be investigated. The limited funding in each locality prohibited the collection of extensive survey material. Instead a variety of different sources of data was employed.

In Lancaster the principal sources for data collection were:

1 *Interviews with representatives of the leading organisations in the locality*, especially employers, trade unionists, local government officers and councillors, employment agencies and leaders of political parties and movements, with informants, therefore, in a wide variety of key positions in the area. The persons interviewed were chosen in terms of the importance their organisation was reputed to have in Lancaster.

2 *Household and employment data*, particularly from the Census of Population and the Census of Employment. The latter was accessed through NOMIS, the National Online Manpower Information Service. This is based in the Department of Geography at the University of Durham and funded by the Department of Employment through the Training Agency. Data based on employers' returns is available on employment by economic sector (1968 SIC for 1971–81 and 1980 SIC for 1981–4) disaggregated by sex and full-time/part-time employment. The Census of Employment was conducted annually between 1971 and 1978 and then every three years. It is increasingly relying upon a sample survey of smaller firms so its accuracy for TTWAs in 1984 is somewhat suspect. Problems of comparison over time for local labour market areas are further compounded by changes in the definition of

TTWAs, the 1971–81 data being available for 1978 TTWAs while 1981–4 data is available for 1984 TTWAs. Despite these problems the Census of Employment data available through NOMIS is a valuable source of local labour market data. Paul Bagguley carried out most of this work.

3 *The OPCS Longitudinal Study (LS)*, which works by linking the individual records of 4/365 of the population from census to census, and with certain NHS Central Register and other Registrar General data. So far the 1971 and 1981 censuses are included. The principal advantage is the availability of longitudinal data for such a large sample population (though at 1% the sample size poses quite severe limits on what can be done for a locality such as Lancaster); but a very major further advantage is flexibility, since in principle any combination of LS variables (that is, virtually all of the variables from each Population Census, plus the NHS and RG data) can be tabulated and/or transformed to create other derived variables, using a self-determined categorisation of values. A further description of the LS, and some of the background to its inception, can be found in Fox and Goldblatt (1982). This part of the work was conducted by Dan Shapiro.

4 *Lancaster Women's Work Histories (LWWHS)*. This data was gathered during 1980–1. A sample of 300 women was drawn from a stratified random sample using the electoral register as the sample frame. The Lancaster TTWA was divided into three main areas – Lancaster, Morecambe and rural wards – randomly selected in order to represent the proportions of the population living in each area. All women aged eighteen or over were eligible for inclusion in the sample, giving a full age spread in the interviewed population. The data was collected by interview using a structured questionnaire.

The data comprises a full work history of each woman interviewed, including occupation, industry, employer and reasons for leaving a particular job. A partial life history was also taken, enabling us, for instance, to discover whether the interviewee had lived in the Lancaster area all her life or not, and to discover educational levels. Some data was collected on other members of the household currently resident, enabling us, among other things, to have a complete picture of household income and of the domestic division of labour.

This data was collected by Anne Green and Sylvia Walby. Financial support was also provided by the Manpower Services Commission.

5 *Household interviews*. In 1986–7 thirty-eight in-depth qualitative interviews were carried out with individuals who, at that time,

were employed in certain key sectors – health, education, tourism, power – in the Lancaster TTWA. The same interview was also carried out with six women, previously interviewed as part of the Lancaster Women's Work Histories project in 1980–1. An extensive and detailed topic list of questions and question areas was used to structure the interviews. The topics covered included: household structure; household income; employment of household members; domestic division of labour; work history; details of current employment; workplace and party politics; involvement in social movements; leisure activities; and some questions on attitudes to the locality as a place to live and work, and changes in the locality. Respondents were treated as 'key informants', with the data providing insights into the way individuals experience restructuring at the level of the household, the workplace and the locality. Where such interviews are quoted in the text they are identified with a number starting with 'KI'. Jane Mark-Lawson conducted these interviews.

6 *Newspapers*. Extensive use was made of a catalogue of articles from the local newspapers for the period 1900–80. Stories relevant to issues of economic restructuring and local political behaviour were abstracted and indexed. This work was carried out by Alison Edmonds and Janni Howker, supervised by Alan Warde. Financial support was also provided by the Manpower Services Commission.

Much of this material has also been written up in the series of Lancaster Regionalism Group Working Papers. Those produced relating to this project are:

WP19 *Economic Restructuring and Employment Change in Lancaster 1971–1981: Manufacturing Industries*, Paul Bagguley.

WP20 *Service Employment and Economic Restructuring in Lancaster: 1971–1981*, Paul Bagguley.

WP21 *Economic Planning and Policy in the Lancaster District*, John Urry.

WP22 *Holidaymaking, Cultural Change and the Seaside*, John Urry.

WP24 *Flexibility, Restructuring and Gender: Changing Employment in Britain's Hotels*, Paul Bagguley.

WP25 *Industrial Restructuring, Local Politics and the Reproduction of Labour Power: some Theoretical Considerations and a Case Study*, Alan Warde.

WP28 *Gender Restructuring: a Comparative Analysis of Five Local Labour Markets*, Paul Bagguley and Sylvia Walby.

WP29 *The Post-Fordist Enigma: Theories of Labour Flexibility*, Paul Bagguley.

WP30 *Conditions of Dependence: Working-class Quiescence in Lancaster in the Twentieth Century*, Alan Warde.

WP32 *Restructuring Theory in Crisis*, Dan Shapiro.

WP33 *Industrial Restructuring and the Transformation of a Local Political Environment: the Case of Lancaster*, Jane Mark-Lawson and Alan Warde.

WP36 *Flexibility and the Changing Sexual Division of Labour*, Sylvia Walby.

Bibliography

Abercrombie, N. and Urry, J. (1983) *Capital, Labour and the Middle Classes*. London: Allen & Unwin.

Acker, J. (1973) 'Women and stratification: a case of intellectual sexism', in Joan Huber (ed.), *Changing Women in a Changing Society*. Chicago: University of Chicago Press. 174–83.

Acker, J. (1980) 'Women and stratification: a review of recent literature', *Contemporary Sociology*, 9 (Jan.): 25–39.

Aglietta, M. (1987) *A Theory of Capitalist Regulation*. London: Verso.

Agnew, J. (1987) *Place and Politics: the Geographical Mediation of State and Society*. Boston: Allen & Unwin.

Anderson, B. (1983) *Imagined Communities*. London: Verso.

Ardill, J. (1988) 'Small is Beautiful for Life in Town'. *Guardian*, 25.3.88.

Artley, A. and Robinson, J. (1985) *The Official New Georgian Handbook*. London: Ebury Press.

Atkinson, J. (1984) 'Manpower strategies for flexible organisations', *Personnel Management*, Aug.: 28–31.

Atkinson, J. (1986) *Changing Working Patterns: How Companies Achieve Flexibility to Meet New Needs*. London: National Economic Development Office.

Atkinson, J.(1989)*Flexibility and Skill in Manaufacturing Establishments*. IMS Manpower Commentary No. 41, Brighton: Institute of Manpower Studies.

Bagguley, P. (1986a) *Economic Restructuring and Employment Change in Lancaster 1971–1981. Manufacturing Industries*. Lancaster Regionalism Group Working Paper No. 19, University of Lancaster: Lancaster Regionalism Group.

Bagguley, P. (1986b) *Service Employment and Economic Restructuring in Lancaster 1971–1981*. Lancaster Regionalism Group Working Paper No. 20, University of Lancaster: Lancaster Regionalism Group.

Bagguley, P. (1987) *Flexibility, Restructuring and Gender: Changing Employment in Britain's Hotels*. Lancaster Regionalism Group Working Paper No. 24, University of Lancaster: Lancaster Regionalism Group.

Bagguley, P. and Walby, S. (1988) 'Gender restructuring: a comparative analysis of five local labour markets'. Lancaster Regionalism Group Working Paper No. 28, University of Lancaster: Lancaster Regionalism Group.

Bagguley, P., Mark-Lawson, J., Shapiro, D., Urry, J., Walby, S. and Warde, A. (1989) 'Restructuring Lancaster', in P. Cooke (ed.), *Localities*. London: Unwin Hyman.

Barlow, J. and Savage, M. (1986) 'The politics of growth: cleavage and conflict in a Tory heartland', *Capital and Class*, 30: 156–82.

Baudrillard, J. (1976) *L'Echange Symbolique et la Mort*. Paris: Gallimard.

Baudrillard, J. (1981) *For a Critique of the Political Economy of the Sign*. St Louis: Telos Press.

Beardshaw, V. (1981) *Conscientious objectors at work, mental hospital nurses: a case study*, London: Social Audit.

Beechey, V. (1977) 'Some notes on female wage labour in capitalist production', *Capital and Class*, 3: 45–66.

Beechey, V. (1978) 'Women and production: a critical analysis of some sociological theories of women's work', in A. Kuhn and A. Wolpe (eds), *Feminism and Materialism: Women and Modes of Production*. London: Routledge & Kegan Paul. 155–97.

Beechey, V. and Perkins, T. (1987) *A Matter of Hours: Women, Part-time Work and the Labour Market*. Cambridge: Polity Press.

Bell, D. (1974) *The Coming of Post-industrial Society*. London: Heinemann.

Benjamin, W. (1975) 'The work of art in the age of mechanical reproduction', in W. Benjamin, *Illuminations*. London: Fontana.

Berman, M. (1983) *All That is Solid Melts into Air: the Experience of Modernity*. London: Verso.

Bhagwati, J. (1987) 'International trade in services and its relevance for economic development', in O. Giarini (ed.), *The Emerging Service Economy*. Oxford: Pergamon Press. 3–34.

Blau, J. R. (1988) 'Where architects work: a change analysis 1970–1980', in P. L. Knox (ed.), *The Design Professions and the Built Environment*. London: Croom Helm. 127–46.

Bourdieu, P. (1984) *Distinction: a Social Critique of the Judgement of Taste*. London: Routledge & Kegan Paul.

Braverman, H. (1974) *Labour and Monopoly Capital*. New York: Monthly Review Press.

Butler, D. E. and Stokes, D. (1974) *Political Change in Britain* (2nd edn). London: Macmillan.

Cabinet Office (Enterprise Unit) (1985) *Pleasure, Leisure – and Jobs. The Business of Tourism*. London: HMSO.

Cameron, A. (1985) 'Bread and roses revisited: women's culture and working-class activism in the Lawrence strike of 1912', in R. Milkman (ed.), *Women Work and Protest: a century of women's labour history*. Boston: Routledge & Kegan Paul.

Carlzon, J. (1987) *Moments of Truth*. Cambridge, Mass.: Ballinger.

Castells, M. (1983) *The City and the Grassroots*. London: Edward Arnold.

Cawson, A. and Saunders, P. (1983) 'Corporatism, competitive politics and class struggle', in R. King (ed.), *Capital and Politics*. London: Routledge & Kegan Paul.

Chivers, T. S. (1973) 'The proletarianisation of a service worker', *Sociological Review*, 21: 633–56.

Christie, G. (1964) *Storeys of Lancaster: 1848–1964*. London: Collins.

Clairmonte, F. and Cavanagh, J. (1984) 'Transnational corporations and services: the final frontier', *Trade and Development*, 5: 215–73.

Clarke, P. F. (1971) *Lancashire and the New Liberalism*. Cambridge: Cambridge University Press.

Cockburn, C. (1983) *Brothers: Male Dominance and Technological Change*. London: Pluto Press.

Cohen, S. and Zysman, J. (1987) *Manufacturing Matters*. New York: Basic Books.

Cooke, P. (1984) 'Region, class and gender: a European comparison', *Progress in Planning*, 22: 89–146.

Cooke, P. (1985) 'Class practices as regional markers: a contribution to labour geography', in D. Gregory and J. Urry (eds), *Social Relations and Spatial Structures*. Basingstoke: Macmillan. 213–41.

Cooke, P. (1987) *Inside the Divided Kingdom: Urban and Regional Change in the 1980s*. London: Economic and Social Research Council.

Cooke, P. (1989) 'Restructuring, flexibility and local labour markets', in J. Morris (ed.), *Labour Market Responses to Industrial Restructuring and Technological Change*. Brighton: Wheatsheaf Books.

Cooke, P. and Morgan, K. (1985) *Flexibility and the New Restructuring: Locality and Industry in the 1980s*. Papers in Planning Research No. 94, Cardiff: University of Wales Institute of Science and Technology, Department of Town Planning.

Coombes, M. G., Green, A. E., Owen, D. W. (1988) 'Substantive issues in the definition of "localities": evidence from sub-group local labour market areas in the West Midlands', *Regional Studies*, 22(4): 303–18.

Cornetz, W. (1988) 'The dark side of the "employment miracle" in the USA', *Intereconomic*, Jan./Feb: 39–48.

Cousins, C. (1986) 'The labour process in the state welfare sector', in D. Knights and H. Willmott (eds), *Managing the Labour Process*. London: Gower. 85–108.

Cousins, C. (1987) *Controlling Social Welfare*. Brighton: Wheatsheaf Books.

Cox, K. R. and Mair, A. (1988) 'Locality and community in the politics of local economic development', *Annals of the Association of American Geographers*, 78: 307–25.

Curtice, J. and Steed, M. (1982) Electoral choice and the production of government: the changing operation of the electoral system in the UK since 1955', *British Journal of Political Studies*, 12: 249–98.

Daniel, W. and Milward, N. (1984) *Workplace Industrial Relations in Britain. The DE/PSI/SSRC Survey*. London: Heinemann Educational Books.

Daniels, P. W. (1985) *Service Industries*. London: Methuen.

Delphy, C. (1984) *Close to Home: a Materialist Analysis of Women's Oppression*. London: Hutchinson.

Dex, S. (1987) *Women's Occupational Mobility: a Lifetime Perspective*. Basingstoke: Macmillan.

Dicken, P. (1986) *Global Shift: Industrial Change in a Turbulent World*. London: Harper & Row.

Dickens, P. (1988) *One Nation? Social Change and the Politics of Locality*. London: Pluto.

Doeringer, P. and Piore, M. (1971) *Internal Labour Markets and Manpower Analysis*. Lexington, Mass.: Heath.

Duncan, S. (1986) 'What is locality?'. Urban and Regional Studies Working Paper No. 51, Brighton: University of Sussex.

Duncan, S., Goodwin, M. and Halford, S. (1988) 'Policy variations in local states: uneven development and local social relations', *International Journal of Urban and Regional Research*, 12: 107–28.

Dunleavy, P. (1980) 'The political implications of sectoral cleavages and the growth of state employment', *Political Studies*, 28: 364–83 and 527–49.

Economic Trends (various years) London: HMSO

Employment Gazette (various dates) London: Department of Employment.

Enderwick, P. (1984) 'Patterns of industrial conflict in private sector service industries: evidence from British survey data', *Service Industries Journal*, 4: 30–47.

Evans, P. B., Rueschmeyer, D. and Skocpol, T. (eds) (1985) *Bringing the State Back In*. Cambridge: Cambridge University Press.

FAST (Forecasting and Assessment in Science and Technology) (1984) *Eurofutures: the Challenges of Innovation*. London: Butterworth/Futurea.

Feifer, M. (1985) *Going Places*. London: Macmillan.

Feldberg, R. and Genn, E. N. (1984) 'Male and female: job versus gender models in the sociology of work', in J. Siltanen and M. Stanworth (eds), *Women and the Public Sphere: a Critique of Sociology and Politics*. London: Hutchinson. 23–36.

Fielding, A. and Savage, M. (1987) *Social Mobility and the Changing Class Composition of Southeast England*. Working Paper No. 60, Brighton: University of Sussex, Graduate Division of Urban and Regional Studies.

Finch, J. and Groves, D. (1983) *Labour of Love*. London: Routledge & Kegan Paul.

Fothergill, S. and Gudgin, G. (1979) 'Regional employment change: a sub-regional explanation', *Progress in Planning*, 12(3): 155–219.

Fothergill, S. and Gudgin, G. (1982) *Unequal Growth: Urban and Regional Employment Change in the UK*. London: Heinemann.

Fox, J. and Goldblatt, P. (1982) *Longitudinal Study 1971–75*. Longitudinal Series No. 1, Office of Population Censuses and Surveys, London: HMSO.

Fröbel, F., Heinrichs, J. and Kreye, O. (1980) *The New International Division of Labour*. Cambridge: Cambridge University Press.

Gaventa, J. (1980) *Power and Powerlessness: Quiescence and Rebellion in an Appalachian Valley*. Oxford: Clarendon Press.

Gershuny, J. (1978) *After Industrial Society*. London: Macmillan.

Gershuny, J. (1986) 'Time use and the dynamics of the service sector'. Mimeo, University of Bath: Department of Sociology.

Gershuny, J. (1987) 'The future of service employment', in O. Giarini (ed.), *The Emerging Service Economy*. Oxford: Pergamon Press. 105–26.

Gershuny, J. I. and Miles, I. (1983) *Social Innovation and the Division of Labour*. Oxford: Oxford University Press.

Giddens, A. (1981) *A Contemporary Critique of Historical Materialism*. London: Macmillan.

Giddens, A. (1984) *The Constitution of Society*. Cambridge: Polity Press.

Gilroy, P. (1987) *There Ain't No Black in the Union Jack: the Cultural Politics of Race and Nation*. London: Martin Robertson.

Giner, S. (1976) *Mass Society*. London: Martin Robertson.

Glucksmann, M. (1986) 'In a class of their own? Women workers in the new industries in inter-war Britain', *Feminist Review*, 29.

Goldthorpe, J. (1983) 'Women and class analysis: a defence of the traditional view', *Sociology*, 17: 465–88.

Goldthorpe, J. (1984) 'Women and class analysis: a reply to the replies', *Sociology*, 18: 491–9.

Green, A. E., Coombes, M. G. and Owen, D. W. (1986) 'Gender-specific local labour market areas in England and Wales', *Geoforum*, 17(3): 339–51.

Gregory, D. and Urry, J. (eds) (1985) *Social Relations and Social Structures*. London: Macmillan.

Griffiths Report (1984) *Social Services Committee (House of Commons) Reports (1983–4). 1st Report from the Social Services Committee: Griffiths NHS Management Inquiry Report*. London: HMSO.

Hakim, C. (1979) *Occupational Segregation: a Comparative Study of the Degree and Pattern of the Differentiation between Men and Women's Work in Britain, the*

United States and Other Countries. Research Paper No. 9, London: Department of Employment.

Halford, S. (1988) 'Women's initiatives in local government: where do they come from and where are they going?', *Policy and Politics*, 16: 251–9.

Hall, S. (1980) 'Encoding/decoding', in S. Hall (ed.), *Culture, Media, Language.* London: Hutchinson. 128–38.

Hannah, L. (1980) 'Visible and invisible hands in Great Britain', in A. Chandler and H. Daems (eds), *Managerial Hierarchies.* Cambridge, Mass.: Harvard University Press. 41–76.

Harvey, D. (1987) 'Flexible accumulation through urbanism: reflections on "postmodernism" in the American city', *Antipode*, 19: 260–86.

Heap, S. H. (1980) 'World profitability crisis in the 1970s: some empirical evidence', *Capital and Class*, 12: 66–84.

Heath, A. (1981) *Social Mobility.* London: Fontana.

Heath, A., Jowell, R. and Curtice, J. (1985) *How Britain Votes.* London: Pergamon Press.

Hewison, R. (1987) *The Heritage Industry: Britain in a Climate of Decline.* London: Methuen.

Hewison, R. (1988) 'The Heritage Business', *Up North* series. Written and presented by Robert Hewison, BBC Newcastle.

Hills, J. and Lovenduski, J. (eds) (1981) *The Politics of the Second Electorate: Women and Public Participation.* London: Routledge & Kegan Paul.

Hirst, P. and Zeitlin, J. (1988) 'A Strategy of Flexible Specialisation'. *Financial Times*, 7.12.88.

Hobsbawm, E. J. and Ranger, T. (eds) (1983) *The Invention of Tradition.* Cambridge: Cambridge University Press.

Hochschild, A. (1983) *The Managed Heart.* Berkeley and Los Angeles: University of California Press.

Howell, D. (1983) *British Workers and the Independent Labour Party 1888–1906.* Manchester: Manchester University Press.

Hymer, S. H. (1975) 'The multinational corporation and the law of uneven development', in H. Radice (ed.), *International Firms and Modern Imperialism.* Harmondsworth: Penguin. 37–62.

Jameson, F. (1984) 'Postmodernism, or the cultural logic of late capitalism', *New Left Review*, 146 (July–Aug.): 53–92.

Jarratt Report (1985) Committee of Vice-Chancellors and Principals: *Steering Committee for Efficiency Studies in Universities Report.* London: HMSO.

Jarrett, D. (1984) *The Electronic Office.* Aldershot: Gower.

Jenkins, S. (1987) 'Art Makes a Return to Architecture'. *Sunday Times*, 15.11.87.

Jessop, B. (1982) *The Capitalist State.* Oxford: Martin Robertson.

Jessop, B. (1988) 'Regulation theory, post Fordism and the state: more than a reply to Werner Bonefield', *Capital and Class*, 34: 147–68.

Johnson, K. and Mignot, K. (1982) 'Marketing trade unionism to service industries: an historical analysis of the hotel industry', *Services Industries Journal*, 2: 5–23.

Johnston, R. J. (1986a) 'Place and votes: the role of location in the creation of political attitudes', *Urban Geography*, 7: 103–17.

Johnston, R. J. (1986b) 'Research policy and review 9. A space for place (or a place for space) in British psephology: a review of recent writings with especial reference to the General Election of 1983'. *Environment and Planning A*, 18: 573–98.

Keat, R. and Urry, J. (1982) *Social Theory as Science* (2nd edn). London: Routledge & Kegan Paul.

Kellner, D. (1987) 'Baudrillard, semiurgy and death', *Theory, Culture and Society*, 4: 125–46.

King, A. (1983) 'Culture and the political economy of building form', *Habitat International*, 7(5/6): 237–48.

King, A. (1984) *The Bungalow: the Production of Global Culture*. London: Routledge & Kegan Paul.

King, A. (1987) 'Making a market in meaning: the national and international reorganisation of domestic architecture'. Nov. British Sociological Association, Sociology and Environment Study Group. London: London School of Economics.

Knox, P. L. (1987) 'The social production of the built environment', *Progress in Human Geography*, 11(3): 354–77.

Krier, L. (1984) 'Berlin–Tagel' and 'Building and architecture', *Architectural Design*, 54: 87, 119.

Lakatos, I. (1970) 'Falsification and the methodology of scientific research programmes', in I. Lakatos and A. Musgrove (eds), *Criticism and the Growth of Knowledge*. Cambridge: Cambridge University Press. 91–196.

Lancashire County Council (1987) *A Strategy for Tourism in Lancashire*. Preston: Lancashire County Council.

Lancashire Evening Post (various dates).

Lancaster DHA (District Health Authority) *Annual Programme and Planning Review*, (various years).

Lancaster Guardian (LG) (various dates).

Lancaster Guardian Property Guide (various dates).

Lash, S. (1984) *The Militant Worker*. London: Heinemann.

Lash, S. (1987) 'Critical theory and postmodern culture: the eclipse of aura', *Current Perspectives in Social Theory*, 8: 197–213.

Lash, S. (1988) 'Discourse or figure? Postmodernism as a "regime of signification" ', *Theory, Culture and Society*, 5: 311–36.

Lash, S. and Urry, J. (1987) *The End of Organized Capitalism*. Cambridge: Polity Press.

Lee, C. (1984) 'The service sector, regional specialisation, and economic growth in the Victorian economy', *Journal of Historical Geography*, 10: 139–55.

Leidner, R. (1987) 'Scripting service work: case studies of fast food and insurance sales'. Paper presented to the Society for the Study of Social Problems, Aug. Chicago.

Levitt, R. and Wall, A. (1984) *The Reorganised National Health Service*. London: Croom Helm.

Levitt, T. (1976) 'Management and the "post-industrial" society', *The Public Interest*, 44: 69–103.

Leyshon, A., Daniels, P. and Thrift, N. (1987) *Internationalization of Professional Producer Services: the Case of Large Accountancy Firms*. Working Paper on Producer Services No. 3, Lampeter: St David's College.

Lickorish, L. J. and Kershaw, A. G. (1975) 'Tourism between 1840 and 1940', in A. J. Burkart and S. Medlik (eds), *The Management of Tourism*. London: Heinemann. 11–26.

Linder, S. (1970) *The Harried Leisure Class*. New York: Columbia University Press.

Lipietz, A. (1987) *Mirages and Miracles: the Crises of Global Fordism*. London: Verso.

Littler, C. (1985) 'Taylorism, Fordism and Job Design', in D. Knights, H. Willmott and D. Collinson, (eds), *Job Redesign: Critical Perspectives on the Labour Process*. Aldershot: Gower.

Local Plan: Lancaster Local Plan. Feb. 1987. See also Building Design Partnership and Donaldsons, *Lancaster City Centre Retail Development: a Report for Public Consultation*. March 1986. Both available from Lancaster City Council, Lancaster.

Lovenduski, J. (1986) *Women and European Politics: Contemporary Feminism and Public Policy*. Amerhurst, Mass.: University of Massachusetts Press.

Lyotard, J. F. (1984) *The Postmodern Condition: a Report on Knowledge*. Manchester: Manchester University Press.

MacInnes, J. (1987) *Thatcherism at Work*. Milton Keynes: Open University Press.

MacIntyre, S. (1980) *Little Moscows*. London: Croom Helm.

Mandel, E. (1963) 'The dialectic of class and region in Belgium', *New Left Review*, 20: 5–31.

Mark-Lawson, J. (1988) 'Women, welfare and urban politics 1917–1936'. PhD thesis, University of Lancaster.

Mark-Lawson, J., Savage, M. and Warde, A. (1985) 'Women and local politics: struggles over welfare, 1918–1939', in L. Murgatroyd et al., *Localities, Class and Gender*. London: Pion. 195–215.

Mark-Lawson, J. and Warde, A. (1987) *Industrial Restructuring and the Transformation of a Local Political Environment: a Case Study of Lancaster*. Lancaster Regionalism Group Working Paper No. 33, University of Lancaster: Lancaster Regionalism Group.

Mark-Lawson, J. and Witz, A. (1988) 'From "family labour" to "family wage". The case of women's labour in nineteenth-century coalmining', *Social History*, 13: 151–74.

Marris, R. (1985) 'The paradox of services', *Political Quarterly*, 56: 242–53.

Mars, G. and Nicod, M. (1984) *The World of Waiters*. London: Allen & Unwin.

Marshall, G. (1986) 'The workplace culture of a licensed restaurant', *Theory, Culture and Society*, 3: 33–48.

Marshall, G., Newby, H., Rose, D. and Vogler, C. (1988) *Social Class in Modern Britain*. London: Hutchinson.

Marshall, J. N. (1985) 'Research policy and review. Services in a postindustrial society'. *Environment and Planning A*, 17: 1155–67.

Marshall, J. N. (1988) *Services and Uneven Development*. Oxford: Oxford University Press.

Martin, J. and Roberts, C. (1984) *Women and Employment: a Lifetime Perspective*. Report of the 1980 DE/OPCS Women and Employment Survey. London: HMSO.

Martin, J. P. (1984) *Hospitals in Trouble*. Oxford: Basil Blackwell.

Martin, R. (1988) 'Thatcherism and Britain's industrial landscape', in R. Martin and B. Rowthorn (eds), *The Geography of Deindustrialisation*. London: Macmillan. 238–90.

Martin, R. and Fryer, R. H. (1973) *Redundancy and Paternalist Capitalism: a Study in the Sociology of Work*. London: Allen & Unwin.

Massey, D. (1978) 'Regionalism: some current issues', *Capital and Class*, 6: 106–25.

Massey, D. (1979) 'In what sense a regional problem?', *Regional Studies*, 13: 233–43.

Massey, D. (1984) *Spatial Divisions of Labour: Social Structures and the Geography of Production*. London: Macmillan.

Massey, D. (1987) 'Heartlands of defeat', *Marxism Today*, July: 18–23.

Massey, D. and Meegan, R. (1982) *An Anatomy of Job Loss*. London: Methuen.

Massey, D. and Meegan, R. (eds) (1985) *Politics and Method: Contrasting Studies in Industrial Geography*. London: Methuen.

McQuail, D., Blumler, J. and Brown, J. (1972) 'The television audience: a revised perspective', in D. McQuail (ed.), *The Sociology of Mass Communications*. Harmondsworth: Penguin. 135–65.

Medlik, S. (1982) *Trends in Tourism: World Experience and England's Prospect*. London: English Tourist Board.

Melling, J. (ed.) *Housing, Social Policy and the State*. London: Croom Helm.

Miller, W. L. (1978) 'Social class and party choice in England: a new analysis', *British Journal of Political Studies*, 8: 257–84.

Miller, W. L. (1984) 'There was no alternative: the British election of 1983', *Parliamentary Affairs*, 37: 364–84.

Milner, M. (1987) 'Where the Squeeze is Not Only On Holidaymakers'. *Guardian*. 20.8.87.

Milward, N. and Steven, M. (1986) *British Workplace Industrial Relations: 1900–84*. London: Gower.

Morley, D. (1980) *The 'Nationwide' Audience*. Television Monograph No. 11, London: British Film Institute.

Murgatroyd, L. and Urry, J. (1985) 'The class and gender restructuring of the Lancaster economy, 1950–1980', in L. Murgatroyd et al., *Localities, Class and Gender*. London: Pion.

Murgatroyd, L., Savage, M., Shapiro, D., Urry, J., Walby, S. and Warde, A. with Mark-Lawson, J. (1985) *Localities, Class and Gender*. London: Pion.

Murray, F. (1987) 'Flexible specialisation in the "Third Italy" ', *Capital and Class*, 33: 84–95.

Nairn, T. (1988) *The Enchanted Glass: Britain and its Monarchy*. London: Radius.

Nelson, K. (1986) 'Labour demand, Labour supply and the suburbanization of low-wage office work', in A. Scott and M. Storper (eds), *Production, Work, Territory*. Boston: Allen & Unwin. 149–71.

NIER (1986) (National Institute for Economic Research), 'Productivity in Services', *National Institute Economic Review*, 115: 44–7.

Noyelle, T. (1986) 'Services and the world economy: towards a new international division of labour', Sept. Cardiff: ESRC Workshop on Localities in an International Economy.

Oberhauser, A. (1987) 'Labour, production and the state: decentralization of the French automobile industry', *Regional Studies*, 21: 445–58.

Offe, C. (1975) *Contradictions of the Welfare State*. London: Macmillan.

Offe, C. (1985a) *Disorganized Capitalism*. Cambridge: Polity Press.

Offe, C. (1985b) 'New social movements: challenging the boundaries of institutional politics', *Social Research*, 52(4): 817–68.

O'Reilly, E.-L. (1987) 'The cheapest Georgian townhouse', *Landscape*, Nov, Vol. 1, no. 2.

Peck, J. A. (1989) 'Reconceptualizing the local labour market: space, segmentation and the state', *Progress in Human Geography*, 13(1): 42–61.

Pelling, H. (1967) *Social Geography of British Elections 1885–1910*. London: Macmillan.

Percy, S. and Lamb, H. (1987) 'The Squalor Behind the Bright Fast Food Lights'. *Guardian*, 22.8.87.

Perkin, H. (1976) 'The "social tone" of Victorian seaside resorts in the North-West', *Northern History*, 11: 180–94.

Perrons, D. (1986) 'Unequal integration in global Fordism: the case of Ireland', in A. Scott and M. Storper (eds), *Production, Work, Territory*. London: Allen & Unwin. 246–64.

Petit, D. (1986) *Slow Growth and the Service Economy*. London: Frances Pinter.

Pickvance, C. (1976) 'On the study of urban social movements', in C. Pickvance (ed.), *Urban Sociology: Critical Essays*. London: Tavistock. 198–218.

Pickvance, C. (1985) 'Spatial policy as territorial politics: the role of spatial coalitions in the articulation of "spatial" interests and in the demand for spatial policy', in G. Rees, J. Bujra, P. Littlewood, H. Newby and T. Rees (eds), *Political Action and Social Identity*. London: Macmillan, 117–42.

Piepe, A., Prior, R. and Box, A. (1969) 'The location of the proletarian and deferential worker', *Sociology*, 3: 239–44.

Pimlott, J. (1947) *The Englishman's Holiday*. London: Faber & Faber.

Piore, M. and Sabel, C. (1984) *The Second Industrial Divide*. New York: Basic Books.

Political, Social, Economic Review (1986) *National Opinion Poll*. 58 (March).

Pollert, A. (1987) *'The Flexible Firm': a Model in Search of Reality (Or a Policy in Search of a Practice?)*. Warwick Papers in Industrial Relations No. 19, Warwick: University of Warwick.

Pudup, M. B. (1988) 'Arguments within regional geography', *Progress in Human Geography*, 12: 369–90.

Punter, J. (1986–7) 'The contradictions of aesthetic control under the Conservatives', *Planning, Practice and Research N, 1*: 8–13.

Purcell, K. (1979) 'Militancy and acquiescence among women workers', in S. Burman (ed.), *Fit Work for Women*. London: Croom Helm. 112–33.

Raban, J. (1986) *Çoasting*. London: Collins Harvill.

Relph, E. (1987) *The Modern Urban Landscape*. London: Croom Helm.

Report (1987) A. Moscardini (Inspector) and E. Emery (Assessor), Lancaster City Council. *Lancaster Local Plan: Report on Objections to the Plan*. Available from Lancaster City Council, Lancaster.

Riley, S. (1974) *Tourism. Its Impact on Retail Trade*. Lancaster University: Tourism Research Unit.

Roberts, E. (1984) *A Woman's Place: an Oral History of Working-Class Women: 1890–1940*. Oxford: Oxford University Press.

Robinson, O. (1988) 'The changing labour market: growth of part-time employment and labour market segmentation in Britain', in S. Walby (ed.), *Gender Segregation at Work*. Milton Keynes: Open University Press. 114–34.

Rose, R. (1984) *Understanding Big Government. The Programme Approach*. London: Sage.

Ross, E. (1983) 'Surreal networks: women's neighbourhood sharing in London before World War One', *History Workshop Journal*, 15: 4–27.

Rubinstein, W. (1977) 'Wealth, elites and the class structure of modern Britain', *Past and Present*, 76: 99–126.

Rustin, M. (1986) 'The fall and rise of public space', *Dissent, Fall*: 486–94.

Rustin, M. (1987) 'Place and time in socialist theory', *Radical Philosophy*, 30–6.

Sabel, C. (1982) *Work and Politics*. Cambridge: Cambridge University Press.

Sabolo, Y. (1975) *The Service Industries*. Geneva: International Labour Organization.

Savage, M. (1987a) *The Dynamics of Working-Class Politics*. Cambridge: Cambridge University Press.

Savage, M. (1987b) 'Spatial mobility and the professional labour market'. Urban and Regional Studies Working Paper No. 56, Brighton: University of Sussex.

Savage, M., Barlow, J., Duncan, S. and Saunders, P. (1987) ' "Locality research": the Sussex programme on "economic change and the locality" ', *Quarterly Journal of Social Affairs*, 3(1): 27–51.

Savage, M. and Fielding, A. (1989) 'Class formation and regional development: the 'service class' in South East England', *Geoforum* 20(2): 203–18.

Sayer, A. (1984) *Method in Social Science: a Realist Approach*. London: Hutchinson.

Sayer, A. (1985) 'Industry and space: a sympathetic critique of radical research', *Environment and Planning D: Society and Space*, 3: 3–29.

Scott, A. J. (1983) 'Industrial organization and the logic of intra-metropolitan location, 1: theoretical considerations', *Economic Geography*, 59: 223–50.

Scott, A. J. (1986) 'Industrialization and urbanization: a geographical agenda', *Annals of the Association of American Geographers*, 76: 25–37.

Scott, A. J. (1988) 'Flexible production systems and regional development: the rise of new industrial spaces in North America and Western Europe'. Mimeo, Los Angeles: University of California, Department of Geography.

Shapiro, D. (1985a) 'Explaining peripheral change', in L. Murgatroyd et al., *Localities, Class and Gender*. London: Pion, 77–95.

Shapiro, D. (1985b) 'Policy, planning and peripheral development', in L. Murgatroyd et al., *Localities, Class and Gender*. London: Pion. 96–120.

Shapiro, D. (1987a) 'Restructuring theory in crisis'. Lancaster Regionalism Group Working Paper No. 32, University of Lancaster: Lancaster Regionalism Group.

Shapiro, D. (1987b) 'The state and restructuring'. Mimeo, University of Lancaster: Department of Sociology.

Shapiro, D. (1989) 'Restructuring and the state', in J. Morris, A. Thompson and A. Davies (eds), *Labour Market Responses to Industrial Restructuring and Technological Change*, Brighton: Wheatsheaf Books.

Skocpol, T. (1985) 'Bringing the state back in: current research', in P. P. Evans et al. *Bringing the State Back In*. Cambridge: Cambridge University Press.

Sparks, L. (1981) 'A note upon retail employment and superstore development', *Service Industries Review*, 1: 44–61.

Stanworth, M. (1984) 'Women and class analysis: a reply to John Goldthorpe', *Sociology*, 18(2): 159–70.

Stauth, G. and Turner, B. (1988) 'Nostalgia, postmodernism and the critique of mass culture', *Theory, Culture and Society*, 5: 509–26.

Stewart, A., Prandy, K. and Blackburn, R. M. (1980) *Social Stratification and Occupations*. London: Macmillan.

Storper, M. and Christopherson, S. (1987) 'Flexible specialization and regional industrial agglomerations: the case of the US motion picture', *Annals of the Association of American Geographers*, 77: 104–17.

Summerfield, P. (1984) *Women Workers in the Second World War*. London: Croom Helm.

Swingewood, A. (1977) *The Myth of Mass Culture*. London: Macmillan.

Taylor, S. (1978) 'Parkin's theory of working class conservatism: two hypotheses investigated', *Sociological Review*, 26(4): 827–42.

Theroux, Paul (1984) *The Kingdom by the Sea*. Harmondsworth: Penguin.

Thomas, D. E. (1987) 'Don't Lie Back and Just Think of England'. *Guardian*, 21.12.87.

Thompson, E. P. (1971) 'The moral economy of the English crowd in the eighteenth century', *Past and Present*, 50: 76–136.

Thrift, N. (1987) 'Introduction: the geography of late twentieth-century class formation', in N. Thrift and P. Williams (eds), *Class and Space*, London: Routledge & Kegan Paul, 207–53.

Thift, N. (1988a) 'Images of Social Change', Open University course D314 *Restructuring Britain*.

Thrift, N. (1988b) 'Serious money'. Seminar paper, 20.5.88, University of Lancaster: Department of Geography.

Tilly, C. (1978) *From Mobilisation to Revolution*. Reading, Mass.: Addison–Wesley.

Todd, N. (1976) 'A history of labour in Lancaster and Barrow-in-Furness c. 1890–1920'. MPhil thesis, University of Lancaster.

Townsend, A. (1986) 'Spatial aspects of part-time employment in Britain', *Regional Studies*, 20: 310–30.

UCNS (1988) *Investing in People*. Aug. Universities' Council for Non-academic Staff, Universities Manpower Review Group.

Urry, J. (1981) *The Anatomy of Capitalist Societies*. London: Macmillan.

Urry, J. (1986) 'Locality research: the case of Lancaster', *Regional Studies*, 20(3): 233–42.

Urry, J. (1987a) *Economic Planning and Policy in the Lancaster District*. Lancaster Regionalism Group Working Paper No. 21, University of Lancaster: Lancaster Regionalism Group.

Urry, J. (1987b) *Holidaymaking, Cultural Change and the Seaside*. Lancaster Regionalism Group Working Paper No. 22, University of Lancaster: Lancaster Regionalism Group.

Urry, J. (1987c) 'Some social and spatial aspects of services', *Society and Space*, 5: 5–26.

Urry, J. (1988a) 'Cultural change and contemporary holidaymaking', *Theory, Culture and Society*, 5: 35–55.

Urry, J. (1988b) 'Society, space and locality', *Environment and Planning D: Society and Space*, 5: 435–44.

Urry, J. (1990) 'Lancaster: small firms, the state and the "locality" ', in M. Harloe, C. Pickvance and J. Urry, *Localities, Policies and Politics*. London: Unwin Hyman.

Van der Pijl, K. (1984) *The Making of an Atlantic Ruling Class*. London: Verso.

Vattimo, G. (1988) 'Hermeneutics as Koine', *Theory, Culture and Society*, 5: 399–408.

Venturi, R. (1972) *Learning from Las Vegas*. Cambridge, Mass.: MIT Press.

The Visitor (various dates).

Volpato, G. (1986) 'The automobile industry in transition: product market changes and firm strategies in the 1970s and 1980s', in S. Tolliday and J. Zeitlin (eds), *The Automobile Industry and its Workers: Between Fordism and Flexibility*. Cambridge: Polity Press. 193–223.

Wainwright, H. (1987) *Labour: a Tale of Two Parties*. London: Hogarth Press.

Walby, S. (1985) 'Spatial and historical variations in women's employment and unemployment', in L. Murgatroyd et al., *Localities, Class and Gender*. London: Pion.

Walby, S. (1986a) 'Gender, class and stratification: towards a new approach', in

Rosemary Crompton and Michael Mann (eds), *Gender and Stratification*. Cambridge: Polity Press. 23–39.

Walby, S. (1986b) *Patriarchy at Work*. Cambridge: Polity Press.

Walby, S. (1987) 'Flexibility and the changing sexual division of labour'. Lancaster Regionalism Group Working Paper No. 36, University of Lancaster: Lancaster Regionalism Group.

Walby, S. (ed.) (1988) *Gender Segregation at Work*. Milton Keynes: Open University Press.

Walker, R. (1985) 'Is there a service economy? The changing capitalist division of labour', *Science and Society*, 49: 42–84.

Walton, J. (1978) *The Blackpool Landlady*. Manchester: Manchester University Press.

Ward, C. and Crouch, D. (1988) *The Allotment. Its Landscape and Culture*. London: Faber & Faber.

Warde, A. (1985a) 'Comparable localities: some problems of method', in L. Murgatroyd et al., *Localities, Class and Gender*. London: Pion. 54–76.

Warde, A. (1985b) 'Spatial change, politics and the division of labour', in D. Gregory and J. Urry (eds), *Social Relations and Spatial Structures*. London: Macmillan. 190–212.

Warde, A. (1988a) *Conditions of Dependence: Working-class Quiescence in Lancaster in the Twentieth Century*. Lancaster Regionalism Group Working Paper No. 30, University of Lancaster: Lancaster Regionalism Group.

Warde, A. (1988b) 'Industrial restructuring, local politics and the reproduction of labour power: some theoretical issues', *Environment and Planning D: Society and Space*, 6: 75–95.

Warde, A. (1989) 'Industrial discipline: factory regime and politics in Lancaster', *Work, Employment and Society*, 3: 49–63.

Warde, A., Savage, M., Longhurst, B., and Martin, A. (1988) 'Class, consumption and voting, an ecological analysis of wards and towns in the 1980 local elections in England', *Political Geography Quarterly*, 7: 339–51.

Wates, N. and Krevitt, C. (1987) *Community Architecture*. Harmondsworth: Penguin.

Watt, I. (1980) 'Linkages between industrial radicalism and the domestic role among working women', *Sociological Review*, 28: 55–74.

Whitelegg, J. (1982) *Inequalities in Health Care*. Retford, Notts.: Straw Barnes.

Whyte, W. F. (1948) *Human Relations in the Restaurant Industry*. New York: McGraw–Hill.

Winckler, V. (1986) *Sector and State in Restructuring: the Case of the Civil Service, 1962–85*. Cardiff: University College Social Research Unit.

Witz, A. (1988) 'Patriarchal relations and patterns of sex segregation in the medical division of labour', in S. Walby (ed.), *Gender Segregation at Work*. Milton Keynes: Open University Press.

Women and Geography (1984) Women and Geography Study Group of the Institute of British Geographers, *Gender and Geography: an Introduction to Feminist Geography*. London: Hutchinson.

Wright, P. (1985) 'The ghosting of the inner city', in P. Wright, *On Living in an Old Country: the National Past in Contemporary Britain*. London: Verso. 215–49.

Younger, G. (1973) *Tourism: Blessing or Blight*. Harmondsworth: Penguin.

Index